Energy, Climate Change & Sustainability in the Global South

The "Global South" emerges as an undeniable force in global energy and climate governance, making substantial contributions to international climate negotiations and sustainable development. Representative of these emerging nations in the Global South, the BRICS+ Countries have fortified their collaboration on sustainable development through the BRICS cooperation mechanism. Actively engaging in the formulation of global energy and climate governance rules, they play a pivotal role in the sustainable development of the Global South and the entire world.

This book series centers on the BRICS+ Countries, delving into their current situations, challenges, and prospects in energy, climate, and sustainable development. It amalgamates the research findings of various experts and scholars to offer profound insights and recommendations on achieving sustainable development in the Global South.

Sustainability stands as the linchpin for achieving economic and social development in Global South countries. This book series selects the BRICS+ Countries as representative research subjects, providing comprehensive insights and suggestions on progressing in energy, climate, and sustainable development for Global South nations. It aims to serve as a theoretical reference and source of experience for advancing the development of the BRICS+ Countries and the Global South, thereby realizing global sustainable development goals.

Xiangyu Dong • Jin Gu

The Belt and Road Initiative and the Global South

A Strategic Partnership for Sustainable Development

Springer

Xiangyu Dong
School of Humanities and Law
Zhejiang A&F University
Hangzhou, Zhejiang, China

Jin Gu
School of Humanities and Law
Zhejiang A&F University
Hangzhou, Zhejiang, China

ISSN 3005-1568 ISSN 3005-1576 (electronic)
Energy, Climate Change & Sustainability in the Global South
ISBN 978-981-92-0143-3 ISBN 978-981-92-0144-0 (eBook)
https://doi.org/10.1007/978-981-92-0144-0

This work was supported by Talent Startup Project Fund of Zhejiang A&F University (Program No. 2022FR022, Program No. 2034020043).

This Springer imprint is published by the registered company Springer Nature Singapore Pte Ltd.
The registered company address is: 152 Beach Road, #21-01/04 Gateway East, Singapore 189721, Singapore

Preface

This book mainly studies the sovereign states in the Global South and explains in detail how the sovereign countries of the Global South set up voting rules for regional international organizations. In addition, the concept of travel restriction measures has been introduced, which combines these measures with the national and social interests of sovereign countries in the Global South so as to promote the sovereign countries of the Global South to find a win-win direction for cooperation in the interests of the community. The book also focuses on and interprets the ways in which sovereign countries in the Global South can collaborate on cultural heritage protection. Of course, for the sovereign countries of the Global South, the most important is the environmental issues, so we have used several chapters to analyze and interpret in detail, from the perspective of carbon dioxide emissions and trading, the protection of marine plastic waste pollution, and the environmental provisions of free trade agreements. This book is characterized by policy analysis, professional interpretation of legal provisions, and a case-oriented approach, which can not only popularize policy theory for social groups but also provide a certain reference for the academic community of sovereign countries in the Global South. Of course, there are also certain shortcomings in the book, and we ask scholars and readers to be more tolerant and welcome criticism and correction.

Hangzhou, China
5 March 2026

Xiangyu Dong
Jin Gu

Competing Interests The authors have no competing interests to declare that are relevant to the content of this manuscript.

Introduction: The Belt and Road Initiative and the Global South: A Strategic Partnership for Sustainable Development

As of October 2025, the Belt and Road Initiative (BRI) has entered its institutionalized 2.0 phase, with 152 countries participating in its infrastructure and trade networks. This section establishes the conceptual framework by defining the Global South's evolving geopolitical identity beyond geographic terms (e.g., BRICS+ expansion to 25 members); analyzing BRI's shift from infrastructure-focused 1.0 phase to institutionalized 2.0 phase post-2023; introducing the triple synergy model: economic connectivity, governance innovation, and cultural exchange. The 2025 New Development Bank (NDB) annual report shows 72% of its $50 billion portfolio now integrates BRI projects with UN Sustainable Development Goals (SDGs).

It transfers trade to value chains and defines infrastructure as development backbone, expanded analysis of key corridors: CPEC Phase II (2025–2030): $75 billion investment in Gwadar Smart Port and SEZs, projected to create 2.3 million jobs; Africa Railway Network: Comparative cost–benefit analysis of Chinese-built vs. Western-funded projects (e.g., Ethiopia-Djibouti Railway vs. India-Mozambique corridor). World Bank 2025 data show BRI countries average 4.2% GDP growth boost versus 2.8% for non-participants. Digital Silk Road Revolution: 5G infrastructure penetration in BRI nations (2025 average: 68% vs. Global South average: 42%) and cross-border e-commerce platforms like Alibaba's Africa Digital Hub processing $28 billion/year; there is some *controversy*: Huawei's role in African digital governance debates (e.g., Kenya's AI surveillance partnership).

Geopolitical reconfiguration occurs beyond Western-centered order. For instance, financial architecture alternatives such as currency De-Dollarization: RMB's 28% share in Africa's trade settlements (vs. 5% in 2015); NDB vs. World Bank: Comparative case studies of Kenya's Lamu Port financing. Security cooperation dynamics as peacekeeping: China's BRI-linked UN missions in South Sudan (3800 troops deployed as of 2025) and anti-piracy: Djibouti's China-supported naval base reducing Gulf of Aden incidents by 63%.

Governance models, including Beijing Consensus 2.0, contain conditional vs. non-conditional aids. Quantitative analysis: 87% of BRI contracts lack human rights clauses vs. 92% of World Bank loans; case study: Sri Lanka's debt restructuring under BRI's debt sustainability framework. Green BRI evolution includes 2025 renewable energy projects: solar capacity additions (120 GW), hydropower (45 GW), and coal phase-out timeline: China's 2025 pledge to halt overseas coal financing.

There are **challenges and future trajectories, including debt sustainability debates**, such as the new 2025 BRI Transparency Index covering 78% of projects and Zambia's debt-for-nature swap with China as a precedent. The expansion risks include BRICS+ fragmentation challenges (e.g., India's hesitance on BRI) and Latin America's Pacific Alliance balancing BRI with U.S. initiatives.

The future will go **toward a multipolar developmental state**. The findings are synthesized through three perspectives: BRI as a post-pandemic global supply chain stabilizer; NDB/AIIB's 2025 $100 billion joint financing capacity; and Confucius Institutes in 140 BRI countries fostering soft power. The 2030 BRI-Global South integration will unfold through three possible pathways (cooperative, competitive, bifurcated).

This monograph approaches geopolitical relations, focusing on countries that form interest communities within the Global South. It conducts in-depth discussions primarily from the perspectives of politics, national security, synchronized development of cultural heritage, environmental protection, and economic development. From a globalization perspective, the Global South and the Global North are divided based on geopolitical angles. Countries included in the Global North are mainly represented by developed countries, while the Global South encompasses more developing countries and least developed countries. In the process of rapid globalization, the problems manifested by the Global South more truly reflect the urgent characteristics of reality and are more worthy of investment of time and energy as research objects. Therefore, Chap. 1 of this monograph focuses on the decision-making methods that different countries in the Global South need to adopt when forming regional organizations or other interest communities. Using international organization voting methods as background, it demonstrates that "consensus-based" voting methods can be applied to improve efficiency. Chapter 2 mainly discusses the historical development of travel visa measures and their relationship with the Global South, introducing from the perspectives of basic concepts, characteristics, and so on. Chapter 3 proceeds from the concept of community and introduces in detail how countries in the Global South can use travel visa measures to protect national interests, security interests, and economic interests. Chapter 4 mainly focuses on cultural heritage protection as the research object, deeply exploring how countries in the Global South can form synchronized development models for subsequent cultural heritage protection and achieve mutually beneficial and win-win results. Chapter 5 explains in detail from the environmental protection perspective the targets that the Global South needs to complete in the process of carbon neutrality, such as achieving carbon neutrality as soon as possible and issuing green bonds to carry out a series of highly effective environmental protection measures. Chapter 6 also focuses on the issue of plastic pollution governance in environmental protection, and by demonstrating the urgency, necessity, and affirmative aspects of plastic pollution governance, further proposes how Global South countries can better participate in the environmental pollution control process. Chapter 7 mainly focuses on explaining the relationship between economic development and the environment in detail, hoping to effectively achieve a sustainable development model that reconciles economic development with environmental protection.

The main characteristics of this monograph are to interpret the Global South from different perspectives, presenting the following features: First, **the diversity of research objects**. This monograph not only involves political perspectives, but also argues from economic, humanistic, and environmental perspectives, attempting to provide a more comprehensive and multifaceted discussion of the emerging topic of the Global South. Second, **the novelty of research content**. The content focused on in each chapter of this monograph are currently popular topics. These topics can provide certain positive impacts for the development of the Global South, and can form theoretical support for the future development of the Global South, possessing active academic value. Third, **the research methodology of this monograph** presents diversified characteristics. In the book, different topics are introduced, and more case elements are incorporated to strengthen the argumentative viewpoints, and many scholars' perspectives are referenced to support the professionalism of the arguments. Furthermore, large amounts of legal norms and policy documents have been searched and referenced, enriching the depth and breadth of the overall arguments, enabling this monograph to present diversified characteristics.

The objectives and purposes of this monograph are to enable readers to generate the following effects based on reading different chapters of the book: First, **to attract more readers** to pay attention to Global South issues and, through examination and reflection on different countries in the Global South, to popularize and promote the concept of the Global South. Second, **to inspire readers** from different perspectives and, through this monograph as a foundation, to conduct more in-depth research on certain content of the Global South. Third, **to hope that some of the perspectives** focused on in this monograph can produce positive impacts on the future development of Global South countries, promote the formation of an interest community of the Global South, and enhance the cohesion, appeal, and influence of the community. To this end, this monograph will be oriented toward different types of audiences: scholars and student groups researching the Global South, political groups from both the Global South and non-Global South regions, and social groups interested in Global South topics. It is hoped that this monograph can produce certain theoretical and practical positive impacts on current globalization development.

Contents

About the Authors

Xiangyu Dong is a lecturer at Zhejiang A & F University, and researcher of Research Academy for Rural Revitalization of Zhejiang Province, Zhejiang A&F University. He received his Ph.D. at Zhongnan University of Economics and Law, with a specialization in international law. With research interests in international law, law of the sea and digital law, he has published extensively in SSCI and CSSCI.

Jin Gu is a lecturer at Zhejiang A & F University, and researcher of Institute of Ecological Civilization, Zhejiang A& F University. She received her Ph.D. degree at the China Institute of Boundary and Ocean Studies (CIBOS) of Wuhan University with a specialization in international law. Her major research interest focuses on international environmental, international water law, and climate change law.

Chapter 1
"Global South" and "Consensus" Voting System

The rapid and profoundly impactful transformation of the global landscape has significantly accelerated the continuous, dynamic, and ever-evolving process of evolution within geopolitical relations across the entire world. As developing countries continue to rise steadily and gain increasingly notable influence on the international diplomatic and economic stage, an emerging cluster of powers—characterized by their shared developmental trajectories and growing collective voice—is gradually emerging as a pivotal new factor that actively shapes and repeatedly reshapes the intricate patterns of global economic trade as well as the broader, more far-reaching political order of the international community. These burgeoning world powers are also widely and formally referred to as the "Global South"—a designation deeply rooted in their geographical distribution, given that the vast majority of these nations are situated within the territorial boundaries of the southern hemisphere.

The term "Global South" typically denotes a highly diverse and multifaceted collective of countries, with most being geographically located in the southern hemisphere and spanning multiple continents and cultural spheres. This expansive and inclusive group encompasses a wide range of nations from Latin America (including both large regional economies and smaller nation-states), the entire African continent (covering nations across sub-Saharan Africa and North Africa alike), various key regions of Asia (such as South Asia, Southeast Asia, and parts of West Asia), and the scattered Pacific Islands, and the vast majority of these countries explicitly fall under the internationally recognized category of developing nations. Importantly, the term "Global South" embodies the meaningful convergence of shared political aspirations (including the pursuit of sovereignty and self-determination), overlapping geopolitical interests (such as advocating for fairer global resource distribution), and common economic characteristics (like relying on primary commodity exports in many cases) among its diverse member states. From a historical perspective, these countries have long grappled with a multitude of formidable and persistent challenges, including widespread poverty that afflicts large

X. Dong, J. Gu, *The Belt and Road Initiative and the Global South*, Energy, Climate Change & Sustainability in the Global South,
https://doi.org/10.1007/978-981-92-0144-0_1

and vulnerable segments of their populations, recurring bouts of political instability that severely disrupt effective governance and social order, and persistent underdevelopment across key sectors such as critical infrastructure, quality education, and accessible healthcare. In recent decades, however, a striking and transformative shift has occurred: the "Global South" has emerged as a robust, resilient, and increasingly influential force in the global arena, with its presence felt across diplomatic, economic, and social domains. It now plays a crucial and irreplaceable role in driving sustained global economic growth (contributing a significant share of global GDP expansion in recent years), spearheading targeted efforts to promote inclusive social development both within its own borders and beyond (through initiatives like south-south cooperation), and earnestly demanding a more equitable, representative, and legally recognized position in major international fora and formal multilateral governance structures (such as the United Nations and its specialized agencies). Influenced by the complex, interconnected, and often fluid dynamics of contemporary geopolitics, these countries in the southern hemisphere frequently find it necessary and strategically advantageous to join forces, pool their resources, and form their own regional organizations—bodies designed to address shared concerns and amplify their collective influence. The establishment of such regional bodies serves a critical and well-defined purpose: it can effectively strengthen the internal cohesion, mutual trust, and collaborative spirit among member states, fostering a strong sense of solidarity and collective purpose that enables them to address shared challenges (such as climate change, cross-border conflicts, and economic crises) more effectively and with greater collective leverage. Yet, amid this active push for regional cooperation and integration, there remains a key area that demands our heightened attention, careful analysis, and deliberate action—specifically, how to enhance the operational efficiency, transparency, and accountability of these organizations to ensure the strict, consistent, and legally binding implementation of their internal decisions, resolutions, and outcomes. When seeking practical, sustainable, and legally sound solutions to this pressing and urgent need, the deliberate design, careful calibration, and formal adoption of a clear, equitable, and procedurally rigorous voting system stands out as an undeniable, evidence-based, and optimal approach for the regional organizations of the "Global South" to forge efficient, unified, and widely accepted results that reflect the collective will of their member states.

As a constitutive legal mechanism for inter-state dialogue, cooperation, and peaceful settlement of disputes under contemporary international law, international organizations have been attracting growing attention and emphasis from countries across the globe. In the past, given that international organizations primarily served as the core platform for political diplomacy among major powers, the predominant legal form assumed by these entities was that of formal intergovernmental organizations established by treaty. Their key focus and missions were predominantly centered on advancing political coordination and driving economic development—prominent examples of this include the founding of the United Nations and the establishment of the World Trade Organization, both of which have played pivotal roles in shaping global governance. Under the dual impetus of the worldwide trend toward multi-polarization and the rising influence of the Global South, the development of international organizations has gradually stepped into a brand-new historical stage. During this phase, international organizations characterized by regional focus (catering to the specific needs of particular geographic areas) and professional specialization (concentrating on niche fields like healthcare, environment, or technology) have begun to emerge and gain increasing prominence on the global stage. The evolving nature and functions of international organizations have also exerted a profound and far-reaching impact on the renewal and advancement of their internal voting systems. Building on the foundation of traditional voting mechanisms such as unanimity voting, majority voting, and weighted voting, the consensus procedure—originally institutionalized in the 1960s as a sui generis decision-making modality—has since acquired customary status in the practice of international organization*s*. This shift is largely driven by the urgent need to better align with the concept of global integration rooted in peace and development, which stands as a core tenet of today' s international political landscape. For instance, the World Trade Organization (WTO), formally established in 1995, has explicitly incorporated the principle of consensus into its fundamental voting rules, making it a cornerstone of its decision-making framework. Similarly, the Shanghai Cooperation Organization (SCO) clearly stipulates in its foundational purposes that all member states must resolve any and all issues through constructive consultation, reflecting the organization' s commitment to this approach. As far as this innovative voting system is concerned, the "mission" it undertakes holds extraordinary significance in the ongoing development of the international community under the current "global integration" pattern. Particularly, under the guidance of the forward-looking international political concept of "Community of Shared Future for Mankind," the "Consensus"voting method is poised to become an increasingly popular and widely adopted applicable rule in international governance. From the perspective of literal interpretation, the term "consensus"encompasses two distinct yet interconnected special definitions: "Consultation" and "Agreement." "Consultation" refers to the act of "engaging in joint discussion with the aim of reaching a common consensus," emphasizing the interactive process of dialogue. "Agreement," on the other hand, mainly denotes a state of "no disagreement," focusing on the unified outcome of such dialogue. Therefore, the term "Negotiation" (a core part of consultation) is primarily embodied as a dynamic, ongoing process, while "Agreement" highlights the final consensus achieved as a result. Since the consensus on the outcome is also an integral part of its process-oriented conclusion, the main core of "consensus"lies firmly in the "Negotiation" process itself. Scholar Davey has specifically described the consultative process as a distinct political process, one that should be clearly separated from the more rigid, legalized panel procedures and formal appeals processes. Indeed, if improvements are deemed necessary in the area of consultation, the direction of such improvements should be focused on increasing the possibility of third-party mediation during the consultation process. This would help create a more neutral and constructive environment to facilitate the resolution of disputes and differences. Of course, in the course of negotiation, there will inevitably be instances where a full consensus cannot be reached immediately. In practice, there are two main ways to address this challenge: One approach is to return to the "Negotiation" process, revisiting the core points of disagreement at hand and making another deliberate effort to find common ground and bridge differences. The other approach is to adopt the method of implied consent—meaning that the absence of a formal objection, in writing or by declaration, shall be deemed to constitute tacit consent under the applicable rules of procedure. For example, the United Nations Convention on the Law of the Sea explicitly provides in the rules governing the Council of the International Seabed Authority that "consensus"means the complete absence of any formal objection. It follows from this that, in most general international organizations, tacit consent serves as the main form of reaching agreement. In other words, an agreement can be considered reached as long as there are no formal or explicit objections raised by any member. With the continuous development and refinement of the rules of procedure of modern international organizations, it has become the primary choice for regional international organizations to supplement and offset the adversarial and majoritarian logic inherent in traditional voting paradigms, which may undermine the principle of sovereign equality through consultative voting. Take the Shanghai Cooperation Organization, which was formally established on June 15, 2001, for instance—one of its core purposes is explicitly stated as: "Upholding equality and mutual benefit, and resolving all problems through mutual consultation." Beyond regional international organizations, the important status of the "Consensus"voting system has also been prominently highlighted in the main voting methods adopted by the WTO. As scholar Pedersen aptly points out: "Every member participates in the process of negotiating issues related to voting, though not every member plays a key role throughout the entire process. However, every member is actively involved in the critical step of approving the final adoption of the resolution." [1] Promoting the transparency and democratization of decision-making through broad and inclusive member participation stands as one of the most important and fundamental elements of the WTO' s operational framework. The Uruguay Round Agreement, a landmark in global trade governance, also explicitly reaffirms the vital importance of the principle of "Consensus"voting—and in fact, the agreement itself was formally ratified through the consensus method, underscoring the practice' s credibility [2]. The development of the "Consensus"voting mechanism represents a clear new trend in the evolution of the voting systems of modern international organizations. This trend signifies that its existence can provide a solid functional and value-based foundation for the orderly, fair, and effective operation of international organizations. However, the inherent diversity of modern voting methods also determines that other voting systems possess unique characteristics and advantages that the "Consensus"voting method does not have. In contrast, the "Consensus"voting system still has several aspects that require further improvement and refinement. For example, it often faces challenges such as high time costs associated with prolonged negotiations, potential ambiguities in the content and scope of voting outcomes, and the risk of the risk of pro forma consensus, wherein apparent unanimity masks underlying reservations or persistent objections not formally recorded. Clarifying the root causes of these shortcomings in the "Consensus"voting system will help further enhance the system' s universal applicability and effectiveness in practical use. In turn, this will play an important and constructive role in establishing a fair, efficient, and democratic voting mechanism—one that takes democratic consultation as its core purpose—within modern international organizations.

1.1 The Advantages of the "Consensus" Voting Mechanism and Its Practical Difficulties

1.1.1 A Brief Analysis of the Advantages of the"Consensus" Voting Mechanism

The consensus voting system has been widely accepted by a growing number of international organizations—including both global multilateral bodies and regional cooperative alliances—and this widespread adoption is primarily attributed to the distinct, inherent advantages that the system inherently possesses and consistently delivers in practice. First and foremost, a "Consensus" voting system is highly effective in softening the inherent antagonisms that are characteristic of traditional majority-based voting systems, which often pit opposing factions against one another. Unlike conventional voting mechanisms that prioritize numerical dominance, the "Consensus" voting system, right from the initial stage of its decision-making process, chooses to move beyond the rigid constraints of traditional voting frameworks and instead forms decisions through structured, inclusive consultative means. This approach fundamentally eliminates the possibility of direct confrontation from the legal perspective of voting participation—replacing the rigid, winner-takes-all model of hard voting with a collaborative, interest-aligned approach centered on reaching consensus through constructive dialogue. In doing so, it constructs a formal platform for amicable and solution-oriented discussion, one specifically tailored to resolve differences that pertain to the core interests at stake in a proposed resolution. At the same time, the "Consensus" voting system breaks new ground by opening up an alternative voting pathway rooted in iterative consultation, one that operates outside the narrow boundaries of traditional yes/no/abstain voting forms. Throughout this structured consultative process, members of an international organization can fully leverage the opportunity of in-depth, issue-specific dialogue to communicate thoroughly on matters involving diverse and sometimes conflicting interests. They can also make appropriate, mutually acceptable concessions—calibrated to balance competing priorities—to bridge gaps and ultimately reach a collective agreement. When compared to the traditional voting system—where the only options available to members are limited to "Yes," "No," or "Abstain," leaving little room for nuance—this consultative approach significantly broadens the scope of choices for members and greatly mitigates the confrontational tensions that often arise from rigid, binary voting procedures. After a "Consensus"vote is conducted, countries are only required to reach agreement on the basic, core points of the negotiated issue; there is no need to resolve every minor, non-essential difference that may arise. Instead, reservations on non-essential elements may be formally entered into the official summary record of the proceedings, and such reservations do not preclude the adoption of the resolution—this is done in strict accordance with the silence-procedure clause commonly embedded in international organizational rules—and a final, binding decision can still be formally adopted by the body. The key insight that can be gleaned from this arrangement is that the outcome of the consultation process is not a hasty, superficial compromise driven by expediency, but rather a well-considered, interest-balanced product of thorough, multi-round discussion among participating states and the collective achievement of agreement on the core, fundamental points that matter most. Secondly, the "Consensus" voting system is well-equipped to meet the specific needs of maximizing legitimate interests among all participating entities, ensuring that no single member's key concerns are unduly sidelined. Under the framework of this system, the adoption of any resolution is not a one-step, rushed process; instead, it requires repeated rounds of detailed consultation, in-depth, issue-specific negotiations, and, when necessary, voluntary concessions of non-core interests from relevant parties—all conducted in good faith. This rigorous, multi-stage process ensures that the original voting matters—once refined and adjusted through substantive, interest-sensitive consultative procedures—become far more readily acceptable to all member states, as each has had the opportunity to voice concerns and shape the outcome. Crucially, this acceptance is not a passive or coerced compliance driven by procedural pressure, but rather a deliberate, voluntary shift in perspective on the part of each member state, reached after careful consideration of both individual national interests and the broader collective interests of the organization. In other words, within the "Consensus" voting mechanism, member states ultimately achieve outcomes that align with their key priorities and protect their essential interests. This, in turn, means that each country has, to a significant extent, maximized its own legitimate interests through the collaborative process, fostering a sense of fairness and ownership in the final decision. Finally, the "Consensus" voting system plays a vital, long-term role in fostering the formation of a strong "Sense of Community" among member states—an intangible but critical asset for effective international cooperation. By its very design and operational logic, the "Consensus" voting system demands repeated, structured consultations, as well as occasional, good-faith exchanges of interests and mutual concessions, among the member states of an international organization. Throughout this ongoing, interactive process of engagement, the views or propositions held by different member states on a specific matter gradually evolve—shifting from an initial state of divergence, or even open conflict, toward a state of relative proximity, mutual understanding, and shared purpose. As communication deepens and inter-member trust builds incrementally, the perspectives of member states on voting issues slowly transcend the narrow framework of their own immediate, short-term national interests and begin to incorporate the broader good of the collective. Over time, this collective shift in mindset gives rise to a preliminary yet meaningful "Community Consciousness," one that binds members together through shared goals, mutual respect, and a recognition of interdependence. This emerging sense of community also lays a solid, trust-based foundation for the smoother, more effective, and more sustainable implementation of the final resolution in the long run, as members are more likely to comply with decisions they helped shape.

1.1.2 The Dilemma of the "Consensus" Voting Mechanism

In the specific and practical application of the "Consensus" voting system, its inherent characteristic of requiring the achievement of collective consensus exerts a continuous and far-reaching impact on the timeline and cut-off points of the entire decision-making process. After going through rounds of repeated consultations, voluntary concessions, and mutual compromises—steps that are essential to narrowing differences— the opinions represented by the participating entities are still frequently constrained by a variety of complex factors. These constraints may stem from the unique national conditions of their respective countries (such as distinct political systems, economic structures, or cultural backgrounds), be driven by the pursuit of specific interest goals (including economic benefits, security guarantees, or strategic advantages), or even result from the need to act as "spokesmen" for certain domestic political parties, interest groups, or social alliances. These aforementioned restrictive conditions, which are deeply rooted in objective realities and subjective demands, cause the "Consensus" voting mechanism to exhibit several noticeable drawbacks in its operation. For instance, the repeated consultations necessary to align divergent views often lead to a significantly high time cost in the voting process, as each round of dialogue and adjustment extends the overall timeline. Additionally, the mechanism's allowance for participants to make interpretations of or reservations about voting matters—while designed to accommodate diverse perspectives—often results in ambiguity regarding the content and scope of the voting matters themselves, making it difficult to form clear and unified standards. Furthermore, in the actual implementation phase of the final decision, the voting results may only present an apparent consistency: on the surface, all parties have reached an agreement, but in practice, there may be hidden disagreements or passive acceptance, which undermines the authenticity of the consensus. If these prominent problems are not properly identified and resolved in a timely manner, they will inevitably give rise to a series of negative consequences in the practical application of the "Consensus" voting system. Specifically, it may lead to persistently low operational efficiency, with decision-making processes dragged out indefinitely; it may result in unclear and ambiguous voting outcomes, making it hard for member states to grasp the core requirements of the resolution; and it may even cause a lack of effective enforcement, as the superficial consensus fails to generate sufficient willingness to implement among participants. Therefore, it is absolutely necessary for the international community to face up to the inherent shortcomings of the "Consensus" voting system with a realistic and proactive attitude. Only by acknowledging these issues and taking targeted measures to address them can the system be optimized and improved, thereby better providing efficient, convenient, and reliable rules of procedure for the growing number of international organizations—organizations that play an increasingly important role in global governance, regional cooperation, and international affairs coordination.

The Voting Process Is Time-consuming and Costly

In the operational stage of the "Consensus" voting mechanism, achieving collective consensus first requires the formation of unity around the basic points of the issue at hand. Yet, within the framework of non-voting rules—where formal ballot-casting is not the core driver of decision-making—the process of building consensus on these basic points relies heavily on repeated, in-depth deliberations among the member states of the international organization. This process also demands sustained efforts from all parties to push for the eventual entry into force of the resolution, and in some cases, may even involve voluntary concessions and mutual compromises on key interests to bridge remaining gaps. Notably, the negotiations between member states are far from simple exchanges of views. For example, due to the long-standing imbalance in economic development between developed and developing countries, their core interest demands often diverge significantly: developed nations may prioritize issues like market access and intellectual property protection, while developing countries tend to focus on fair trade terms and support for industrialization. This inherent divergence means that when it comes to identifying and aligning shared interests during joint negotiations, the two sides must go through repeated rounds of adjustment and adaptation—fine-tuning their positions to find common ground. Nevertheless, as long as the process of reconciling these interests adheres to the principle of fairness, ensuring that neither side is forced to bear an unreasonable burden, a stable consensus can still be achieved within the framework of the "Consensus" voting system [3]. In the voting process of the World Trade Organization (WTO), the application of a majority voting system typically consumes far less time. This is because majority voting yields only two clear outcomes: either the proposal is approved or it is rejected, with no room for ambiguous middle ground. This binary result structure significantly streamlines the decision-making process, thereby greatly boosting the efficiency of majority voting. However, this gain in efficiency is accompanied by a notable paradox of non-reciprocity. For developing countries, the realization of their economic interests often depends on the preferential treatment extended by developed countries—such as reduced tariffs on their exports or technical assistance for capacity-building. In the context of voting, this inherently unequal relationship between the strong and the weak ultimately relegates developing countries to the role of bystanders in multilateral trade negotiations: their voices are often overshadowed by the numerical advantage of developed nations, leaving them unable to effectively safeguard their own core interests [4]. Beyond the time spent on reconciling interests to build consensus, the "Consensus" voting process also inevitably incurs additional time costs because each member state is entitled to make corresponding explanatory statements during the consultations. These statements—while crucial for clarifying positions and addressing concerns—require time for delivery, discussion, and response, which in turn exerts a negative delaying effect on the efficiency of final voting results. In contrast, the traditional voting system requires participants to do no more than cast an abstention if they are unwilling to take a clear stance; this simple act of abstention has no delaying impact on the overall progress of the voting process. Therefore, when compared to voting-based methods, the primary reason for the relatively low efficiency of the "Consensus" voting method lies in its core requirement: to achieve genuine consensus, the mechanism must fully take into account the opinions of participants who hold opposing views on the voting matter. The process of persuading these dissenting participants to adjust or change their positions—whether through further dialogue, interest adjustments, or compromise—is directly and positively correlated with the total time consumed by the voting process: the more persistent the dissent, the longer the time needed to resolve it. In a traditional voting system, by virtue of the "minority subject to the majority" principle, the number of participants holding opposing views only needs to be smaller than that of those in favor to ensure the resolution is adopted; the dissent of the minority has no bearing on the final outcome. In the "Consensus" voting mechanism, however, failing to account for the concerns of dissenting participants will directly hinder the efficiency of the voting process—since even a single unresolved objection can prevent the formation of the required consensus. Thus, within the "Consensus" voting mechanism, time cost and voting efficiency exhibit a clear negative correlation: the more time invested in addressing dissent and building consensus, the lower the immediate efficiency of the process, and vice versa. This inherent relationship is the fundamental root cause of the high time cost associated with the "Consensus" voting mechanism.

The Content of the Vote is not Clear

The ambiguity inherent in the "Consensus" voting mechanism is primarily a relative concept, defined in contrast to the clarity and straightforwardness of traditional voting systems. First and foremost, from the perspective of disputes tied to voting matters, participating entities of international organizations operating under a traditional voting system have a limited set of ways to express their positions regarding controversial issues. They can only convey their stance by directly exercising the right to cast an opposing vote on the disputed matter; alternatively, casting an abstention also serves as a formal means of expressing a position—yet under this traditional framework, an abstention holds no material impact on whether the voting matter is ultimately adopted. In sharp contrast, within a "Consensus" voting process, while the elimination of explicit objections stands as a critical prerequisite for moving a matter forward to a final decision, member states still retain the right to offer interpretations of or make reservations about the disputed aspects of the voting matter. Importantly, these interpretations or reservations do not hinder the eventual adoption of the voting matter itself. During this process, member states may naturally hold divergent views on the specific content of the resolution. To safeguard their own core interests, they often need to interpret existing differences in ways that align with their priorities and attach targeted reservations to address unmet concerns. This practice, however, virtually increases the frequency of inconsistencies in the overall content of the resolution, as each member state' s tailored interpretations and reservations introduce subtle variations in understanding—ultimately leading to ambiguity in the final resolution' s content [5]. Secondly, when analyzing the context in which voting mechanisms permit interpretations and reservations, it is essential to recognize that the principle of national sovereignty stands as one of the foundational and inviolable principles guiding international organizations. This principle explicitly allows sovereign states to offer interpretations of voting matters or attach reservations to them during the voting process. As a result, member states that choose to provide interpretations or make reservations regarding a voting matter will not be materially bound by the parts of the resolution they have questioned or qualified. In contrast, other member states that fail to explicitly declare their own interpretations or reservations will be fully bound by the terms of the resolution. This distinction in binding effects actually amplifies the generality of the resolution' s content: the text must be broad enough to accommodate potential interpretations and reservations, which in turn dilutes the specificity of its provisions and reduces the clarity of the final resolution outcome. Finally, from the practical perspective of implementation, the "Consensus" voting mechanism tends to yield outcomes that are more readily accepted by member states—precisely because these outcomes are the product of a thorough, multi-round interest game, where each party' s concerns have been (at least partially) addressed through negotiation. Nevertheless, challenges arise during the implementation phase: if an excessive number of member states choose to invoke their right to interpret the resolution, the scope of the resolution' s effective implementation will inevitably shrink. Each interpretation may narrow the application of the resolution to fit a member state' s specific circumstances, creating fragmented enforcement. This issue becomes particularly pronounced when major developed countries are involved in offering interpretations. Given their significant influence in global governance and resource capabilities, their interpretations often carry disproportionate weight—leading to situations where the implementation of the basic consensus resolution fails to deliver substantive, unified results. Instead, it plunges the implementation process into a state of ambiguity, as different interpretations clash or weaken the resolution' s core intent. In turn, this ambiguity ultimately erodes the clarity of the content of the basic consensus resolution that was initially agreed upon.

The Apparent Consistency of the Voting Results

In the face of the highly complex and ever-evolving international situation, as well as the intricate web of international relations, it is inevitable that uncontrollable factors will arise within international organizations—especially those founded by member states with diverse and often conflicting interest demands. By contrast, voting mechanisms such as "unanimity" and "majority voting" rely explicitly on the number of votes cast as the core basis for recognizing a decision. These mechanisms hold certain legal validity under international law, with clear and binding rules that leave little room for ambiguity. As a result, there are very few instances where the formal outcome of these votes conflicts with the actual intentions of participating states, meaning cases of duplicity (where words or actions contradict true intentions) are rare. However, the "Consensus" voting mechanism operates on a fundamentally different logic. Throughout its process, in addition to the primary goal of reaching collective consensus on a resolution, member states are also entitled to offer interpretations of the corresponding issues being discussed. While this right to interpret is designed to accommodate diverse perspectives and clarify potential ambiguities, it inadvertently creates a subtle "window" for member states to express implicit opposition to the resolution. Instead of openly rejecting the proposal—which would block the formation of consensus—states can use interpretations to dilute the resolution' s impact, qualify their acceptance, or even undermine its core intent, all without formally opposing it. When examining the phenomenon of "apparent consensus" (where a resolution seems to have broad support but lacks genuine unity), we can further analyze it by linking it to the inherent characteristics of the "Consensus" voting mechanism: First, due to the profound differences in economic interests between countries—particularly the gap between developed and developing nations—resolutions formulated within international organizations led by developed countries are more likely to see an increase in the probability of "apparent consensus." In practical operations, the implicit threat of resorting to a formal vote on reservations (a measure that could disrupt the consensus process) can sometimes deter non-cooperating states from abusing their potential veto power. Yet, this same dynamic can also thwart the majority of states' desire to use the consensus principle to reach a truly inclusive and effective general agreement [6]. A typical example of this occurred in 1974, when the Sixth Special Session of the United Nations General Assembly adopted the Programme of Action for the Establishment of a New International Economic Order through a consensus vote. Despite the formal adoption of the programme, the United States and several European developed countries promptly put forward interpretive reservations regarding key provisions of the action programme. These reservations ultimately rendered the adopted resolution ineffective, as they created insurmountable barriers to its practical implementation [7]. Second, when a proposed resolution touches on the interests of small, less powerful countries—interests that directly conflict with those of major power groups—countries in disadvantaged positions often have no choice but to compromise on the resolution. This phenomenon is far from an isolated case within international organizations; it is a common reality shaped by power asymmetries. Many less developed countries, when faced with a "Consensus" voting scenario, frequently opt for temporary compromises. Their decision to do so is driven by the need to avoid open conflict with influential major power groups, as such conflict could jeopardize critical practical interests—including subsequent economic aid, technical support, or preferential trade terms that are vital to their development. This choice of temporary compromise typically leads small-country groups to respond to the resolution by offering interpretations or attaching reservations. While these measures allow them to safeguard their core interests to some extent, they also inadvertently increase the probability of "apparent consensus," as the formal unity of the consensus masks the underlying dissent and dissatisfaction of the disadvantaged states. Professor Wang Junmin also points out in his research that "Consensus" voting outcomes are often not the product of the true, free expression of will of all participating countries. Instead, they are more frequently the result of tedious reconciliation processes and reluctant compromises between conflicting parties. In this dynamic, what truly shapes the final outcome are the opposing major powers or powerful country groups, while other, weaker countries are subject to the influence of these dominant pressure groups. In other words, the choices made by many countries in the consensus process are not entirely voluntary; they are often shaped by the need to align with "general consent" (a surface-level agreement driven by power dynamics) rather than their own genuine preferences [8]. On the whole, the inherent design of the "Consensus" voting mechanism makes it particularly prone to leading to superficial consistency or even falsity in voting outcomes. The core root of this dispute, however, still lies in the divergent interest demands between countries—a divide primarily caused by the long-standing unbalanced economic development across the globe. Until this fundamental imbalance is addressed, the risk of "apparent consensus" within the "Consensus" voting mechanism will remain a persistent challenge for international organizations.

1.2 Theoretical Interpretation of the Causes of the Dilemma of the "Consensus" Voting Mechanism

Based on a systematic and in-depth analysis of the dilemmas faced by the "Consensus" voting mechanism, it becomes clear that the inherent deficiencies of this mechanism stem primarily from the frequent, iterative communication and interactive exchanges between participating entities. These ongoing interactions, while essential to building understanding, often give rise to phenomena such as interest-based compromises, strategic concessions, and reciprocal exchanges of benefits—dynamic processes that, while sometimes bridging differences, also introduce inefficiencies and ambiguities. On one hand, this mode of mechanism construction, with "communication and consultation" at its very core, fully showcases the unique advantages of the "Consensus" voting mechanism. For instance, it enables the formulation of resolution matters through a fully democratized process, where every participant's voice is heard and considered; it ensures that the adoption of voting matters is far more easily accepted by all participating subjects, as their concerns are addressed through dialogue rather than imposed by a majority; and it effectively avoids the confrontational tensions that often arise among participating subjects in traditional voting systems, fostering a more cooperative decision-making atmosphere. On the other hand, this communication-centered model also lays bare the internal origin of the "Consensus" voting mechanism's deficiencies. Specifically, the dynamic cycles of communication and interaction inherently give rise to complex interest games—where participants advocate for their own priorities—alongside interest transactions and reluctant compromises. These elements, while part of the process to reach consensus, can lead to delays, superficial agreements, or unclear outcomes. Therefore, it is essential to systematically summarize and refine the theoretical paradigms that underpin the mechanism's dynamic evolution. Only by clarifying these theoretical foundations can we more effectively identify the root causes of its shortcomings and put forward targeted, practical countermeasures to optimize its operation. The core principles and key operational points involved in the "Consensus" voting system bear a close and inherent connection to Habermas' Theory of Communicative Action—a framework that emphasizes rational dialogue and mutual understanding as the basis for legitimate social decisions. During the stage of dynamic change in communication and negotiation between international subjects (such as member states of an international organization), the "Consensus" voting process intersects with three core components of Habermas' theory: the rationalization of communicative action (where interactions are guided by reason and mutual respect), the liberalization of the negotiation principle (where participants enjoy equal opportunities to express views), and the theoretical norm of consensus truth (where agreements are rooted in shared, valid reasoning). It is within the interplay of these theoretical elements that the "Consensus" voting system both manifests its distinct advantages and exposes its inherent limitations. Accordingly, this paper draws on the analytical framework of the Theory of Communicative Action to dissect and explain the underlying causes of the dilemmas faced by the "Consensus" voting mechanism.

1.2.1 High Cost of Voting Time: The Time Limit of "Rationalization of Communicative Action"

As the core and foundational idea of Jürgen Habermas' social theory, "The Rationalization of Communicative Action" primarily elaborates on the constructive interactive relationship that emerges between different subjects through effective, meaningful communication. A critical and non-negotiable standard for this kind of interaction is rationalization—this requirement mandates that the linguistic dialogue exchanged between subjects and the specific interactive behaviors they engage in must align with shared, similar standards, and this alignment is achieved through sustained, reciprocal communication between the two sides. When it comes to rational participants (whether individuals or collective entities like states), they may be willing to accept certain costs or even bear losses of specific benefits for the sake of broader cooperation. In some cases, they might even agree to a transaction that is generally disadvantageous to their own immediate interests—all on the condition that the transaction itself is widely recognized as fair, with its terms and outcomes reflecting a balance of interests rather than one-sided advantage [9]. This dynamic is clearly observable in the course of deliberations on legal resolutions within the World Trade Organization (WTO). There are instances where legal resolutions that seem unfavorable to developing countries may emerge from the negotiation process. However, these developing countries—acting as rational actors that weigh long-term interests against short-term drawbacks—will almost certainly judge such resolutions to be fair in the broader context of global trade rules. As a result, they will ratify these resolutions (or at the very least, refrain from exercising a veto to block them), thereby acknowledging the legitimacy of the content of WTO law. In other words, to achieve the overarching goal of the rationalization of communicative action, there are three primary and feasible pathways: First, engaging in dialogue through language that is appropriate and accessible to all communicating parties. This means avoiding overly technical jargon that excludes some participants or ambiguous expressions that could lead to misinterpretation, ensuring that every subject can fully understand and engage with the discussion. Second, all participating parties must recognize and voluntarily abide by a set of common norms. These norms—whether derived from international law, organizational charters, or shared ethical principles—serve as the foundation for orderly communication, preventing chaos and ensuring that interactions remain focused on resolving issues rather than escalating conflicts. Third, all parties work together to form a genuine consensus through equal dialogue and interactive exchange. This equality means that every participant' s voice carries equal weight, with no single subject dominating the conversation, and that decisions are reached through mutual understanding rather than coercion [10]. Dialogue is an inherent and unavoidable component of the "Consensus" voting system. It is not limited to conversations between international subjects that hold conflicting views on the resolution at hand; it also encompasses interactions between other international subjects that have no substantive disputes regarding the resolution. Importantly, the disputes that arise among international subjects during the consultation and voting process usually do not escalate into extreme or confrontational conflicts. Even so, the fundamental purpose of the consultation remains centered on eliminating objections—this goal serves as the guiding framework for all discussions. In this process, there are two main approaches to eliminating objections: One is the approach of coercive conquest, which relies on power or pressure to force opposing parties to concede. This dialogue model between conflicting subjects carries a certain degree of coercive effect; its only advantage is that it can quickly achieve a formal, surface-level "consensus," even if that consensus lacks genuine acceptance from all parties. The other is the approach of compromising reconciliation, which focuses on mutual accommodation and give-and-take. This approach not only addresses disputes between the directly conflicting international subjects but also includes other participants who are not part of the core conflict. These non-conflicting international subjects are primarily the entities that need to be consulted when making interest concessions and compromises—their input ensures that the final agreement does not overlook broader interests. Only after completing this consultation stage can a truly inclusive and authentic consensus be achieved. For any opinion where no final agreement is reached but no explicit objection is raised, participants may further offer explanations or attach reservations to clarify their positions. After the above-mentioned pathways to rationalization are implemented, the subjects of international organizations still need to further elevate and refine the rationalization of their communicative behaviors by recognizing and complying with common norms. The elevation at this stage is mainly manifested in the rational recognition of the content of the resolution matters (i.e., understanding and accepting the logic and purpose behind the resolution) and voluntary compliance with its provisions (i.e., committing to implementing the resolution in good faith). From the perspective of deductive reasoning, the necessary and sufficient condition for the conclusion of "communicative rationality in recognition and compliance" to be valid is that both the major premise and the minor premise are true. Specifically, this means that international subjects must have reached the rational stage of communicative behavior throughout the entire process of the emergence and development of the resolution matters. The "Consensus" voting system, from the very initial stage of addressing the resolution issue, is already immersed in a process of continuous, rational interaction—every discussion, adjustment, and compromise is guided by the goal of achieving a reasonable and acceptable outcome. These legal formal elements (such as the requirement for rational dialogue and compliance with norms) are by no means the product of a brief, intuitive, or perceptual cognitive process. Instead, they are the result of a thorough and multi-round game between subjects with diverse interest demands—each party advocates for its own priorities, adjusts its positions, and seeks a balance that can be accepted by all. Therefore, the final conclusion of the "Consensus" voting process must inherently possess communicative rationality, and the "Consensus" voting system itself can also be regarded as the legal manifestation of the product of communicative rationality. The key value and utility of this system lie in the legitimacy it bestows upon decision-making results: because the resolution is reached through rational dialogue and broad consultation, it is more likely to be recognized as legitimate by all participants. Although the decision-making process associated with this system often takes a long time—due to the need for repeated discussions and compromises—there is a positive correlation between this time investment and the legitimacy of the outcome: the more thorough the consultation, the stronger the legitimacy of the final resolution [11]. Therefore, rational participants in international organizations must carefully weigh and consider the time constraints throughout the entire process. The inclusion of these time costs in the voting process is certainly not a hasty, overnight conclusion; instead, it requires repeated negotiations that are as meticulous as "peeling a cocoon to draw out the thread"—gradually narrowing differences and refining agreements. As a result, the concluding observations related to the voting matter are inevitably influenced by the theoretical paradigm of "Communicative Rationalization," leading to the characteristic of delay in the decision-making process.

1.2.2 The Voting Content Is Not Clear: The Discussion Mechanism of the "Negotiation Principle" Is Constrained

The original purpose behind Jürgen Habermas' introduction of the Discourse Principle was to derive the core content of the Democratic Principle through the institutionalization of legal forms—translating abstract democratic ideals into concrete, rule-bound systems. In turn, the connotation of the Democratic Principle further endows the legislative process with the inherent power to shape and establish legitimacy: laws and resolutions crafted through democratic procedures are more readily recognized as authoritative and binding by the public or participating entities [12]. This theoretical framework offers a substantive-level summary of the power logic origin of the Democratic Principle. Specifically, when tracing the roots and evolution of the Democratic Principle, the overlapping and mutual reinforcement of the Discourse Principle and legal forms emerge as its primary result-oriented goal. This means that democratic values can only be fully realized when rational dialogue (the core of the Discourse Principle) is embedded within formal legal structures. A similar logic applies to the stage of state formation: a state founded on democratic principles typically requires a relatively unified and coherent social governance mechanism. This is because in pluralist societies—societies that are sharply divided into nearly independent sub-societies, each with distinct values, interests, and identities—the flexibility essential to sustaining democracy may be lost. In such fragmented contexts, majority rule not only fails to embody democratic ideals but also poses inherent dangers. Minority groups that are consistently denied political power and marginalized will inevitably feel excluded and discriminated against; worse still, when they are unable to advocate for and realize their legitimate interests through existing negotiation mechanisms, they may gradually lose their sense of loyalty to the ruling regime, threatening social stability [13]. Therefore, the Negotiation Principle (a practical manifestation of the Discourse Principle) serves as an indispensable and necessary stage in the realization of the Democratic Principle. It acts as a bridge between diverse interests, ensuring that even minority voices are heard and considered. Within the content scope of the Discourse Principle, three key aspects of critical information stand out: First, within the framework of the Discourse Principle, the formation of collective opinions and shared wills can only be achieved through the equal participation of all subjects. Every participant must be granted equal opportunities to engage in dialogue, express views, and influence decisions—this equality is the foundation for safeguarding political autonomy (the right of each subject to shape collective outcomes) and ensuring the legalization of decisions (the process of rendering outcomes formally binding). Second, in the process of internalizing the Discourse Principle—i.e., integrating its values into daily decision-making—each subject is able to exercise their equal rights to freedom to the greatest extent possible. This freedom includes the right to articulate personal opinions, defend individual interests, and challenge existing viewpoints, all without fear of coercion or exclusion. Third, the Discourse

Principle also provides a clear interpretation of citizens' basic rights from the perspective of legal protection. It not only defines the scope and content of these rights but also offers specific, enforceable legal guarantees in the essential fields covered by civil rights—such as freedom of speech, equality before the law, and the right to participate in public affairs. For the key information outlined above, the "Consensus" voting system demonstrates a high degree of compatibility at the content level: First, the "Consensus" voting system guarantees equal opportunities for all international subjects to express their views on the matter at hand. As long as clear objections are eliminated through continuous, constructive exchanges of views, a valid consensus can be formed. This core procedural mechanism—centered on inclusive dialogue and objection resolution—can be succinctly summarized as a "discussion mechanism." In specific negotiation processes, when international subjects participating in the voting face controversial focal points, they are not forced to adhere to the rigid framework of traditional voting systems (which often prioritize the interests of the majority while ignoring the minority). Instead, the "Consensus" system encourages the consideration of all interests, ensuring that the concerns of even a small number of countries are not overlooked. Second, the primary theoretical basis of the "Consensus" voting system lies in the pursuit of shared interests among participating subjects. This focus on common ground ensures that subjects within international organizations can exercise their rights on an equal basis while maximizing their freedom of will—each party can advocate for its own interests without being overshadowed by more powerful entities. Meanwhile, resolutions negotiated and adopted under this system also possess practical operational and enforcement value: since they reflect the balanced interests of all participants, they are more likely to be voluntarily implemented by member states. Third, the "Consensus" voting system allows international subjects to offer interpretations of or attach reservations to voting matters. This provision is not only a flexible safeguard of rights but also essentially returns the right of active choice to the international subjects themselves. Beyond excluding explicit objections to ensure consensus, the system grants participants selective legal rights—such as the right to qualify their acceptance of a resolution through reservations. This design is a concrete legal guarantee rooted in the full respect for the free will of each subject.

In general, the ambiguity inherent in the "Consensus" voting mechanism bears a close and inherent connection to the discussion mechanism within the "Discourse Principle" theory. Although subjects with divergent interests may be unable to reach a final, comprehensive consensus through consultation alone, they can still form a valid voting conclusion by means of interpretations or reservations. This very flexibility—while a strength in terms of inclusivity—undoubtedly becomes a key source of ambiguity in the system. This dynamic is evident in the practice of voting on legal resolutions within the European Union (EU). When member states encounter conflicts of fundamental interests, and no consensus can be reached (nor any realistic expectation of reaching consensus in a specific area), the disputed issue is often separated from the EU' s collective decision-making process and returned to the individual member states for independent negotiation [14]. This approach aligns precisely with the deliberative mechanism advocated by the "Discourse Principle" theory: dialogue between subjects must be based on equal opportunities. However, this emphasis on equality also overlooks the inherent limits of equality in inter-subject dialogue—i.e., equality of opportunity cannot be absolute; it requires a reasonable scope or "interval" that accounts for differences in power, resources, and interests. In practical operations, the judgment of this reasonable interval is constrained by the degree of freedom that voting subjects have to make interest concessions and compromises during discussions. Due to the subjective nature of interest assessment and the complexity of power dynamics, this interval cannot be clearly defined or uniformly interpreted. As a result, each voting participant tends to prioritize the maximization of their own interests as the primary standard in negotiations. Even though they may make certain concessions and compromises during the dialogue process, they still retain the right to offer interpretations of or attach reservations to the resolution matters at hand. This practice, while protecting individual interests, also becomes a direct cause of the uncertainty surrounding voting outcomes in the "Consensus" system.

1.2.3 The Consistency of Representation: The Limitation of the Validity of the Speech of the Theory of consensus Truth

Within the operational framework of the "Consensus" voting system, if a final, binding consensus is to be achieved among all participating entities, the theoretical foundation that applies most fittingly is the Theory of Consensus Truth. According to this foundational theory, "truth" (in the context of collective decision-making) refers to a specific type of "validity claim" embedded in interpersonal linguistic communication—it is essentially the claim of authenticity that accompanies descriptive speech acts, where statements are expected to align with shared facts, logical reasoning, or mutually accepted values. When analyzing the "Consensus" voting system through the lens of this theory, it becomes clear that there exists an inherent, interconnected relationship between the two in the substantive decision-making process. On one hand, when an international subject (such as a member state of an international organization) puts forward a position on a specific issue, this stance tends to resonate with and attract the support of other international subjects that hold similar views or share overlapping interests—gradually forming a collective consensus view that transcends individual positions. On the other hand, for any international body that adopts the "Consensus" voting system, the minimum and non-negotiable requirement for a resolution to be formally adopted is the complete elimination of explicit objections. This means that even if most subjects agree, a single unresolved objection can block the formation of a valid consensus. A notable example of this dynamic is the General Agreement on Tariffs and Trade (GATT)—the direct predecessor of the World Trade Organization (WTO). The GATT' s entire institutional framework and operational logic were built on a foundation of substantive, continuous basic consensus among its member states. This consensus ensured that its trade rules and dispute-solving mechanisms could function smoothly over decades, laying the groundwork for the modern global trade system [15]. In terms of linguistic form—the medium through which consensus is built—the internal international subjects involved in the "Consensus" voting system must engage in sincere exchanges of opinions or provide authentic, unambiguous interpretations of their positions. These linguistic interactions are not mere formalities; they are the driving force that propels the negotiation process forward and ultimately leads to the final resolution result. Just as the truth of a logical proposition is conveyed to the listener through active listening, clear statement, and valid reasoning, the "truth" (or legitimacy) of a position in a "Consensus" vote must also be communicated through genuine, effective language. For subjects that hold different standards or conflicting views on the matter at hand, they must use transparent, evidence-based language to explain their perspectives to others, supplementing their arguments with corresponding reasons (such as legal principles, interest considerations, or practical feasibility). Only when the listener fully understands and no longer holds objections to the view can the core criterion for reaching consensus be met. Moreover, this kind of consensus must also satisfy the condition of "rationality"—it cannot be the product of coercion, emotional impulse, or superficial compromise. Specifically, under the premise of pursuing consensus, international subjects are expected to conduct in-depth, critical thinking about the issue at hand: they should look beyond superficial appearances to raise reasonable doubts about existing positions, feedback these doubts to the subject that put forward the view, and then the original speaker must respond with real, valid reasons to address the concerns. This cycle of questioning, feedback, and response continues to deepen and refine the dialogue, ultimately promoting both sides to reach a consistent, rational consensus through this ongoing cycle of verbal exchange and critical reflection. Another key reason for the emergence of the Theory of Consensus Truth lies in its role as a response to the inherent defects of the Correspondence Theory of Truth—a traditional theory that defines truth as the correspondence between a statement and an objective reality. Habermas, a leading proponent of the Theory of Consensus Truth, argues that the Correspondence Theory of Truth suffers from three major flaws: first, it creates an artificial duality between the "real world" (objective facts) and the "linguistic world" (human expressions of those facts), ignoring the role of language in shaping how we perceive reality; second, it assumes that the "subject of judgment" (the person or entity making a truth claim) can stand outside of reality to make an objective judgment—a position that is philosophically untenable; third, it insists on the "identity of propositional statements," assuming that a statement can have only one true meaning, which fails to account for the ambiguity and context-dependence of language [16]. These three flaws all lead to the fragmentation of rational consensus: they make it impossible for different subjects to reach a shared understanding of "truth" through dialogue. In fact, this limitation of the Correspondence Theory of Truth indirectly confirms the advantages of the Theory of Consensus Truth—its ability to bridge differences through inclusive, rational communication. When applied specifically to the "Consensus" voting system, the Correspondence Theory of Truth essentially represents a potential form of "non-consensus." Under this theoretical framework, international actors could, in theory, pass a resolution without reaching a genuine collective consensus—for example, by relying on majority voting to impose a decision that aligns with an "objective truth" (as defined by the majority). However, this approach is fraught with risks: it is likely to lead to a dual phenomenon where the resolution' s conceptual goals conflict with practical implementation difficulties (since minority subjects may resist implementation); it makes it hard to maintain a neutral, impartial judgment model (as the majority' s definition of "truth" may dominate); and it can trigger self-limiting independent identity problems (minority subjects may feel marginalized and assert their distinct identities to resist the resolution). These issues are direct manifestations of the three flaws of the Correspondence Theory of Truth in practical decision-making. In contrast, the guiding role of the Theory of Consensus Truth endows the "Consensus" voting system with the maximum degree of democracy. Before a final decision is formed among voting participants, the system requires full, inclusive consultation, careful balance of conflicting interests, and reciprocal exchange of benefits—ensuring that the adopted voting matters reflect the collective will of all subjects, not just the powerful or the majority. On the flip side, however, the adoption of resolutions between different interest subjects is also constrained by the Theory of Consensus Truth. Since the theory requires genuine, universal agreement, it becomes difficult to reach a resolution if subjects cannot form a completely unanimous conclusion. As scholar Jackson points out: "When one country supports a decision that serves its own narrow interests rather than the common interests of all countries, other countries will inevitably unite to form a consensus to oppose it." [17] In other words, the consensus reached by participants in the voting process may not be absolute; it can also accommodate alternative interpretations or targeted reservations, as long as a formal, surface-level agreement is achieved. Even after going through full democratic consultation, the subject participating in the voting still retains the right to explain or reserve its core interests—all in the pursuit of maximizing its own interests. Yet, the Theory of Consensus Truth imposes a critical constraint: it requires that all linguistic expressions (including interpretations and reservations) must meet the standard of "real validity." This requirement limits the participants' ability to express their inner will freely—they cannot make arbitrary claims or false justifications. As a result, making flexible interpretations or offering reserved concessions has become the optimal way for subjects to balance the need for consensus with the protection of their own interests. Unfortunately, this very practice has also become the fundamental root cause of the "apparent consistency" of voting results—where the formal consensus masks underlying differences and unresolved conflicts.

1.3 Countermeasures to the "Consensus" Voting Mechanism

In the analysis and deconstruction of the "Consensus" voting mechanism, we can analyze this new voting mechanism in depth more comprehensively, however, the main reason for the use of the system is still to maximize the advantages of the system. How to put forward the corresponding countermeasures through the above analysis is the key to determine the development trend of "Consensus" voting mechanism in international organizations in the future. In order to overcome the shortcomings of the "Consensus" voting mechanism, we can improve it from the following aspects.

1.3.1 "Common Interests" Should be Taken as the Criterion for Member States to Participate in the Voting

As a key indicator to measure the efficiency of decision-making in international organizations, if there are different views on the interests represented by member states, it will inevitably lead to an increase in the time cost of decision-making, the result is the ambiguity of decision-making objectives. Therefore, following the screening rule of "Common interest appeal" can enhance the decision-making efficiency of international organizations and clarify the resolution matters. This rule can also be called "Concentric Zone Model" [18]. The model was originally created by Burgess and used to study the layout of the functional areas within the city and the invasion and inheritance between functions. The scholar Blackhurst developed this theory and used it to study the institutional functioning of WTO consultations and negotiation groups. In addition, this model also has an important reference for the establishment of international organizations based on the principle of "Common interest appeal", gradually spreading outwards and constantly identifying and including new members with the same objectives, thereby reducing the degree of disagreement on matters to be voted on, in order to more effectively solve the "Consensus" voting mechanism prone to high time cost and uncertainty. In the process of specific consultations and deliberations, the time cost of voting is often high in the situation where the interests do not reach basic agreement, that is, when the resolution matters of specific international organizations are in progress, there are still voting participants who hold opposing opinions, which is an important basis for affecting the efficiency of voting results. The reason why the voting system has some advantages in the efficiency of the results is also the benefit of the principle of "The minority is subordinate to the majority". According to the analysis of "Consensus theory", under the condition of democratic consultation, voting system is lack of substantive legitimacy compared with "Consensus" voting, that is to say, voting system can not make all international subjects reach a consensus on the acceptance and recognition of the resolution matters, and it only meets the conditions on the formal legitimacy of the formulation process. On the other hand, the "Consensus" voting mechanism can meet the conditions of substantive legitimacy on the basis of formal legitimacy. However, the satisfaction of substantive legality was achieved in exchange for a lengthy and complex voting process that did not address the issues addressed in the resolution in a prompt and effective manner. Therefore, in order to solve the problem of long-delayed timeliness and improve the efficiency of voting under the framework of "Consensus" voting mechanism, we must start from the root to avoid the drawbacks of voting. Therefore, it is necessary to add purposive norms in the result-oriented "Consensus" voting mechanism by means of causal inversion, that is, through the establishment of "Concentric circles" model of the "Community of interest demands" international organizations, to reduce the impact of subject to time costs. Its essence is to establish common core values in the area of shared interests [19]. The criteria for the inclusion of member states adopted by most of today' s regional international organizations all have similar or similar interest demands, and on this basis, the rules of procedure for consultation have been established as the main voting mechanism, the most typical case is the establishment of the Shanghai Cooperation Organization, which has established the principle of solving all problems through mutual consultation. The establishment of the Shanghai Cooperation Organization also highlights the essence of "Cooperation", and strives to promote the steady economic development of member states in regional development. At the same time, the organization also stipulates the identification of the organizational philosophy and the purpose of consensus in the requirements of membership. All of the above-mentioned processes demonstrate an innovative model for overcoming the high time cost of voting. As long as the interests of one member state are harmed, the result of the resolution can not be adopted between member states holding similar interest claims [20]. Therefore, the content certainty is guaranteed in the operation of the system. These characteristics also avoid from the side of the international organizations in the application of the "Consensus" voting system arising in the resolution of the matter is not clear.

In the context of the global trend toward multi-polarization and the ongoing reform of regional integration, international organizations, while conforming to this broader international backdrop, find it necessary to increasingly adopt the "Consensus" voting mechanism as their primary rule of procedure. However, to overcome the challenges of high time costs and uncertainties inherent in the negotiation process, it is essential to address the root cause of these issues. A key step in this direction lies in the selection of international subjects during the establishment of such organizations: the selection must be grounded in the "Common Interest Perspective." This ensures that member states share foundational interests, laying the groundwork for the efficient and clear adoption of resolution matters. Some scholars refer to this shared foundation as "the common interests of the international community"—defined as the general interests essential for the survival and development of the international community that transcends the boundaries of individual sovereign states [21]. Under the framework that fully upholds the principle of sovereign equality, participants in international organizations are encouraged to make every effort to identify points of interest convergence. By focusing on these shared interests, they can more quickly reach consensus following democratic consultation. The process of gradually identifying common ground amid interest-based negotiations—ultimately leading to compromise and consensus—will also serve as an important basis for the future implementation of resolutions. In this way, participants will be better able to accept and recognize one another' s positions, and the formation of clear, unified opinions to guide efficient completion of resolution matters will become a normalized mechanism within international organizations.

1.3.2 Follow the Negotiation Method of "Whether to Realize the Optimization of Interests" to Measure the Resolution Items

In view of the lack of genuine consistency in resolution matters—often manifesting as mere "apparent consistency"—the root cause lies with the stakeholders involved in voting matters. While these stakeholders can render a resolution effective by avoiding formal objections, this outcome amounts to no more than an agreement to eliminate explicit dissent, rather than a sincere, comprehensive consensus. Due to the persistent imbalance in economic development across countries, nations still prioritize maximizing their own interests as the primary criterion when pursuing goals. Compounding this, the "Consensus" voting mechanism permits interpretations and reservations, which in practice provide voting participants with superficial room for compromise. Even after subsequent resolutions are negotiated and adopted, they remain ineffective for the participants that have made reservations—these entities are not bound by terms they have qualified. Since interpretation is inherently a continuation of the "consultation" process and does not alter the final vote outcome, this dynamic is particularly evident when developed country participants (as mentioned earlier) make reservations. In such cases, the resolution' s adoption only achieves the effect of formal "unanimity," lacking substantive unity. To address this, it is essential to explore new rules that minimize the risks of such apparent unanimity. Drawing on Habermas' "Discourse Principle," subjects can only find a mutually recognized balance point—and thus a threshold for maximizing interests—through continuous dialogue conducted on the basis of equal opportunities. Within game theory, there exists a pivotal theorem known as the Pareto Efficiency Rule, which emphasizes the practical optimization of interests. In a unanimity voting system, a valid outcome must leave all countries in a better position than they were previously—and this outcome stands as a key manifestation of Pareto superiority [22]. It is widely accepted that in economic interactions, a "win-win" goal is achieved when all parties secure the maximum possible benefits. However, this goal has a critical threshold: once this peak is crossed, further pursuit of gain for one party will harm the other. This aligns with what scholar Bacchus terms the "Bicycle Theory," which states: "If protectionist pressures accumulate and the world fails to move steadily toward freer trade, the global trading system will topple and collapse." [23] Both the Pareto Efficiency Rule and the Bicycle Theory leverage the maximum potential of resource allocation, ensuring that resources are optimized to achieve the best interest distribution before reaching a peak beyond which decline begins. Introducing the "Pareto Efficiency Criterion" into the "Consensus" voting mechanism thus offers dual benefits: it not only enables the optimal allocation of interests among participants but also minimizes the risk of superficial negotiations that lack genuine commitment. The application of this negotiation approach can be outlined as follows: First, within the framework of the Discourse Principle, participants engage in multiple rounds of dialogue and interest-based games to identify the critical point of Pareto efficiency—the peak at which interests are maximized for all. Second, each participant integrates diverse interest factors to reach a consensus, and this consensus must represent the best possible plan for realizing the interests of every participant. This aligns with the concept of "tacit consent" as defined by scholar Robert Berger in his work: for routine, largely uncontroversial, or low-priority matters, tacit approval is adopted to enhance efficiency [24]. Finally, the application of this rule is verified against the "Pareto Efficiency Criterion" to form a final conclusion. The key condition for validating this conclusion is whether participants can achieve a result of substantive interest maximization. If every participant secures optimal interest allocation within the scope of this rule, the risk of superficial consensus is eliminated, and benefits can truly extend to all involved. The Shanghai Cooperation Organization (SCO), from its very establishment, has fully embodied the outcomes of interest optimization. Its core purpose—maintaining regional security and peace to combat terrorism, separatism, and extremism, while striving to build a regional national security alliance—ensures that no apparent consistency arises during the application of the "Consensus" voting process. The reason for this lies in the fact that the matters under negotiation align with the maximum security interests of all participating states, fostering genuine unity. Beyond the SCO, other professional international organizations—such as the International Committee of the Red Cross, the International Union Against Cancer, and the World Meteorological Organization—also embody resolution rules centered on interest optimization. The establishment of these organizations not only reflects specialized focus but also achieves optimal resource allocation, thereby avoiding the problem of resolutions failing to be truly implemented due to superficial consensus.

1.3.3 Apply the Dual" Consensus Truth Theory" to Clarify the Content of the Vote

The ambiguity inherent in the "Consensus" voting mechanism stems from two key, distinct factors that collectively undermine the clarity and certainty of its outcomes. First, unlike the well-defined "majority rule" in traditional voting systems—where the final outcome and its core, non-negotiable content are clearly articulated and confirmed during the formal voting process—the agreements reached through "Consensus" voting often lack such explicit clarity in their formation phase, leaving room for varying interpretations of key provisions. Second, the mechanism explicitly permits voting subjects (i.e., member states or participating entities of an international organization) to make corresponding legal interpretations and formal reservations regarding the adopted resolutions; this common practice significantly diminishes the practical enforceability and operational value of the resolution' s substantive content and directly gives rise to the problematic phenomenon widely referred to as "consensus confusion." Consequently, it inadvertently provides convenient loopholes for participants who propose such interpretations or reservations to obscure the original, intended true intent of the resolution, thereby weakening its effectiveness. Among these two interrelated factors, the second one remains the most critical and impactful driver of ambiguity within the consensus mechanism, as it directly affects the post-adoption implementation of resolutions. To proactively address this pressing issue, it is essential to foster a unified, coherent opinion among all participants who have made interpretations or reservations regarding the resolution. Specifically, this requires re-applying the established consensus-based consultation rules—consistent with those used in the initial resolution-forming process—to achieve a shared, mutually acceptable viewpoint even under the conditions of existing interpretations or reservations—a deliberate process that transitions participants from fragmented, individual positions to collective, unified agreement. The application of these specific, rule-based procedures can be divided into two distinct, sequential levels, each with a clear objective: At the first level, focused primarily on participants who have not made any interpretations or reservations regarding the resolution, consensus is reached through in-depth, issue-specific negotiations, reciprocal exchanges of interests, and voluntary concessions on non-core matters. This structured process ensures that this group of participants fully aligns on the core, fundamental content of the resolution, eliminating potential disagreements among non-reserving members. Subsequently, at the second level, targeted efforts are made to build internal consensus among participants who have formally put forward interpretations or reservations. However, these participants are often driven by the goal of maximizing their own legitimate national or organizational interests, which inherently complicates the consensus-building process and may lead to prolonged negotiations. To effectively navigate this challenge, a "reverse exclusion rule" should be formally adopted to clearly define and clarify the minimum interest demands that each participating subject can reasonably accept without compromising their essential priorities. This proposed approach bears notable similarity to the well-established "reverse consensus" mechanism utilized by the World Trade Organization (WTO) in its dispute settlement and rule-making processes: in all matters involving interpretations or reservations, the relevant parties engage in good-faith consultation, open exchange of views, and voluntary concessions of non-essential interests. The overarching end goal is to finalize resolution content to which no party with an interpretation or reservation has explicitly objected—either formally or informally—and this mutually agreed content is then formally recognized as the internal consensus for this specific level of negotiation. The combination of these two structured, sequential processes constitutes the dual rule framework of the "Consensus Theory of Truth," which serves as the theoretical basis for resolving ambiguity. The final outcome of this comprehensive consultation process—unified, unreserved consensus among all participants, both those with and without prior interpretations or reservations—should serve as the formal concluding link in the overall resolution-forming process, ensuring the resolution's clarity and enforceability. Given the inherent existence of exceptions or reservations within the "Consensus" voting mechanism, and to proactively reduce the diversity and complexity of reservations embedded in the resolution' s final content, it is necessary for all parties involved in making interpretations or reservations to reach additional, supplementary consensus through further targeted consultation. This critical step is indispensable to minimizing the risk of ambiguity in the resolution' s substantive content and enhancing its practical effectiveness in implementation.

In the process of applying the dual "Consensus Theory of Truth," a key accompanying effect is the gradual improvement of trust between participating entities. Once the first stage of consensus-building begins, participants can work together to identify a balanced solution to the core issue—this initial alignment lays the groundwork for mutual understanding. On this basis, further efforts to deepen consensus can strengthen the mutual confidence that all participants place in the final resolution outcome, and this enhanced trust, in turn, helps improve the clarity of the voting matters themselves. The role of "consensus" as a confidence-building measure is closely tied to the concept of free will. As Rousseau famously stated, freedom lies in obeying "la loi qu'on s'est prescrite" (the law one prescribes for oneself)—meaning that true autonomy comes from adhering to rules one has voluntarily agreed to [25]. The "Consensus" voting mechanism embodies this idea: it fully solicits and listens to member states' suggestions on how to implement the resolution, allowing countries to naturally forge a bond of trust through inclusive dialogue. Additionally, it provides sufficient time for all participants to familiarize themselves with the specific content of the resolution, thereby building a bridge of trust between each entity and the voting matters at hand. This dynamic is clearly reflected in the World Trade Organization (WTO): WTO decisions primarily rely on the "Consensus" voting mechanism, and since these decisions are mostly collections of economic policies and legal norms—documents that require strict compliance—internal consensus is not just important, but essential. To ensure the effectiveness of a resolution, its guiding principles must be accepted by all member states. This means that even after an initial internal consensus is reached, specific details of the issue still need to be revisited and discussed in a subsequent consensus stage. Crucially, these decisions cannot be imposed through heteronomous resolutions dominated by certain forces; they must retain a degree of autonomy, with every participant having a say in the final outcome. These requirements align perfectly with the core purpose of "consensus" itself. Through this kind of participatory autonomy, the level of trust between international subjects can be enhanced at the level of will autonomy—each entity feels its voice is respected, and its interests are considered. This not only brings greater clarity to the voting matters (as trust reduces the need for ambiguous interpretations or reservations) but also plays a positive role in boosting effective compliance with the resolution after it is adopted: when countries voluntarily agree to a decision, they are far more likely to implement it sincerely.

1.3.4 Establishing a "Consultative Representation System" to Improve the Efficiency of the Adoption and Implementation of Resolutions

To avoid the high time costs inherent in the "Consensus" voting system and the negative impact these costs exert on the voting process, it is imperative to introduce a practical and effective mechanism to enhance voting efficiency. Posner and Sykes, in their academic paper, put forward a notable hypothesis: the weaknesses of international organizations do not stem (or do not entirely stem) from the anarchy of international relations, mutual distrust between states, or power-related considerations. Instead, the core flaw lies in the lack of a system capable of reliably translating the hidden preferences of states—their unspoken interests or priorities—into tangible, effective outcomes [26]. Furthermore, the paper clarifies that one way to achieve such effective outcomes under a voting mechanism is through a strategic approach: subjects with the most intense interest conflicts may "purchase" the votes of subjects less directly involved in the dispute. This transactional dynamic ultimately evolves into a final vote contest game, where competing interests vie for numerical advantage. Drawing inspiration from this insight, we can pose a thought-provoking question: Is it feasible to establish a "Consultative Representation System" within the framework of the "Consensus" voting mechanism to address long-pending, unresolved issues? From Habermas' theoretical perspective, concepts such as "the rationalization of communicative action," "the Discourse Principle," and "the Theory of Consensus Truth" all serve as practical pathways to solve real-world problems. Similarly, international law itself is inherently a problem-solving process, designed to resolve conflicts and coordinate interests among states [27]. From the perspective of essential attributes, the ability to solve problems efficiently represents the closest link between theory and practice. Thus, the establishment of a "Consultative Representation System" can leverage the opportunity of consultation to identify representative entities that stand for the interests of the majority of participants. These representatives then engage in efficient consultations with representatives of other interest groups, focusing on resolving the most prominent differences or conflicting interest demands. This targeted approach allows for the rapid fulfillment of the conditions required for formal consensus, creating a favorable environment for the eventual formation of effective negotiation outcomes. Crucially, this system retains the core features of the "Consensus" mechanism: it still requires the elimination of explicit objections and permits interpretations or reservations on resolution matters. However, a key transformation occurs: the original decentralized consultation structure—where every participant engages directly—evolves into a centralized consultation model led by representatives. As a result, the focus of disputes becomes more concrete and focused, and the formation of the final consensus conclusion grows increasingly clear, with stronger enforceability in practice. In the application of the "Consultative Representation" rule, the primary task to address is the classification of demands among participants. This involves grouping participants with identical or highly similar demands into the same interest group. From each group, a representative entity is then selected through an internal consultative process. A key point to clarify during this selection is the number of distinct demand groups, as this figure serves as an important indicator of how efficiently the matter can be adopted. Through direct interaction between the elected representatives, the time-cost barrier imposed by the original "Consensus" voting mechanism—where large numbers of participants slow down dialogue—can be significantly reduced. Finally, when representatives clarify their views on the voting matters, the number of participating entities is minimized to the core group of representatives. This means the time spent on exchanging interests and making compromises to resolve key sticking points is drastically reduced. In turn, the efficiency of reaching a consensus vote is significantly higher compared to the initial stage when the "Consultative Representation System" was not in place.

Stark, a renowned scholar in the field of international law, has explicitly pointed out: "Recent voting systems within the international community have, to a certain extent, tended to reflect the power dynamics and interest demands of those states—states that are particularly affected by the activities of international organizations, or upon which the effective implementation of these organizations' resolutions ultimately depends." [28] Among all the challenges faced by international organizations, the implementation phase of resolutions stands out as the most critical. Given that resolutions adopted by international organizations often rely on self-execution (with no centralized enforcement authority to compel compliance), a key dynamic emerges: the more states are able to participate equally in establishing the rules contained in these resolutions, the more consciously they will abide by and implement those rules. This is because equal participation fosters a sense of ownership, making states more willing to honor commitments they helped shape [29]. As discussed earlier, the establishment of a "Consultative Representation System" is designed to address the core interest games among key participants. By taking democratic consultation as its cornerstone, this system helps reach a stable basic consensus while effectively cutting down on the time wasted in scattered, unfocused negotiations. In the face of complex and ever-shifting international relations, international organizations have long struggled to find effective solutions for the implementation of their resolutions. This difficulty becomes particularly pronounced when resolutions touch on the real, tangible interests of member states. The root cause of this implementation gap lies in the fact that interest conflicts during the resolution' s formation phase were not fully reconciled—unresolved tensions resurface later, undermining compliance. The "Consultative Representation System" directly addresses this by proactively arranging for interest coordination at the very stage of resolution formulation. By converging fragmented demands into clear, focused interest priorities, the system enhances the efficiency of the voting mechanism itself. And as the legitimacy and acceptability of resolutions are strengthened through this coordinated interest alignment, the efficiency of their subsequent implementation is also significantly improved.

Under the influence of the "Global South", countries try to form different regional organizations to achieve close solidarity and unity. How can these united regional organizations play a role in improving the efficiency of decision-making among countries? I believe that through the demonstration of "Consensus" voting system, we will see the advantages and disadvantages of this system. Although there are some shortcomings in the "Consensus" voting system, this system can allow each country to fully express its own views in the implementation process, which is conducive to the unity between countries, ensure the smooth implementation of decisions. In legal practice, it is necessary to minimize the drawbacks brought about by the high inherent time cost of law, and to conform to the trend of social development through the renewal of ideas and systems. International law should be the "Pioneer", which represents not only the adjustment of the domestic legal system, but more importantly the result of the profound impact of globalization. The evolution of the voting system of international organizations from the development of the traditional voting system to today' s new method of "Consensus" voting is not only an innovation of the system, behind it is the new trend of international relations brought about by globalization. The WTO and the European Union, for example, agree on the legality of applying a "Consensus" vote [30]. International cooperation is increasingly becoming a national vision, and its strengthening depends on a platform where countries can engage in constant negotiation and consensus-building on key issues, furthermore, they can deepen the acquaintance and understanding of each other, promote the establishment of trust mechanism, and finally form effective resolutions of international law and guide the practice. The above process is the core step of consensus voting. I believe that with the deepening of globalization, in solving the problems brought about by globalization, deepening the cooperation and exchanges between the forces of the "Global South", and establishing a long-term mutual consultation and trust mechanism through the concept of "A community of shared future for mankind", the "Consensus" voting model will certainly play its important value function.

References

1. Pedersen PN (2006) The WTO decision-making process and internal transparency. World Trade Rev 5(1):103
2. Jackson JH (1998) Designing and implementing effective dispute settlement procedures: WTO dispute settlement, appraisal and prospects. In: Krueger AO (ed) The WTO as an international organization. The University of Chicago Press, Chicago, pp 161–180
3. Steinberg RH (2002) In the shadow of law or power? Consensus-based bargaining and outcomes in the GATT/WTO. Int Organ 56(2):339
4. Carreau D, Juillard P (2005) Droit International Economique, 2nd edn. Dalloz, Paris, p 225
5. Zhengchao W (1988) On the 'consensus' system. Law Polit 6:43
6. Szaz P (1979) Improving the international legislative process. Georgia J Int Comp Law 9:519–533
7. Huikang H (1984) Voting systems in modern international organizations. Soc Sci 6:49
8. Junmin W (1998) The principle of consensus in international conferences and international organizations. Foreign Law Rev 3:95
9. Howse R (Undated) How to begin to think about the "Democratic Deficit" at the WTO'. pp 4–12. Accessed 28 May 2008

10. Hanjian Y (2016) Habermas's theory of communicative action and its implications for handling international relations. Jiangnan Forum 5:22
11. Nettesheim M (2004) Decision-making in the EU: identity, efficiency and democratic legitimacy. Eur Rev Public Law 16(1):197
12. Habermas J (Germany) (2003) Between facts and norms: contributions to a discourse theory of law and democracy (trans: Tong Shijun). SDX Joint Publishing Company, Beijing, p 122
13. Lijphart A (1999) Patterns of democracy. Yale University Press, New Haven, pp 32–33
14. Scharpf, F. W. (1997). Demokratische Politik in Europa. In: Hesse, J. J., Jochimsen, R., & Scharpf, F. W. (eds) Staatswissenschaften und Staatspraxis: Festschrift für Dieter Grimm. Baden-Baden: Nomos Verlagsgesellschaft, pp. 87–88.
15. Jackson JH (1967) The puzzle of GATT: legal aspects of a surprising institution. J World Trade Law 1(2):138
16. Zhidan L (2012) Habermas's consensus theory of truth. Guangxi Soc Sci 8:45
17. Jackson JH (2001) The WTO "constitution" and proposed reforms: seven 'mantras' revisited. J Int Econ Law 4(1):74
18. Blackhurst R (2000) Reforming WTO Decision Making: Lessons from Singapore and Seattle, Working Paper No. 63. Center for Research on Economic Development and Policy Reform
19. Esty DC (2002) The World Trade Organization's legitimacy crisis. World Trade Rev 1(1):15
20. Kielmansegg, P. G. (1995). Lässt sich die Europäische Union verfassen? In: Weidenfeld, W. (ed) Reform der Europäischen Union: Materialien zur Revision des Maastrichter Vertrages 1996. Gütersloh: Bertelsmann Stiftung, pp. 238–239.
21. Hua L (2011) On the 'consensus' voting system and its development trend. J Huazhong Agric Univ (Social Sciences Edition) 1:116
22. See generally James M. Buchanan & Gordon Tullock, The Calculus Of Consent (1962)
23. Bacchus J (2003) The bicycle Club: arming the American interest in the future of the WTO. J World Trade 37(3):429–430
24. Henry M, Robert (U.S.A.) (2011) Robert's rules of order newly revised, 11th edn (trans: Yuan Tianpeng and Sun Di). Shanghai People's Publishing House, Shanghai, p 40
25. Jaimetijmes-LHL (2009) Consensus and majority voting in the WTO. World Trade Rev 8(3):422
26. Posner EA, Sykes AO (2014) Voting rules in international organizations. Chic J Int Law 15(1):Article 10.224
27. Mullersonr (1994) International law, rights and politics. Routledge, London, p 55
28. Starkejg (1994) An introduction to International Law, 11th edn. Butterworths, London, p 557
29. Giuseppe Barile, The way of negotiation at the third United Nations conference on the law of the sea. In: Rozakis CL, Stephanou CA (eds) The New Law of the Sea, p 21
30. Krajewski M (2001) Democratic legitimacy and constitutional perspectives of WTO law. J World Trade 35(1):169

Chapter 2
"Global South" and Tourist Visa Measures

Countries of the "Global South" face the dual, interconnected task of not only joining forces—through regional alliances and cooperative frameworks—to advance the political and economic development of their shared region but also addressing a critical, time-sensitive question: how to ensure that this hard-won economic development moves steadily, sustainably toward a path of long-term security and stability. For this fundamental reason, security safeguards stand as the most essential, fundamental, and pressing issue for all countries involved in the "Global South" cooperation framework, as any lapse in security can undermine decades of developmental progress. A core, non-negotiable element of these security measures is the urgent need to prevent the emergence of destabilizing factors within the "Global South" region—factors that can disrupt supply chains, erode investor confidence, and threaten social order. These factors arise from a wide range of diverse, context-specific scenarios—for instance, long-standing challenges related to the implementation of large-scale cross-border infrastructure projects (such as unexpected delays due to regulatory hurdles, disputes over equitable resource allocation among participating nations, or unforeseen safety hazards in construction), significant risks to the security of regional capital flows (including excessive volatility in foreign direct investment, sudden capital flight triggered by geopolitical tensions, or unequal benefit distribution that exacerbates economic disparities between nations), and the inherent complexity of developing and integrating different industries across borders (such as mismatched industrial policies that create trade barriers, uneven technological capabilities that widen competitive gaps, or unbalanced market access that favors more developed regional economies). Among this broad diversity of potential risks, it is essential to identify and prioritize the most critical, far-reaching elements that pose the greatest threat to regional stability. If monitoring and management efforts are scattered, unfocused across too many scenarios without clear prioritization, the effectiveness of implementation across the "Global South" will be significantly diminished, as limited financial, human, and institutional resources are

X. Dong, J. Gu, *The Belt and Road Initiative and the Global South*, Energy, Climate Change & Sustainability in the Global South,
https://doi.org/10.1007/978-981-92-0144-0_2

spread too thin to address any single risk adequately. In general, under international law and customary practice, the two primary ways for a sovereign state to exercise its jurisdiction are territorial jurisdiction (the authority to apply its domestic laws and regulations within its clearly defined geographical borders) and personal jurisdiction (the power to govern its own citizens, legal entities, and nationals regardless of their physical location outside the state's territory). Notably, the legal object of territorial jurisdiction also explicitly includes specific individuals—whether citizens of the state or foreign nationals—who are physically present within the state's territorial boundaries at any given time. This legal principle makes clear that how to better manage and regulate the relevant personnel within the "Global South" region is a key, determining factor in realizing the secure and stable development of countries in this bloc. The types of personnel in question are highly complex, diverse, and dynamic—ranging from low-skilled and high-skilled migrant workers employed in cross-border industries, cross-border traders engaged in regional commerce, and technical experts providing specialized services to international students pursuing academic opportunities, tourists visiting for cultural or leisure purposes, and diplomatic staff representing their home nations in regional capitals. As such, effective management approaches must fully, thoughtfully take into account the unique identity attributes of these different groups (such as their stated purpose of stay, legally approved duration of residence, professional backgrounds, and potential impact on local communities) to ensure targeted, proportionate, and effective governance that balances security needs with the facilitation of legitimate cross-border movement. The above-mentioned system of managing and regulating personnel—encompassing entry, exit, and stay—can be collectively referred to as travel visa measures under international law and administrative practice. The main, overarching purpose of these measures is to safeguard the national security, public order, and public health of each country while ensuring the orderly cross-border movement of people between nations. By formally regulating who can enter, exit, or stay within a country's borders—and under what specific, legally defined conditions (such as visa validity periods, entry restrictions, and reporting requirements)—travel visa measures lay the necessary, legal groundwork for the normal, uninterrupted operation of economic and trade development between nations. This foundational role is particularly important in the context of the "Global South," where cross-border cooperation in trade, investment, and labor mobility is a major, irreplaceable driver of regional economic growth, and orderly, predictable personnel movement is essential to sustaining and deepening these cooperative ties over time. To gain a more comprehensive, nuanced, and in-depth understanding of travel visa measures—including their legal design, administrative implementation, and practical impact on regional cooperation—it is necessary to begin with a systematic overview of their historical evolution within the "Global South" context. Tracing how these measures have developed over decades, adapted to changing regional economic and security needs, and responded to past security crises and economic challenges (such as pandemics, financial downturns, or political unrest) will provide critical, contextual insight for analyzing their current role and future relevance in the "Global South" cooperation framework.

2.1 The "Global South" and the Historical Development of Travel Visa Measures

In the 1990s, as a punitive response to Iraq's military invasion of Kuwait, the United Nations imposed a rigorous and far-reaching economic blockade on Iraq through comprehensive sanctions. The core intention behind these sanctions was to take decisive punitive action against Iraq's aggressive act: in accordance with Article 41 of Chapter VII of the Charter of the United Nations [1], the international community sought to sever nearly all forms of engagement with Iraq, thereby pressuring its government to reverse course. Yet, while these comprehensive sanctions succeeded in achieving their primary goal of punishing Saddam Hussein's regime in Iraq, they simultaneously inflicted severe, unintended harm on innocent Iraqi civilians. A critical consequence was the disruption and cutoff of essential daily life supplies—this led to an acute shortage of food, clean water, medicine, and other basic necessities for ordinary people [2]. Directly tied to the imposition of these comprehensive sanctions, the number of Iraqi refugees (forced to flee their homes due to hardship and instability) and the death toll (from starvation, disease, and a collapse of public services) rose sharply.

This devastating humanitarian disaster sparked profound reflection within the United Nations and among its member states. It highlighted the inherent flaws of broad, untargeted sanctions—measures that failed to distinguish between a rogue regime and the vulnerable civilians under its rule. Marked by this pivotal moment of reckoning, targeted sanctions gradually emerged as the preferred foreign policy tool to replace the blunt instrument of comprehensive sanctions.

In the wake of this shift, three key international conferences were held to refine and institutionalize targeted sanctions: the Interlaken Process (hosted in Switzerland), the Bonn-Berlin Process (held in Germany), and the Stockholm Process (convened in Sweden). Each process had a distinct, focused mandate:

The Interlaken Process centered primarily on addressing the institutional framework for financial sanctions, aiming to design rules that would disrupt illicit financial flows linked to targeted entities without crippling an entire country's economy [3]. The Bonn-Berlin Process focused heavily on the institutional construction of sanctions related to arms trade restrictions, travel bans, and aviation limitations—seeking to create clear, enforceable norms for these specific measures [4]. The Stockholm Process, by contrast, directed its discussions toward the concrete implementation plans of the aforementioned targeted sanctions, ensuring that the frameworks designed in earlier processes could be put into practice effectively [5]. As a result of these three collaborative processes, three influential and detailed reporting manuals were developed. These manuals formalized best practices, legal standards, and operational guidelines for targeted sanctions—marking a critical step in the evolution of this policy tool. This development also signified that the international legal system governing targeted sanctions had gradually taken shape. For the United Nations and its member states, this emerging legal framework provided invaluable international legal reference points, enabling them to apply targeted sanctions more precisely, humanely, and in line with international law. Against this backdrop, to fully understand the origin and development of travel visa measures (a key component of targeted sanctions, particularly in the context of the "Global South"), it is essential to trace and analyze the specific content of travel visa-related provisions outlined in the Bonn-Berlin Process and within the broader framework of targeted sanctions. This historical and legal context is critical to grasping how travel visa measures evolved into a tool for balancing security needs with humanitarian considerations.

2.1.1 Tourist Visa Measures in the Berne-Berlin Report Manual

The main sponsors of the Bonn Conference, held in Germany, were the United Nations Secretariat and the German Federal Foreign Office. While the reporting manual produced by this conference primarily focused on addressing the implementation of arms embargoes within the framework of targeted sanctions, it also encompassed a wide range of solutions for the practical execution of travel visa measures. Undoubtedly, this content provides invaluable reference value for how to better utilize travel visa measures as a foreign policy tool in real-world scenarios. As explicitly stated in a report by the United Nations Secretariat, future sanctions regimes should be designed with two core objectives: first, to maximize the likelihood of compliance with United Nations Security Council resolutions, and second, to minimize the adverse impacts of sanctions on innocent civilians, neighboring countries, and other states indirectly affected by the measures [6]. The ultimate purpose of such sanctions is to assist the United Nations in collectively safeguarding international peace and security—and crucially, to avoid a recurrence of the devastating humanitarian catastrophes that resulted from the earlier use of comprehensive sanctions. To advance these goals, the Bonn Expert Seminar set out three key tasks for participants to address: Conduct an in-depth and comprehensive analysis of the shortcomings and gaps in the current implementation of arms embargoes, travel bans, and aviation restrictions. This included identifying inefficiencies, loopholes, and unintended consequences of existing measures. Present and discuss a broad spectrum of proposals aimed at enhancing the effectiveness of arms embargoes, travel bans, and aviation restrictions. These proposals sought to make sanctions more targeted, enforceable, and aligned with humanitarian principles. From the wide array of proposals put forward, identify those that would benefit from further, more thorough review by the International Peace Institute (IPI)—an independent organization focused on global security and conflict resolution [7]. Before formulating targeted recommendations for each of these three tasks, the seminar first took a critical preliminary step: defining key terms. Specifically, it provided clear definitions for arms embargoes, travel visa measures, and aviation sanctions within the context of targeted sanctions. This step was essential to ensure that different groups of experts could engage in discussions based on a shared understanding of the concepts, laying a solid theoretical foundation for subsequent deliberations. According to the definition outlined in the Bonn-Berlin Process reporting manual (developed by the expert panel), travel-related targeted sanctions are understood as measures that prohibit specific individuals or designated categories of persons from traveling to, or transiting through, the territory of any state other than the "target state" (the state or entity the sanctions aim to pressure). Building on this definition, the expert panel then put forward four detailed recommendations regarding the design and implementation of travel visa measures: [8] First, on the scope of application: The expert group emphasized that travel visa measures would only be meaningful if they were applied to individuals or specific categories of individuals who intend to engage in international travel (such as official trips, business travel, or leisure travel) and/or benefit from the services of international commercial flights. Applying the measures to individuals with no such travel plans would be unnecessary and ineffective. Second, on the implementation methods: The panel clarified that travel visa measures could take multiple forms, including (but not limited to): preventing designated individuals from entering or transiting through the territory of the sanctioning state; imposing a temporary ban on these individuals departing from the sanctioning state's territory; and prohibiting them from traveling from the sanctioning state to the target state of the sanctions. Additionally, the panel reached a key consensus: travel-related restrictions should be framed as a "travel ban" rather than a "visa ban." This distinction was important because a "travel ban" directly restricts movement, while a "visa ban" only blocks the issuance of travel documents—leaving open loopholes if individuals already hold valid visas. Third, on assessing effectiveness: The expert group argued that the effectiveness of travel-related sanctions should never be evaluated in isolation. Instead, these measures often serve as a "prelude" to other types of sanctions (such as financial or trade restrictions) and operate in conjunction with them. Targeted travel sanctions can exert both psychological and practical impacts: on the one hand, they stigmatize the designated individuals, creating reputational pressure that incentivizes them (or the entities they represent) to make policy changes; on the other hand, they disrupt the individuals' ability to conduct business, attend meetings, or engage in activities that support the target regime. Furthermore, travel visa measures can indirectly facilitate the implementation of trade and financial sanctions by limiting the movement of individuals involved in illicit transactions. Fourth, on distinguishing target objects: The panel stressed the need for precise differentiation between the individuals subject to travel visa measures. During the Security Council's deliberations on sanctions, members must first clarify critical questions: Who qualifies as a "member" of the target group? Which individuals "support" the target regime through their official functions or actions? For example, if the target includes government officials, the panel noted that it is essential to specify exactly which government actors fall under the travel restrictions—since applying the measures to every government employee would undermine the "targeted" nature of the sanctions. After extensive discussion, the group identified specific categories of officials that could be targeted, including: Heads of government, cabinet ministers, and lower-level government officials with decision-making authority; Members of national parliaments or legislative bodies; Heads or senior personnel of security forces, intelligence agencies, gendarmeries, and paramilitary police units; Heads or senior managers of state-owned or state-controlled enterprises (covering sectors such as banking, transportation, manufacturing, public utilities, media, and insurance); Members of the ruling political party (especially those in leadership roles); Other relevant personnel (this may include senior managers of state-owned enterprises, family members of key officials, and even lower-level staff performing critical functions—such as certain accountants, procurement officers, or technical experts who support the target regime's operations) [9]. These recommendations largely cover the key issues commonly encountered in the implementation of travel visa measures. While the expert group did not address the specific ways in which travel visa measures could be coordinated with other types of sanctions (such as financial or trade restrictions), the proposals nonetheless provide a solid foundation and clear guidelines for the practical application of travel visa measures in targeted sanctions regimes.

2.1.2 Travel Visa Measures Under Targeted Sanctions

According to scholars such as Thomas J. Biersteker, targeted sanctions can be categorized into six distinct types, namely sanctions against individuals and entities, diplomatic sanctions, arms embargoes, commodity sanctions, transportation sanctions, and financial sanctions [10]. Among these, sanctions against individuals and entities primarily apply to specific individuals, corporate entities, and political parties; diplomatic sanctions involve restrictions on the diplomatic activities of governing bodies, encompassing measures like limiting the number of accredited diplomatic personnel, imposing constraints on their travel, and temporarily suspending participation in intergovernmental organizations; arms embargoes refer to either comprehensive or partial moratoriums on the international supply of arms or dual-use goods (which can be used for both civilian and proliferation-related purposes) to designated countries or regions; commodity sanctions focus on restricting trade in specific resources (such as oil, minerals, or agricultural products) with targeted countries or regions; transportation sanctions prohibit carriers (whether by sea or air) from conducting international transportation services to or from the target country; and financial sanctions mainly include measures like investment bans, restrictions on banking services provided to the target country, and limitations on the operation of its sovereign wealth funds, with the implementation of these financial measures often exerting a significant impact on the core economic sectors of the target country. Within this classification framework of targeted sanctions, travel visa measures fall under the category of sanctions against individuals, which means that travel visa measures are generally restricted to specific groups of people rather than being applied universally—this characteristic is fully aligned with the "targeted" nature that defines targeted sanctions in the first place. It is precisely based on this type of targeted restrictive measure that international subjects (such as the United

Nations, regional organizations, or sovereign states) have developed different types of legal systems (including relevant resolutions, treaties, and domestic laws) to regulate their application and have proceeded to implement these measures in practical international affairs.

While travel visa measures and targeted sanctions share a strong inherent correlation, they still possess both notable commonalities and distinct individual differences—yet the differences between these two are far less apparent than those between travel visa measures and unilateral economic sanctions, especially given that travel visa measures are inherently a component of targeted sanctions. Since both travel visa measures and targeted sanctions have only been widely recognized by the international community as the most optimal alternatives to traditional economic sanctions in recent years, there remain numerous aspects within the practical field that are worthy of in-depth discussion and systematic research; therefore, clarifying the intrinsic relationship between targeted sanctions and travel visa measures not only facilitates the proper handling of complex diplomatic relations but also enables the functional value of targeted sanctions in shaping international relations to be exerted in a timely manner. In light of this, our analysis should begin with a thorough exploration of the concept of targeted sanctions. According to scholar Surya P. Subedi, targeted sanctions—also referred to as "targeted" sanctions—are "unfriendly" acts that a state carries out when exercising its inherent sovereign rights. These sensible or targeted sanctions cover a wide range of specific measures, including the severance of diplomatic relations, the declaration of diplomats as persona non grata, the suspension of overseas development assistance, the refusal to recognize a new government that has come to power through a military coup or other undemocratic means, the cessation of trade or investment with the target country, the termination, suspension, or restriction of diplomatic relations, the recall of ambassadors, the suspension of the operation of a treaty itself, or the restriction or impediment of trade within the limits set by the Vienna Convention on the Law of Treaties—all of which must be implemented without violating obligations under WTO law [11]. They also include the imposition of visa bans or the freezing of assets of blacklisted government officials who have violated human rights, committed other internationally wrongful acts, or engaged in economic or financial misconduct such as money laundering. From this concept of targeted sanctions, it is clear that they may include common measures like diplomatic restrictions, asset freezes, adjustments to overseas aid, financial and trade restrictions, and travel visa bans; these measures are less intense than the restrictions imposed by unilateral economic sanctions, which is why they are regarded as "unfriendly" acts rather than the threatening or coercive pressure defined by unilateral economic sanctions—pressure that aims to force a change in the behaviour of the sanctioned state. As a concept falling within the scope of targeted sanctions, the "unfriendly act" of travel visa measures primarily focuses on imposing restrictions on the free movement of specific groups of people, and the relationship between the two is largely one of inclusion (with targeted sanctions as the broader category and travel visa measures as a subset). In view of this, the similarities between targeted sanctions and travel visa measures are significant, and these similarities can be fully understood through a clear definition of the concept of targeted sanctions—though the author can only provide a brief summary and induction here. First and foremost, the two measures are consistent in terms of application intensity: whether it is targeted sanctions or travel visa measures, the choice of implementation mode tends to be based on maintaining the stable and orderly development of the international order within the framework of international law norms, rather than leveraging advantages in economic, political, or other areas of development to take ultra-limit illegal acts that interfere with the autonomy of other countries. Secondly, both are applied within the framework of international law norms: in the case of targeted sanctions, their content is limited to measures such as severing diplomatic relations, ceasing investment in the target state, or restricting trade, and they must not violate obligations under WTO law—this reveals that these sanctions actually set a minimum standard, namely that they cannot exceed the boundaries of international law norms. Meanwhile, the restrictive measures of travel visa measures are still based on the premise of maintaining national security and the stability of social public order. Therefore, both fall within the scope of permissible adjustment by international law norms in their application. Finally, the applicable objects of the two measures are restrictions in specific fields: the main reason targeted sanctions are also called "targeted" is that their applicable objective is to restrict a specific area—for example, in the case of diplomatic sanctions, the key measures mainly involve the recall of personnel from embassies and consulates stationed in each other's countries or the termination of diplomatic relations. On this basis, travel visa measures leverage the targeted nature of targeted sanctions by imposing restrictions on the free movement of specific groups of people linked to the purpose of the sanctions, which allows both to better align with basic concepts in international law such as the free exercise of state sovereignty and non-interference in internal affairs. Of course, beyond the above-mentioned commonalities, other shared features can also be identified, but when inducing concepts, individual components can actually reflect their particularity. Therefore, the author believes that analyzing the differences between travel visa measures and targeted sanctions will enable travel visa measures to better exert their unique functional value during the application process.

Based on the above summary of these two concepts, the author holds the view that the differences between targeted sanctions and travel visa measures can be analyzed from the following key aspects: first, the two differ in their scope of application, with the distinction in their "scope characteristics" being a particularly prominent feature—targeted sanctions serve as a general, overarching term for all targeted sanction measures, boasting a broad and comprehensive scope of application, while travel visa measures are a specific, narrow subset of targeted measures, thus falling entirely within the broader scope of application covered by targeted sanctions. Secondly, the two vary in their objectives of application: the core objective of implementing targeted sanctions remains to alter the existing behaviors of the target state, yet in terms of the intensity of implementation and the applicable legal norms, they align more closely with the fundamental values of international law; in contrast, although travel visa measures do carry the intention of influencing the target country's actions, their primary role leans more toward serving as a warning and punitive tool. A typical illustration of this lies in the case where, after the United States imposed economic sanctions on Cuba, the Trade Sanctions Reform and Export Enhancement Act of 2000 further prohibited U.S. citizens from traveling to Cuba for tourist purposes and barred the provision of financing for the sale of U.S. agricultural products to Cuba—[12] essentially, these travel-related measures were designed to amplify the impact of economic sanctions, thereby achieving the goal of warning and punishing Cuba. This dynamic between the two can also be understood as a logical, progressive relationship: if the initial targeted sanctions fail to produce the desired behavioral changes in the target state, the corresponding supplementary punitive measures (such as travel visa restrictions) will then be implemented. Thirdly, the two are grounded in different bases for application: due to the diverse range of forms in which targeted sanctions can be implemented, their application in practical scenarios relies on a variety of different legal and regulatory bases—for instance, diplomatic sanctions that involve cutting off the movement of diplomatic personnel are primarily based on the relevant provisions outlined in the Vienna Convention on Diplomatic Relations, while trade-related sanctions are subject to the rules and frameworks established by the World Trade Organization (WTO); on the other hand, the basis for applying travel visa measures is relatively singular, as it mainly draws from legal norms centered on safeguarding national security, maintaining public order, and regulating entry and exit procedures. Examples of such bases include the U.S. executive order titled "Protecting the Nation from Terrorist Attacks by Foreigners," which incorporates visa restrictions on citizens of specific countries seeking to enter the United States, and the aforementioned Trade Sanctions Reform and Export Enhancement Act of 2000, which similarly includes prohibitions on U.S. citizens traveling to Cuba for tourism and other related travel restrictions. Of course, when viewed from different analytical perspectives, the individual differences between targeted sanctions and travel visa measures extend far beyond the three aspects outlined above; however, these three distinct characteristics related to their application represent some of the more crucial and practically relevant individual differences in real-world practice. Ultimately, the fundamental purpose of all sanction measures remains to serve and facilitate the management of diplomatic relations between nations. Therefore, it is only by selecting and applying different types of sanctions (such as targeted sanctions in general and travel visa measures in particular) to achieve specific, intended effects that the value and functional role of sanctions within the framework of international law can be fully realized.

From the various different analytical perspectives discussed above, it becomes clear that the primary purpose of travel visa measures throughout their developmental process is to prevent the global economic order from being disrupted by the excessive generalization or overreach of economic sanctions. Beyond this preventive role, we can also recognize a more positive impact: the implementation of travel visa measures has, to a certain extent, helped curb the escalation of conflicts between countries. By focusing on restricting the mobility of specific groups of people rather than resorting to more severe economic and trade sanctions, this alternative approach can also effectively screen out individuals with potentially dangerous statuses from the target country. In doing so, it safeguards the stability of a country's economic and social development through measures such as issuing warnings or denying entry to such individuals. When considering the "Belt and Road" initiative, which involves a network of close and friendly partner countries, the travel visa measures applied between these participating nations can be designed with more relaxed conditions—conditions that clearly distinguish them from the measures applied to non-Belt and Road countries. This differentiated and flexible approach to travel visas is also a key factor in attracting more countries to join and participate in the Belt and Road Initiative. That said, travel visa measures still possess some unique attributes in the course of their practical application. It is only by fully understanding and grasping these specific characteristics that we can make more effective use of travel visa measures, thereby enabling them to better serve the exchanges and cooperation between the countries involved in the Belt and Road Initiative.

2.2 Characteristics of Travel Visa Measures

On the basis of the above discussion concerning the historical development of travel visa measures, one can identify that, in comparison with other types of targeted sanctions measures, travel visa measures possess distinct and unique characteristics in three key aspects: the subjects they target, the modes through which they are exercised, and the procedures they follow. The core purpose and value behind these unique characteristics lie primarily in two mutually reinforcing goals: on one hand, to ensure the effective implementation of counter-terrorism efforts, and on the other hand, to better safeguard the national interests of the countries involved in the Belt and Road Initiative—striking a balance between security needs and cooperative interests.

2.2.1 The Applicable Subjects of Travel Visa Measures are Extensive

In comparison with other types of international sanctions—such as trade embargoes, asset freezes, or arms restrictions—travel visa measures stand out for having a notably wide range of applicable subjects, spanning individual citizens, diplomatic personnel, and even specific groups of professionals. This characteristic becomes even more prominent when contrasted specifically with unilateral economic sanctions, which tend to target entire economies or key sectors rather than diverse individual or group entities. The implementation of unilateral economic sanctions itself demands the fulfillment of three distinct, legally and practically binding key conditions: first, it depends on the sufficient economic strength of the subject initiating the sanctions, including access to global markets, currency influence, and resource control; second, it relies on the existence of relevant international treaties, customary international law, or formal legal norms to provide a valid legal basis for the sanctions' imposition; third, it hinges on the degree of economic, political, or strategic influence the sanctioned country exerts on the sanction-initiating country, which directly impacts the potential costs and benefits of the sanctions. The first condition is primarily intended to emphasize that unilateral economic sanctions must be underpinned by commensurate economic strength to ensure their practical effectiveness—without such strength, the sanctions risk being ignored or circumvented by the target country. The second condition serves as a critical legal distinction between unilateral sanctions and multilateral sanctions: multilateral sanctions typically require broader international legal authorization, such as resolutions adopted by the United Nations Security Council (UNSC), while unilateral sanctions may rely on the initiator's domestic legal frameworks but still need to align with basic principles of international law to avoid being deemed unlawful. The third condition acts as a pragmatic criterion for determining whether to launch unilateral economic sanctions, meaning the sanction initiator must conduct a thorough assessment of the potential economic, political, and diplomatic costs of imposing such sanctions on the target country before taking formal action. Under the strict constraints of these three interrelated conditions, unilateral economic sanctions have evolved into a measure that only a small number of economically powerful countries—such as major global economies or regional hegemons—are capable of initiating proactively. First and foremost, the economic strength of the implementing subject mainly refers to the tangible material resources (including financial reserves, industrial output, and natural resources) and intangible economic leverage (such as control over key supply chains, currency dominance, or access to international financial institutions) required to launch and sustain unilateral economic sanctions. In general, the implementation of unilateral economic sanctions tends to be an inherently asymmetric measure—for instance, the comprehensive economic embargo imposed by the United States on Cuba since the early 1960s could only be effectively applied because the U.S. possesses far greater economic strength, global market access, and currency influence than Cuba. Without such a significant economic advantage, imposing unilateral economic sanctions would likely backfire, becoming a self-defeating "shooting oneself in the foot" act that harms the initiator's own economic interests as much as the target's. This inherent imbalance in economic power thus greatly reduces the likelihood that least developed countries (LDCs) within the Global South will be able to initiate or effectively implement unilateral economic sanctions, as they often lack the necessary resources and leverage. Secondly, the driving force behind multilateral sanctions is centered on the United Nations Security Council, which serves as the primary international body exercising legal authority in this regard under the UN Charter. Other UN member states are then obligated to provide cooperation and assistance in enforcing the sanctions, including implementing trade restrictions and asset freezes. This scenario underscores the fact that within the framework of multilateral sanctions, the dominant power to impose sanctions is not accessible to every country—only the UNSC, through its formal resolution process, can authorize such measures.

Moreover, the entire process of multilateral sanctions must strictly align with established international law norms: it must be carried out within the explicit parameters of relevant UN resolutions or binding international treaties and regulations. Any deviation from this legal framework—such as imposing additional restrictions not authorized by the UNSC—would exceed the permissible scope of UN sanctions or multilateral sanctions, thereby classifying the measure as part of the unilateral sanctions system instead. In contrast, within the unilateral sanctions system, the country initiating the sanctions may overstep its legal authority when implementing the measures—for example, imposing extraterritorial sanctions on entities not under its jurisdiction—or target a specific country based solely on its own political or economic interests rather than broader international consensus. These practices pose significant challenges for UN member states that only hold a general voice in international affairs, such as most Global South countries, as they lack the political or economic power to counter such arbitrary actions. Only the permanent members of the UN Security Council (China, France, Russia, the United Kingdom, and the United States), which possess the "one-vote veto" power over UNSC resolutions, can shield themselves from adverse impacts stemming from the decision-making process on sanction-related resolutions. Finally, the extent to which the actions of the target country affect the economic, political, or strategic interests of the sanction-initiating country is of crucial importance and serves as a key practical factor in deciding whether to launch unilateral economic sanctions. A notable historical example of this is the long-standing sanctions imposed by the United States on Cuba: while the U.S. has long held a hostile stance toward Cuba's socialist political and economic policies, this ideological difference alone was not the decisive factor in triggering the sanctions. Instead, it was only after Cuba announced the nationalization of large-scale properties, industries, and assets owned by U.S. citizens and corporations within its territorial borders in the late 1950s and early 1960s that the United States formally responded by announcing unilateral economic sanctions and imposing a comprehensive economic embargo on Cuba [13]. Through this case, we can observe that the deterioration of diplomatic relations between a sanctioned target country and a sanction-initiating country often begins with the escalation of concrete economic conflicts, rather than mere ideological differences. When the core economic interests of the sanction-initiating country—such as the protection of its citizens' property rights or corporate assets—are infringed upon, unilateral economic sanctions become a primary tool for the initiator to strike back at the target country. Conversely, Cuba also paid a heavy price that fell outside the scope of specific international law regulation as a consequence of its nationalization of U.S. citizens' industries, including limited access to global markets and foreign investment. This example vividly illustrates that economic conflicts between weaker countries (such as Cuba) and stronger countries (such as the U.S.) frequently become a pretext for stronger countries to take punitive action against weaker ones, and it further highlights the critical importance of the implementing subject's economic strength in determining the feasibility and impact of unilateral economic sanctions.

Based on the analysis of the above three conditions, it is evident that the state initiating unilateral economic sanctions must be a country with substantial economic influence in the international community; otherwise, it will be unable to bear the series of consequences that accompany the implementation of unilateral economic sanctions—consequences that may include retaliatory trade measures from the target country, disruptions to its own domestic industries dependent on trade with the sanctioned state, and potential diplomatic backlash from other nations opposed to unilateral action. In contrast, travel visa measures require relatively little consideration of a country's economic strength, as their enforcement relies more on a state's inherent authority over its borders than on its economic leverage. This means their restrictive impact on the sanctioning subject is far less severe than that of unilateral economic sanctions, which often demand significant financial resources and trade power to be effective. Moreover, the application process of travel visa measures is shaped by specific factors that contribute to the formation of a broad range of applicable subjects, making them accessible to a much larger number of states, including smaller or less economically powerful nations. First and foremost, the inherent restrictive nature of travel visa measures—focused on regulating who may enter or exit a country—dictates that their applicable subjects are extensive. While travel visa measures may take various forms, such as temporary entry bans, visa application denials, or transit restrictions, their ultimate core function lies in the deprivation (or limitation) of an individual's right to free movement—regardless of the duration of this deprivation—and enforcing such measures does not demand an excessively high level of difficulty or specialized resources. This is because the right to free movement is closely intertwined with the principle of state sovereignty, a foundational concept in international law that grants each recognized state exclusive authority over its own territory and the people within it. The principle of state sovereignty primarily encompasses two factors that are most directly linked to free movement: first, the state's fundamental obligation to protect its own territorial integrity, which includes controlling access to its borders to prevent threats to national security; second, the state's authority under the principle of sovereignty to exercise jurisdiction over both its citizens within its territory and those residing outside its borders, allowing it to set rules for the movement of individuals connected to it. These two factors collectively enable any state recognized under international law—whether large or small, economically strong or weak—to impose restrictions on the movement of individuals in accordance with the principle of state sovereignty—a legal foundation that best supports the broad application of travel visa measures across different subjects. However, such restrictions on movement must be tied to legitimate considerations of national security, public health, or public order to ensure further compatibility with the provisions of international law, such as those outlined in the International Covenant on Civil and Political Rights; otherwise, they may risk violating the internationally recognized right to freedom of movement, leading to legal challenges or damage to the state's diplomatic reputation.

Secondly, the restrictive purpose inherent in travel visa measures is a key factor that determines the extensiveness of their applicable subjects. When examining the core purpose of these restrictions, it becomes clear that travel visa measures limit the freedom of movement not to intervene in or attack the economy of the sanctioned target country, but rather to deter potential acts that could harm national interests (of the country imposing the measures) and undermine international peace and security. Guided by this restrictive purpose, the scope of subjects eligible to apply travel visa measures can be extended to any country that bears the obligation to maintain international peace and security—a duty enshrined in foundational international law. In accordance with the provisions of Article 1, Paragraph 1 [14], and Article 2, Paragraph 6 [15], of the Charter of the United Nations, the responsibility to maintain international peace and security is not limited to United Nations Member States alone; it also extends to non-Member States, which are required to uphold this obligation in their international conduct. These Charter provisions further emphasize the importance of resolving disputes peacefully and effectively to prevent the escalation of conflicts—principles that align closely with the functional goal of travel visa measures. From this perspective, since travel visa measures serve as a tool for states to proactively impose restrictions on acts that threaten international interests or disrupt international peace and security, and this function directly aligns with the obligation to maintain global stability outlined in the UN Charter, the range of states that can legitimately apply these measures becomes broad. In short, the alignment between the restrictive purpose of travel visa measures and the core objectives of the United Nations Charter is what ultimately makes their applicable subjects extensive.

Finally, it is the restrictive effects of travel visa measures that serve as a decisive factor in determining the extensiveness of their applicable subjects. The restrictive effects of travel visa measures, by and large, revolve around specific measures: these include cutting off the free movement of people, imposing visa restrictions, and prohibiting unrestricted entry and exit. First and foremost, these measures do not entail a direct economic impact on the sanctioned target state—and this key trait sets them apart from unilateral economic sanctions, which demand that the country imposing the sanctions possesses higher economic strength than the target state. On the other hand, these restrictive measures are of a targeted nature, meaning the effects of the restrictions can be controlled; as a result, they will not bring about greater negative impacts, which in turn reduces the possibility of violating the rules of international law. Thirdly, the application of these measures is in line with the purpose of maintaining national peace and security as stipulated in international law norms. To a certain degree, they are restrictive measures that are implemented within the framework permitted by the United Nations, and for this reason, they hold a certain level of legitimacy. The case in which four Arab countries imposed travel visa measures on Qatar also serves to illustrate the feature that the effect of the restrictions determines the extensiveness of the applicable subjects. From a geographical perspective, once the four Arab countries had imposed the travel visa measures on Qatar, they cut off Qatar from the outside world in geographical terms—but this cutoff had no direct connection to economic impact. The suspension of personnel movement primarily took place in areas such as airspace, territorial sea, and land border crossings; for the four Arab states, this suspension did not depend on economic restrictions. Instead, it focused solely on regulating the specific entry and exit of individuals to and from Qatar. What is more, the intensity of the sanctions could be further increased by imposing a ban on certain Qatari individuals transiting through their territories. Meanwhile, Qatar, in its role as the sanctioned state, also imposed visa restrictions on Egypt after being hit with the travel restrictions from the four Arab countries—and this development serves to confirm the extensive nature of travel visa measures. This type of targeted restrictive effect is not limited to application by the country that initiates the measures; the targeted country can also apply such measures in response. The four Arab states imposed sanctions on Qatar due to Qatar's support for terrorism, a reason that is consistent with the objective of international law to maintain international peace and security. The joint sanctions launched by the four states on the basis of this objective also hold full justification, and the characteristics of these joint sanctions further serve to illustrate the wide range of applicable subjects within the scope of travel visa measures.

The extensiveness inherent in the applicable subjects of travel visa measures plays a defining role in the context of "Belt and Road" economic and trade exchanges—it enables relevant countries involved in these exchanges to make clear distinctions between different types of partners. Specifically, based on the extensiveness of the applicable subjects of travel visa measures, these countries can identify which nations are friendly cooperative partners and which fall under the category of countries covered by the Belt and Road Initiative's policies during the process of their economic and trade interactions. In contrast, for those countries that are not involved in the Belt and Road Initiative, the flexible adjustment of travel visa measures can also serve a practical purpose: it can create favorable conditions to facilitate the smooth progress of economic and trade exchanges between the adjusting country and these non-participating nations.

2.2.2 There Is Diversity in the Way the Measures Are Applied

In terms of the manner in which travel visa measures are enforced, their core mechanism for achieving travel restriction effects lies in severing the free movement of individuals between the enforcing state and the sanctioned state. While this restrictive effect is primarily oriented toward preventing acts of terrorism and other conducts that may potentially impair national interests under international law, such a purpose does not exhaust the full scope of its functional roles—indeed, the enforcement modalities of travel visa measures exhibit distinct diverse characteristics as recognized in practice. The specific manifestations of this diversity are as follows: First, the invocation of such sanctions may generate indirect restrictive impacts on the economic sphere. As a form of targeted restrictive measure under the framework of international sanctions law, travel visa measures do not impose a direct impact on the sanctioned state's economy, and this attribute constitutes the intrinsic distinction between travel visa measures and economic sanctions (which are explicitly designed to disrupt the sanctioned state's economic system). Nevertheless, the modality through which travel visa measures sever human mobility may still inflict adverse economic consequences on the targeted state, depending on the latter's economic development model. In particular, if the sanctioned state's economic structure is predominantly reliant on the tourism and service sectors, its economic sectors will inevitably be constrained by tourist-oriented travel visa measures, as the free movement of individuals is a foundational prerequisite for the operation of such industries. A case in point is the travel visa measures imposed on Qatar by four Arab states during the Gulf crisis: as a geographically insular state, Qatar faced inherent geographical disadvantages relative to the four enforcing states. Upon the imposition of these travel visa measures, the influx of visitors to Qatar experienced a drastic decline, primarily attributable to potential travelers' legitimate concerns regarding the destination's security—a direct consequence of the sanctions regime. The four Arab states had initially intended, through the imposition of sanctions against Qatar (including travel restrictions), to compel Qatar to comply with the terms of the 2014 agreement [16], to dissociate itself from Iran (a state subject to international scrutiny over nuclear-related issues), and to align with the collective effort to counter the threat of terrorism as mandated by international counter-terrorism norms. However, these measures were steadfastly opposed by Qatar; consequently, in mid-2017, the four Arab states imposed comprehensive travel restrictions on Qatar, encompassing land, maritime, and air routes—a move that exerted a severe detrimental impact on Qatar's tourism industry, which was a key pillar of its economic diversification strategy. Even prior to the sanctions' invocation, Qatar had formally designated tourism as one of the five priority sectors for advancing economic diversification, a policy decision rooted in its recognition of the inherent risks of a single-resource economic model. Although Qatar is endowed with substantial oil and gas reserves, the over-reliance on such finite resources entails significant structural vulnerabilities: once its oil and gas reserves are depleted, Qatar's monolithic economic model will be forced into an unplanned and disruptive transformation. Qatar had explicitly acknowledged the imperative of proactively adjusting its economic structure, recognizing that a voluntary restructuring of its existing economic development model is far preferable to a passive and crisis-driven transformation. The most salient enabling condition for this restructuring was the natural tourist resources associated with Qatar's geographical location—Qatar had been actively pursuing economic development through the cultivation of commercial and leisure tourism, which was designated as a core component of its strategy to reduce dependence on oil and gas revenues, in line with international best practices for sustainable economic development. To this end, Qatar had established clear quantitative targets: it aimed to host 5 million tourists by 2023 and had formulated a long-term objective of welcoming 10 million tourists by 2030. Regrettably, this positive trajectory of economic transformation and development was manifestly disrupted and halted by the sanctions regime imposed by the four Arab states.

According to official statistical data released during that period, the number of international tourists visiting Qatar in the first half of 2018 plummeted by one-third compared with the same period in 2017—a sharp decline that directly reflected the impact of travel restrictions. Concurrently, the average occupancy rate of hotels across Qatar dropped to 60 percent, a figure significantly lower than the industry's typical operational benchmarks for profitability. Alongside this, the average revenue per hotel room decreased by 235 Qatari riyals, which is approximately equivalent to $65 when converted at the prevailing exchange rate; this drop in per-room revenue further strained the financial viability of Qatar's tourism-related businesses [17]. Hamad International Airport, a critical travel hub in the Middle East that had previously facilitated transit and direct travel for millions of passengers annually, was closed to air travel involving Qatar as part of the sanctions. This closure resulted in a daily loss of roughly 27,000 passengers for the airport, and hundreds of regularly scheduled weekly flights to and from Qatar were formally cancelled due to the enforced travel restrictions. These disruptions had a cascading knock-on effect on the entire ecosystem of Qatar's airport services industry: airlines were forced to incur substantial losses from compensating passengers for cancelled flights, while terminal operators saw a drastic reduction in revenues generated by duty-free shops, on-site restaurants, and other auxiliary services that rely on passenger foot traffic. From this sanctions case, three key and unambiguous conclusions can be drawn: First, the travel restrictions imposed on Qatar by the four Arab countries were grounded exclusively in measures designed to sever the free movement of individuals entering and exiting Qatar's borders. Notably, these measures did not involve direct interference in Qatar's economic system, such as trade embargoes on key commodities or restrictions on financial transactions—distinguishing them clearly from traditional economic sanctions. Second, Qatar's long-standing single-reliance economic development model, which was heavily dependent on oil and gas exports, had already highlighted the urgency of its economic transformation prior to the sanctions. Before the travel restrictions were imposed, Qatar had proactively formulated and begun implementing plans to shift from this over-reliance on hydrocarbon resources to a more diversified economic structure, with tourism and high-value service industries identified as core growth drivers. The severance of cross-border people flow caused by the travel visa measures thus directly undermined Qatar's efforts to build these new income sources, creating significant obstacles to its planned economic diversification. Third, the travel visa measures implemented by the four Arab countries against Qatar directly contributed to a measurable decline in Qatar's overall economic revenues, particularly in sectors tied to tourism, aviation, and hospitality. These three conclusions, when considered collectively, provide concrete evidence that travel visa measures—even when not explicitly designed as economic tools—can nonetheless produce a tangible indirect restrictive effect on the economic field of the sanctioned state. Second, the enforcement of such travel visa sanctions also carries a distinct restrictive effect that hinders cross-border interpersonal and cultural communication. In his influential case analysis of sanctions imposed on Rhodesia, scholar Johan Galtung proposed a well-known framework that categorizes sanctions into three primary types, and one of these categories is communication sanctions [18]. Importantly, such communication sanctions are, in essence, a direct derivative of the restrictive effect of travel visa measures, as they function by severing the close interpersonal ties that are sustained through cross-border travel, family visits, and face-to-face interactions. A prominent real-world example of this dynamic is found in the long-standing and comprehensive embargo that the United States has imposed on Cuba for decades. This embargo has included strict travel restrictions that have effectively prevented ordinary citizens of the United States and Cuba from traveling freely between the two countries for non-official purposes. Behind this restrictive effect on mobility lies an implicit ban on the informal cross-border exchange of goods, services, and cultural practices that often accompany personal travel. As scholar Galtung detailed in his analysis, the severance of people-to-people flow between the two nations has also created a painful breakdown in familial connections: particularly for Cuban nationals who reside in the United States, many have been forced to endure prolonged periods of estrangement from their immediate relatives and close friends still living in Cuba, with no clear path to regular in-person reunions. Conversely, U.S. citizens who are in Cuba not only face strict regulatory measures that require them to transfer certain categories of property to the Cuban government but also lack the ability to return to their home country on short notice to reunite with their families and friends in times of need or for important life events. Over time, this sustained estrangement can deepen emotional distances and erode the cultural and familial bonds that once connected communities across the two borders. While the widespread severance of the free movement of persons is intended to serve the core objective of travel visa measures—such as pressuring a target state to change its policies—it has, in practical terms, inadvertently impeded the natural communication between individuals across national or regional borders. Therefore, the restrictive effect of travel visa measures is not limited to the narrow scope of severing people flow alone but also manifests in other far-reaching forms that impact social and cultural connections. Third, the enforcement of travel visa sanctions also imposes unintended restrictive effects on the sanction-initiating state itself, creating consequences that extend beyond the target state. Travel visa measures, by their very design, typically operate on a two-way severance basis rather than a one-sided one. This means that on one hand, they explicitly prohibit citizens of the sanction-initiating state from traveling to the target state for specified purposes, and on the other hand, they impose strict restrictions on citizens of the target state from traveling to the sanction-initiating state—creating a mutual barrier to mobility that affects both sides.

This two-way severance of mobility serves a critical defensive function: it enables pre-emptive prevention and restriction of terrorist acts, transnational criminal activities, and other conducts that pose a potential threat to the national interests of the sanction-initiating state or to the maintenance of international peace and security as enshrined in international law. At the same time, this two-way approach is also essential for safeguarding the legitimate personal rights and interests of the sanction-initiating state's citizens—such as protecting their safety while abroad—and upholding the state's core national security interests, which are fundamental to its sovereign existence. However, it is important to note that this two-way restrictive effect is not without drawbacks; it also imposes certain negative consequences on the sanction-initiating state itself, creating unintended costs that extend beyond the targeted state. A clear illustration of this dynamic is seen in the travel visa measures unilaterally imposed by the United States against Cuba: the U.S. ban on its own citizens traveling to Cuba not only reduced the number of international tourists visiting Cuba (as intended) but also inflicted a tangible negative impact on the U.S. tourism and related industries. To quantify this impact, scholars have cited key data: for instance, a 2008 estimate released by the United States International Trade Commission (USITC)—a federal agency tasked with analyzing trade and economic matters—projected that if the U.S. travel ban on Cuba were lifted, the number of American citizens traveling to Cuba annually would range between 1.1 million and 2.8 million, representing a significant untapped market for U.S. travel service providers. Additionally, according to estimates from U.S. tourism industry analysts referenced by scholar Peters, in the very first year after the sanctions on travel to Cuba were lifted, approximately 1 million American tourists would visit Cuba—a figure that underscores the immediate economic potential of resuming such travel. Beyond the increase in American tourist numbers to Cuba, the lifting of the travel ban would also yield substantial benefits for the broader U.S. economy, as it would stimulate activity across interconnected sectors such as aviation, hospitality, and travel planning [19]. To further explore this economic link, scholars including Ed Sanders have conducted in-depth analyses of the relationship between lifting the U.S. travel ban on Cuba and U.S. economic interests, and in their research, they have outlined three distinct scenarios for how the travel ban could be lifted—each with varying implications for U.S. industries [20]. The first scenario involves lifting the ban on American citizens traveling to Cuba but retaining the comprehensive embargo measures that fully block other forms of economic engagement. Under this scenario, the United States would still prohibit any U.S.-based entities from providing transport services to Cuba or offering destination guidance services related to Cuba; this means U.S. commercial airlines would be barred from operating flights carrying passengers to Cuba, and U.S. travel agencies would be forbidden from arranging trips to Cuba for American citizens. Instead, U.S. citizens wishing to travel to Cuba would be forced to do so indirectly—by transiting through other countries and booking flights with foreign-flagged airlines, a cumbersome process that would limit the growth of travel volumes and the corresponding economic benefits for U.S. businesses. The second scenario focuses on the specific economic benefits that would accrue to the United States if it allowed U.S. airlines and U.S. travel agencies to directly provide services for American residents traveling to Cuba. Importantly, this scenario does not involve eliminating the broader embargo or other sanctions against Cuba; it only permits these two specific sectors—aviation and travel planning—to engage with Cuba. Under this framework, other U.S. industries, such as hotel service providers and hospitality companies, would still be prohibited from making direct foreign investments in Cuba or entering into management contracts with Cuban entities to operate hotels or tourism facilities on the island, meaning the economic gains would be limited to a narrow subset of U.S. businesses.

In the context of Scenario III—a comprehensive policy shift aimed at normalizing U.S.-Cuba relations—the scope of policy adjustment expands further to encompass the complete dismantling of long-standing trade restrictions: the comprehensive trade embargo that has for decades constrained and disrupted U.S.-Cuba economic relations would be completely lifted, removing all remaining legal, regulatory, and administrative barriers to unfettered commercial engagement between the two nations. Under this scenario, any United States-based company—regardless of its industry sector, whether it be tourism (including tour operators and travel booking platforms), hospitality (such as hotels and restaurants), manufacturing (ranging from consumer goods to industrial equipment), or professional services (including legal, financial, and consulting services)—would be legally permitted to establish physical or virtual operations in Cuba, enter into formal business partnerships with Cuban state-owned or private entities, or sell a full range of goods and services in the Cuban market without the prior restrictive conditions, licensing requirements, or prohibitions imposed by the embargo. This full, unconditional normalization of economic ties would unlock the maximum potential economic benefits for the United States economy as a whole, as well as for U.S. workers employed in sectors that would gain direct access to the Cuban market and U.S. investors seeking new, untapped opportunities for growth and profit in a previously restricted market. Turning to the specific, quantifiable economic impacts of each scenario, Scenario I—characterized by its limited lifting of the travel ban (restricted to specific traveler categories) and retention of the broader trade embargo—would yield relatively modest, narrow benefits for the U.S. economy in its first year of implementation. According to rigorous economic analyses conducted by policy research institutions, this policy framework would support approximately $23.9 million in total economic activity (encompassing direct revenue and indirect spending) and create 239 new jobs across the United States, distributed primarily across the travel and tourism sector; these gains would be primarily driven by the revenue generated by U.S. travel agencies that would now be able to provide basic, targeted services to American citizens planning authorized trips to Cuba, such as personalized agency consulting, detailed itinerary advice, and assistance with navigating the indirect travel routes (via third countries) required under the scenario—excluding the far larger income gains, job creation, and market expansion that would be possible under the more comprehensive Scenario III. In contrast, the economic benefits to the United States under Scenario II—which expands travel permissions to include all U.S. citizens and lifts restrictions on direct travel—would see a significant, multi-fold increase in the first year, thanks to the expanded legal permission for U.S. commercial airlines to operate direct flights between U.S. and Cuban cities and U.S. travel agencies to offer end-to-end travel packages to Cuba. When accounting for both direct economic effects (such as revenue from airline tickets, travel agency service fees, and related travel products) and indirect and induced effects (such as increased demand for goods and services from businesses that support the aviation and travel sectors—including aircraft maintenance providers, fuel suppliers, and food service vendors—and higher consumer spending from workers employed in these industries, which circulates through local economies), this scenario would generate an additional $523 million in total economic revenue for the United States and create 3224 new jobs in the first year alone, with the majority of these jobs concentrated in transportation, tourism, and retail sectors. A thorough, data-driven analysis of these three distinct scenarios for lifting U.S. travel visa measures against Cuba reveals a key, counterintuitive insight: the restrictive effects of travel visa measures are not one-sided or limited to the target country—they may also produce a "boomerang effect" that rebounds on the sanction-initiating state, inflicting unintended, negative economic costs on its own industries and workers. However, it is important to note that such rebound effects do not occur universally or across all sectors; they are limited to specific, interconnected areas, and these areas directly correspond to the restricted domains that the travel visa measure was designed to target in the first place. This correlation also implies a broader, generalizable pattern: [David L. Edgell, Sr., Tourism Policy: The Next Millenium, (Sagamore Publishing, Champaign, Illinois, 1999), P18.]when a sanction-initiating state imposes travel visa measures on a country that possesses significant, marketable tourism resources (such as cultural heritage sites, natural landscapes, or unique cultural experiences), and in doing so restricts the development of the target country's tourism economy and its associated service industries (such as hospitality, ground transportation, local commerce, and tour guiding services), these restrictive effects will, in turn, have adverse, ripple consequences for the tourism economy-related industries of the sanction-initiating state itself. This is because the travel restrictions cut off not only the target country's access to the initiator's tourists and tourism-related services but also the initiator's own industries from the substantial revenue, market share, and business opportunities that would come from serving travelers to the target country—effectively denying domestic businesses a valuable market for their goods and services.

To summarize the restrictive effects of the three types of sanctions discussed above, it becomes clear that the restrictive effects of travel visa measures extend far beyond the simple act of severing the movement of individuals from the sanctioned country. While cutting off cross-border people flow constitutes the core direct effect of these measures, this direct effect in turn triggers a series of derivative changes—changes that encompass the three distinct restrictive effects analyzed earlier (the indirect impact on the economic field, the hindrance to cross-border communication, and the rebound effect on the sanction-initiating state). Crucially, however, all these derivative changes remain inherently tied to and guided by the fundamental restrictive effect centered on disrupting people's movement; they do not exist in isolation from this core mechanism. It is this interplay between the core direct effect and its multiple derivative impacts that gives rise to the defining characteristic of travel visa measures: the diversity of their restrictive effects. Beyond their role in sanctions, this diversity of travel visa measures also offers a valuable pathway to facilitate economic and trade exchanges between countries participating in the Belt and Road Initiative. Specifically, countries that depend heavily on tourism resources—for which the smooth flow of international travelers is a lifeline—can leverage the flexible, diverse nature of travel visa measures to implement differentiated policies for Belt and Road partner countries. For instance, they can introduce more convenient tourist visa procedures tailored to citizens of Belt and Road involved nations, such as shortening visa processing times, simplifying application materials, or offering visa-on-arrival services. In some cases, this flexibility can even lead to the implementation of mutual visa exemption agreements between pairs or groups of Belt and Road countries [21]. By tailoring travel visa policies to the cooperative context of the Belt and Road Initiative, these countries not only remove unnecessary barriers to people-to-people exchanges but also create more favorable conditions for the growth of tourism-related trade, investment, and cultural cooperation—ultimately strengthening the overall collaborative framework of the Initiative.

2.2.3 Flexibility in the Procedures for Travel Visa Measures

The flexibility and effectiveness of travel visa measures in their practical application are primarily manifested through three key aspects, with the first being the unilateral nature of these measures—a trait that directly underpins their flexibility and effectiveness. This unilateral character means that when a sanction-initiating country imposes restrictions on the free movement of individuals from the target country, such an action constitutes a unilateral measure directed at the target state, rather than one requiring collective authorization. In other words, when the sanction-initiating country decides to implement travel restrictions, it is not legally obligated to base this decision on authorization from the United Nations Security Council or strict adherence to specific provisions of international law. To contextualize this, Article 41 of the United Nations Charter explicitly permits the Security Council to order the severance of economic and other non-forcible relations between states, with the overarching aim of swiftly restoring international peace and security. Travel visa measures, in essence, fall under the category of "other relations" referenced in this article, yet their restrictive intensity is notably weaker than the full severance of economic ties outlined in the Charter. When examining the current state of international relations, unilateral economic sanctions often operate in a legal "vacuum"—while they may be framed as tools to uphold international peace and security, they can also exceed this stated mission and become instruments of hegemonism and power politics for certain nations seeking to advance their own strategic interests. By referencing relevant international legal provisions, it can be concluded that travel visa measures, due to their lower restrictive intensity, occupy a more permissive legal space than unilateral economic sanctions: at the very least, they operate in areas not explicitly prohibited by international law norms. This legal positioning means that travel visa measures can be independently applied by individual states, without being tied to or dependent on multilateral sanctions initiatives led by the United Nations. Of course, this independence does not imply that multilateral sanctions overseen by the UN Security Council would completely exclude the application of travel restrictions. A notable example is the UN-imposed sanctions on Sudan over its alleged ties to terrorism: in response to these multilateral sanctions, Sudan subsequently adjusted its national policies regarding the implementation of travel visa measures, including border blockade-related restrictions. In this case, the goal of countering terrorism—central to the UN sanctions—was also aligned with the functional effectiveness of travel visa measures, as restricting cross-border movement helped mitigate potential terrorist threats [22]. In fact, there exists an inclusive relationship between travel visa measures and multilateral sanctions: while travel visa measures can be incorporated into broader multilateral frameworks, they also retain the ability to operate independently of such frameworks, along with their inherent unilateral character. Furthermore, the restrictive impact of travel visa measures, though unilateral, is not arbitrary; it primarily relies on the principles and statutes of international law to justify actions aimed at safeguarding national interests and upholding international peace and security. This unique combination of unilateral applicability, legal permissibility, and alignment with core international law objectives fully embodies the flexibility and effectiveness of travel visa measures in practical international relations.

Secondly, the core effect of blocking cross-border people flow is a key factor that endows travel visa measures with notable flexibility in practice: blocking the free movement of individuals stands as the primary and most direct effect of implementing travel visa measures, and it is precisely this blocking effect that enables travel visa measures to generate a range of differentiated impacts tailored to specific objectives, such as by restricting the entry of tourists or service industry workers to exert targeted pressure on the sanctioned country's tourism and service sectors—a critical economic pillar for many nations—while through the negative ripple effects on these sectors, the broader economic development of the sanctioned country is indirectly constrained (as these industries often drive employment, consumer spending, and related industrial activity), and the blocking of entry and exit also disrupts the smooth operation of border trade (including the movement of cross-border traders, transportation of small-scale goods, and coordination of border-based business activities), which in turn undermines the stable country's economic stability, especially for nations relying heavily on cross-border commerce; notably, within the framework of visa restrictions that block people flow, measures can be further refined to target groups with distinct needs to enhance flexibility for specific policy goals—for example, visa restrictions on academic activities (denying visas to researchers, students, or university staff) can sever educational exchanges, restrictions on family visit or leisure travel visas can hinder cultural exchanges by preventing personal interactions and familial ties, and these restrictions can even extend to business travel, religious activities, and humanitarian missions, with cutting off people flow in these domains achieving the effect of limiting engagement in specific international interactions; a concrete illustration is the sanctions imposed on Qatar by the four Arab countries: by blocking people flow to and from Qatar to counter its alleged support for terrorism, the measures not only disrupted Qatar's oil and gas logistics (via restricting personnel in energy operations) but also harmed its tourism industry (a core of its economic diversification), prompting Qatar to adopt adaptive responses like relaxing visa requirements for foreign investors, seeking partners to attract tourists from Russia, China, and India, and rolling out incentives for domestic tourism—and this dynamic, where travel visa measures can exert targeted pressure and prompt counter-adjustments, directly confirms their flexible and effective nature in practical application [23].

Finally, the two-way restrictive purpose inherent in travel visa measures is another key factor that enhances their flexibility in practical application, and this two-way restrictive purpose can be succinctly summarized by the phrase "one restriction, double prevention": "one restriction" refers to the entry and exit restriction measures embedded in travel visa measures, which are inherently two-way—meaning they restrict both the entry of individuals into the sanction-initiating state and the exit of its own citizens to the sanctioned target state—while "double prevention" denotes that such two-way restrictions serve two core defensive and strategic goals: on one hand, they prevent the "importation" of individuals who may pose threats to the sanction-initiating state's national interests, public security, or citizens' rights, and on the other hand, they prevent the state's own domestic personnel from traveling to the sanctioned country, with these two prevention goals adapting to different scenarios to reflect the measures' flexibility. Specifically, preventing the entry of foreign individuals (from the sanctioned state) is generally the primary means of sanctions, as its core purpose is to block relevant personnel from the target country—such as those linked to potential security risks or harmful policies—from entering the sanction-initiating state and endangering its national interests or the legitimate rights of its citizens; meanwhile, preventing domestic personnel from traveling to the sanctioned country encompasses two distinct types of restrictions: one type is implemented to safeguard the personal safety of the state's own citizens, typically adopted when the sanctioned target state is in a situation of low security (such as ongoing conflicts, high crime rates, or public health crises), with the restriction on citizens' travel to that country serving to avoid exposing them to safety hazards, and the other type is driven by political or economic strategic purposes, where the sanction-initiating state imposes targeted travel restrictions on specific groups of domestic personnel (such as government officials, business representatives, or technical experts) traveling to the target state, aiming to exert pressure on the sanctioned state and force it to adjust its political stance or economic strategies in line with the initiator's demands. In addition to the two-way restrictions initiated by the sanction-initiating state, there are also scenarios where the sanctioned target state takes the initiative to implement entry and exit restrictions, and such actions are usually self-remedial measures adopted in response to the restrictive actions of the sanction-initiating state—a manifestation of the flexible application of travel visa measures from the target state's perspective. A typical example of this is the situation after the United States withdrew from the Iran Nuclear Agreement in 2018 and imposed a new round of strict sanctions on Iran: [24] these U.S. sanctions not only included sweeping economic sanctions (such as restricting Iran's oil exports and access to the international financial system) but also incorporated targeted travel restrictions, which put Iran under unprecedented economic and diplomatic pressure. To mitigate this pressure and find ways to increase national revenue while reducing foreign currency outflows, Iran implemented a series of countermeasures, including raising taxes on citizens' outbound travel: it increased the exit tax from $20 per trip in 2017 to approximately $60 per trip, and further stipulated that if a citizen continued to travel abroad multiple times within a 12-month period, the exit tax would increase incrementally with each subsequent trip [25]. Through this restrictive measure, the Iranian government aimed to achieve two key goals: on one hand, it sought to reduce the frequency of Iranian citizens traveling abroad for consumption, thereby curbing the outflow of foreign currency (a critical resource for Iran under sanctions) and easing pressure on its foreign exchange reserves, and on the other hand, it intended to redirect domestic consumer demand toward the local market, promoting the development of Iran's domestic tourism industry. Iranian officials also publicly stated that a portion of the additional revenue generated from the increased exit tax would be allocated to developing tourism infrastructure (such as upgrading scenic spots and transportation facilities) and protecting cultural heritage sites—further linking the restrictive measure to long-term economic development goals [26]. This case clearly illustrates that the application of entry and exit restrictions in travel visa measures is not limited to being a one-sided tool used by a single sanction-initiating state against a target state; instead, there are multiple flexible ways to apply these measures (including proactive use by sanctioned states as countermeasures), and these flexible application methods often play a positive and effective role in helping the implementing state achieve its intended policy or sanctions purposes.

The flexibility in the application of sanctions enables the measures to have multiple functions, including containment, suppression and maintenance, and these functions will have their own primary and secondary effects depending on the economic situation of the target state, ultimately, it has a positive effect on the protection of national interests and the maintenance of international peace and security. Under the "Belt and Road" initiative, the alliance between countries is closely linked, but in the process of realizing the purpose of friendly exchanges between countries, we also need to guard against the occurrence of incidents that wantonly undermine the national security of the two countries. The implementation of travel restrictions can flexibly screen the relevant personnel, and achieve the purpose of security in the process of national economic and trade development through the emergency activation of different procedure.

References

1. Article 41 of the Charter of the United Nations states: The Security Council may decide what measures not involving the use of armed force are to be employed to give effect to its decisions, and it may call upon the Members of the United Nations to apply such measures. These may include complete or partial interruption of economic relations and of rail, sea, air, postal, telegraphic, radio, and other means of communication, and the severance of diplomatic relations
2. von Braunmühland C, Kulessa M (1995) The Impact of UN Sanctions on Humanitarian Assistance Activities: Report on a Study Commissioned by the United Nations Department of Humanitarian Affairs, *Berlin*. Gesellschaft für Communication Management Interkultur Training mb H – COMIT
3. Swiss Confederation, United Nations Secretariat and Watson Institute for International Studies (2001) Targeted financial sanctions: a manual for design and implementation. Bonn University, Bonn

4. Design and Implementation of Arms Embargos and Travel and Aviation Related Sanctions, Bonn International Center for Conversion (BICC), German Foreign Office and the United Nations Secretariat, 2001
5. Wallensteen P, Staibano C, Eriksson M (eds) (2003) Making Targeted Sanctions Effective: Guidelines for the Implementation of UN Policy Options – Results from the Stockholm Process on the Implementation Targeted Sanctions, p 146
6. Report of the Secretary-General on the work of the Organization, A/55/1, New York, 2000, p. 13
7. Smart Sanctions. The Next Steps: Arms Embargoes and Travel Sanctions: Proceedings of the 'Bonn-Berlin Process'. Nomos Verlagsgesellschaft, Baden-Baden
8. Brzoska M (2001) Design and implementation of arms embargoes and travel and aviation and related sanctions: results of the Bonn-Berlin process. Bonn International Center for Conversion, Bonn. (Model Security Council Resolution on Travel Bans, With Commentary; Comment 6: The Resolution needs to provide precise wording for the target category, e.g. 'the government of' where a state actor is concerned, or an appropriate designation such as 'Junta', 'faction', 'movement', 'front', 'terrorist group' where a non-state actor is targeted)
9. Brzoska M (2001) Design and implementation of arms embargoes and travel and aviation and related sanctions: results of the Bonn-Berlin process. Bonn International Center for Conversion, Bonn. Comment 6: The Resolution needs to provide precise wording for the target category, e.g. 'the government of' where a state actor is concerned, or an appropriate designation such as 'Junta', 'faction', 'movement', 'front', 'terrorist group' where a non-state actor is targeted
10. Biersteker TJ, Eckert SE, Tourinho M (2016) Targeted sanctions: the impacts and effectiveness of United Nations action. Cambridge University Press, New York, pp 25–26
11. Subedi SP (2021) Unilateral sanctions in international law. Hart Publishing, an imprint of Bloomsbury Publishing, Oxford/New York
12. 'Unilateral sanctions as a means of political and economic coercion against developing countries', Report of the Secretary-General, UN Doc A/72/307 of 9 August 2017
13. Gordon J (2016) Economic sanctions as "negative development": the case of Cuba. J Int Dev 28(4):473–484
14. Article 1, Paragraph 1 of the Charter of the United Nations states: The Purposes of the United Nations are: To maintain international peace and security, and to that end: to take effective collective measures for the prevention and removal of threats to the peace, and for the suppression of acts of aggression or other breaches of the peace, and to bring about by peaceful means, and in conformity with the principles of justice and international law, adjustment or settlement of international disputes or situations which might lead to a breach of the peace
15. Article 2, Paragraph 6 of the Charter of the United Nations states: In order to achieve the purposes set forth in Article 1, the Organization and its Members shall act in accordance with the following Principles: ... The Organization shall ensure that states which are not Members of the United Nations act in accordance with these Principles so far as may be necessary for the maintenance of international peace and security
16. Pursuant to the Riyadh Agreements of 2013 and 2014, Qatar committed, among other things, to refrain from interfering in the internal affairs of other Gulf states, not to support the Muslim Brotherhood or opposition groups in Yemen, and to prevent Al Jazeera (headquartered in Qatar) from being used to challenge the Egyptian government
17. Seyfi S, Michael Hall C (2020) Tourism, sanctions and Boycotts, published by Routledge. Source: Adapted from the Middle East Eye (2017) and Sergie and Odeh (2018), p 65
18. Galtung J (1967) On the effects of international economic sanctions: with examples from the case of Rhodesia. World Politics, 19, 3, 378-416. JSTOR, 2003
19. Farahani BM, Shabani M (2013) The Impact of Sanctions On Iran's Tourism, The Open Access Journal of Resistive Economics (OAJRE)/ Economic Sanctions 1(1), Published Online August 2013
20. Ed Sanders and Patrick Long, Economic benefits to the United States from lifting the ban on travel to cuba, Cuba Policy Foundation Economic Impact Study, June 2002, p 21

21. Edgell DL Sr (1999) Tourism policy: the next millenium. Sagamore Publishing, Champaign, Illinois, p 18
22. Xiangyin Y (2002) Why Did the UN Lift Sanctions on Sudan?. West Asia and Africa 1:39–42
23. Middle East Eye (2017) Qatar tourism sector starts to feel squeeze of block-ade: Hotels recorded lower-than-expected visitor numbers over the Eid festival on Sunday. Reuters, 27 June. Retrieved from www.middleeasteye.net/news/qatar-tourism-sector-starts-feel-squeeze-blockade
24. Seyfi S, Hall CM (2018c) The future(s) of tourism in Iran. In: Seyfi S, Hall CM (eds) (2019) Tourism in Iran: challenges, development and issues. Routledge, Abingdon
25. Bezhan F (2017) Flight fight: Proposed tripling of "departure tax" roils Iranians. Retrieved from www.rferl.org/a/iran-skyrocketing-departure-tax-proposal-anger-tourism/28914103.html
26. Seyfi S, Michael Hall C (2020) Tourism, Sanctions and Boycotts, published by Routledge

Chapter 3
The Impact of Community-Based Travel Visa Measures on the "Global South"

In the process of cross-border exchanges and multi-sectoral cooperation among "Global South" countries—encompassing economic, political, cultural, and social domains—it is essential to adhere to the fundamental principles of consultation, co-construction, and sharing as the overarching guiding framework for all interactions. This framework is anchored in the core goal of advancing systematic collaboration across five key, mutually reinforcing dimensions: policy coordination (aligning national strategies to avoid conflicts), infrastructure connectivity (building cross-border transportation, energy, and digital networks), unimpeded trade (reducing tariffs and non-tariff barriers), financial integration (facilitating cross-border capital flows and currency cooperation), and people-to-people bonds (promoting cultural, educational, and professional exchanges) among these nations. Through sustained joint efforts in these interconnected areas, "Global South" countries aim to collectively build a cohesive community characterized by shared interests, shared responsibilities, and a shared future—one where mutual political trust is continuously deepened through dialogue, economic integration is strengthened via complementary partnerships, and cultural inclusiveness is promoted by celebrating diverse traditions. This community concept not only fully demonstrates the tangible, measurable positive outcomes generated by the practical implementation of "Global South" cooperation policies (such as increased trade volumes and joint infrastructure projects) but also serves as a powerful catalyst for fostering greater internal cohesion among all participating countries, uniting them around common, long-term development objectives that transcend individual national interests. However, in the actual process of translating this community concept into concrete actions and tangible results, challenges and issues inherent to different fields are inevitable and require deliberate attention—for instance, disparities in national policy priorities (where some countries prioritize infrastructure while others focus on trade), gaps in infrastructure development levels (between countries with advanced networks and those with underdeveloped systems), or persistent barriers to

X. Dong, J. Gu, *The Belt and Road Initiative and the Global South*, Energy, Climate Change & Sustainability in the Global South,
https://doi.org/10.1007/978-981-92-0144-0_3

cross-border trade (including cumbersome customs procedures and inconsistent regulatory standards). These issues demand careful, issue-specific attention and proactive, collaborative resolution as we work to drive inclusive and sustainable economic development among "Global South" participating countries. The progression from initial policy communication (including bilateral and multilateral dialogues) to the eventual deepening of people-to-people bonds (such as student exchanges and cultural festivals) is a gradual, multi-stage process that cannot be achieved by any single country acting in isolation. Instead, it requires sustained, long-term, and collective efforts from all "Global South" nations, with each stage building incrementally on the progress and achievements of the previous one to ensure continuity and momentum. A critical, foundational factor in forging and consolidating this collective cohesion lies in the practical realization of shared interests among all participating countries—only when each nation perceives tangible, direct benefits from cooperation (such as expanded market access or improved infrastructure connectivity) will the foundation for stable, long-term collaboration be truly solidified and resilient to external disruptions. Significantly, the travel visa measures analyzed in the preceding chapter provide precisely such a vital safeguard for countries involved in "Global South" initiatives, particularly in two interconnected, high-priority areas: safeguarding common security (by enabling targeted, risk-based regulation of cross-border mobility to mitigate threats such as transnational crime or public health risks) and advancing common economic development (by facilitating the smooth, orderly flow of people essential for trade, tourism, and professional exchanges—including business travelers, technical experts, and tourism workers). Therefore, by integrating a comprehensive understanding of the historical development trajectory (from early border control mechanisms to modern, facilitative visa policies) and inherent characteristics of travel visa measures (such as flexibility and adaptability to regional needs) as discussed earlier, we can systematically identify and extract three distinct, actionable pathways through which travel visa measures exert a direct and indirect impact on the exchanges and cooperation among "Global South" countries.

3.1 The Impact of Travel Visa Measures on the National Interests of the Global South

The travel visa measure is implemented primarily by authorizing the issuance of a visa corresponding to the person's application, which requires a specific review process, in this process, it can effectively prevent the relevant personnel who endanger national security interests from entering their own region, and thus play a positive preventive role in their own national interests and the national interests of the "Global South" community. The specific arguments are as follows:

The interests that drive interactions between sovereign states are primarily embodied in the inherent need to uphold national interests and maintain international peace and security—a norm that is not only universally recognized in international relations but also explicitly enshrined in the United Nations Charter as a core purpose of the organization, making it a binding requirement for all member states. Safeguarding national interests and international peace and security also aligns with the fundamental tenets of the concept of a community with a shared future for mankind: international peace and security are not abstract ideals but the solid cornerstone upon which the survival, development, and prosperity of all human societies depend—without this cornerstone, global cooperation, economic growth, and cultural exchange would lose their foundation and be unable to sustain. In this context, the restriction on human mobility imposed by travel visa measures serves as a relatively intuitive and operable diplomatic strategy. By selectively cutting off the free movement of specific types of individuals—such as those linked to terrorist organizations, transnational criminal networks, or activities that threaten state sovereignty and regional stability—these measures can effectively block actors who attempt to undermine the concept of a community with a shared future for mankind from disrupting the operation of the positive international order centered on the theme of "peace and development." For travel visa measures themselves, as a targeted sanction tool distinct from broad economic sanctions or military interventions, the way they interrupt human movement not only exerts direct impacts on the interests of the sanction-initiating state and the target state but, more importantly, plays a crucial practical role in safeguarding the broader framework of international peace and security. Its specific core functions are detailed as follows: First, cutting off the movement of specific groups helps reduce the probability of public hazards that threaten domestic and international security. A typical example is the travel ban implemented by the U.S. Trump administration under the banner of "protecting the nation from foreign attack"—in essence, this was an administrative measure designed to lower the incidence of domestic public hazards by restricting the free movement of foreign nationals, with the ban specifically targeting countries identified as having high risks of terrorist activities. Whether it is acts of terrorism, large-scale public health emergencies, or other dangerous events with public safety implications, such threats all rely on the movement, assembly, and collaboration of human actors; therefore, restricting the free movement of specific groups associated with countries where potential terrorist acts or public hazards may originate is undoubtedly one of the most direct and effective preventive measures. As the U.S. Supreme Court has explicitly recognized in its rulings, in an era plagued by persistent terrorism and increasingly sophisticated transnational crime, travel bans are of great significance to protecting the safety of American citizens, and the rigorous visa issuance process—including in-depth background checks, verification of travel intent, and cross-referencing with global anti-terrorism and criminal databases—also plays an irreplaceable role in identifying individuals with terrorist links or criminal records and preventing them from entering U.S. territory [1]. The combination of these measures—including targeted travel bans, rigorous visa screening, and cross-border information sharing—not only creates a safe and stable operational environment for safeguarding U.S. national interests (such as territorial integrity, public order, and the physical safety of citizens) but also exerts an indirect yet far-reaching impact on the maintenance of international peace and security. After all, the United States is a developed country with strong comprehensive national strength, encompassing economic, military, and technological dominance, and it maintains close, interdependent economic, trade, and diplomatic ties with most countries around the world—ranging from major global economies to small regional partners. Once its national interests are severely damaged—such as by a large-scale terrorist attack (like the 9/11 incident) or a widespread public safety incident (such as a transnational public health crisis)—it will inevitably trigger a cascading chain reaction: this includes disrupting the economic stability of countries that have close trade links with the U.S. (such as Mexico, China, and Canada), causing bottlenecks in global supply chains for key commodities (like semiconductors, agricultural products, and energy), and even destabilizing regional security frameworks (such as NATO or bilateral defense alliances). In the current international context where "one factor affects the whole body" due to deep globalization and interconnected markets, no country—whether developed or developing—can remain completely insulated from such shocks, as economic and security risks transmit rapidly across borders. Second, cutting off the free movement of key individuals in the target state—those with decision-making authority or influence over policies harmful to international peace—creates targeted, proportional pressure, forcing these specific groups to use their internal leverage to influence the reversal of adverse national policies that harm international peace and security. For instance, the travel restrictions imposed by the UN Security Council on Sudan in the early 2000s, pursuant to Resolution 1591 (2005), were not applied to the country's entire civilian population but specifically targeted key Sudanese government officials, senior military commanders, and leaders of armed groups (such as the Janjaweed) who were formally accused of supporting international terrorism and committing serious human rights abuses—including genocide and crimes against humanity—in the Darfur region. The core goal of these legally binding restrictions was to issue a strong, unified warning and deterrent to Sudan's decision-making elite: by limiting the ability of these key individuals to travel internationally—preventing them from attending high-level diplomatic conferences (such as UN General Assembly sessions), accessing foreign bank accounts or assets held abroad, or engaging in international networks that support their policies—the UN aimed to compel them to use their political and military influence within Sudan to promote tangible changes to policies that were detrimental to international peace and security. This targeted, precision-based approach had a clear, legally and morally defensible advantage: it avoided inflicting widespread harm on Sudan's civilian population (a common flaw of broad economic sanctions that often lead to shortages of food, medicine, and basic services, triggering humanitarian crises) while still applying effective, focused pressure on the specific decision-makers responsible for formulating and implementing harmful policies. In subsequent developments over the following decade, this strategy yielded measurable positive results: Sudan took concrete, verifiable actions to distance itself from terrorist organizations (such as expelling extremist groups), actively participated in international anti-terrorism cooperation (including sharing intelligence with UN counter-terrorism bodies), and adjusted its policies in line with UN resolutions (such as allowing humanitarian access to Darfur). These steps led the UN Security Council to eventually lift the travel restrictions on relevant personnel in 2020, following a comprehensive review of Sudan's compliance. Third, blocking the free movement of people through two-way, reciprocal entry and exit restrictions effectively protects the safety and legitimate interests of citizens of the sanction-initiating state. Since the entry and exit restrictions inherent to travel visa measures are inherently two-way in practice—restricting both the entry of foreign individuals into the initiator's territory and the exit of the initiator's domestic citizens to the target state—from the perspective of regulating the exit of its own citizens, these measures play a strong, proactive protective role for the citizens of the sanction-initiating state, thereby safeguarding their fundamental rights and legitimate interests under international law. Take the U.S. sanctions on Iran over its nuclear program, particularly during the 2010s, as a concrete example: at the time, Iran's domestic social order was relatively turbulent due to prolonged, multi-layered sanctions; in addition to unilateral U.S. sanctions (such as those under the Iran Sanctions Act), it was also subject to restrictive measures from the UN Security Council (under Resolutions 1737, 1747, and 1803) and the European Union, which severely hindered its domestic economic development (including limiting oil exports and access to the SWIFT financial system), led to shortages of daily necessities (such as medicine and imported consumer goods) in some areas, and caused innocent Iranian people to suffer great hardships. In this tense, resource-constrained context, there was a realistic, evidence-based risk that some Iranian citizens might harbor resentment toward citizens of the sanction-initiating states (including the U.S., EU member states, and their allies), increasing the potential danger faced by foreign citizens residing in or traveling to Iran—such as the risk of arbitrary detention, harassment, or targeted violence. Therefore, restricting U.S. citizens from traveling to Iran at this time served a clear "dual-purpose" effect under U.S. foreign policy: on one hand, it expressed the U.S. government's firm opposition to Iran's nuclear policy by imposing targeted restrictions on Iran's tourism economy, which relies heavily on international travelers for revenue; on the other hand, it was a practical, risk-mitigation measure to protect U.S. citizens, preventing them from facing an increased risk of violence, crime, or arbitrary treatment in Iran's unstable social and political environment caused by multi-party sanctions on the nuclear issue. Finally, travel visa measures have a significant, empirically supported positive effect on the prevention and control of transnational crimes that threaten global security, such as the smuggling of contraband (including illegal drugs, weapons, and endangered species), aircraft hijacking, and human trafficking (particularly of women and children). The core, indispensable prerequisite for the successful implementation of these transnational crimes is the ability of perpetrators to move freely across national borders without effective supervision or interdiction; without such unrestricted free movement—including the ability to forge travel documents or exploit weak border controls—the planning, coordination, and execution of such crimes would be severely hindered, if not rendered impossible. In the case of smuggling crimes, for example, the key operational link in transporting smuggled goods (such as cocaine from South America to Europe, weapons from the Middle East to Africa, or counterfeit luxury goods from Asia to North America) is to evade inspection by customs authorities or border control agencies of transit and destination countries. If a country tightens entry and exit restrictions as part of its anti-smuggling strategy—by enhancing verification of travel documents (such as using biometric technology to detect forgeries), conducting more thorough cargo inspections (including using X-ray scanners and sniffer dogs), and strengthening real-time information sharing with other countries' law enforcement agencies (such as Interpol)—the probability of smuggling activities successfully passing through border checkpoints will be greatly reduced. This not only directly protects the national interests of the implementing state (such as safeguarding domestic market order from counterfeit goods, preventing the spread of harmful substances like illegal drugs, and ensuring tax revenue from legitimate trade) but also provides an effective, collective guarantee for regional and international security by curbing the cross-border spread of organized crime networks. The 9/11 incident that shocked the world in 2001 is another stark, tragic example: the terrorist attack, which killed nearly 3000 people, was carried out by 19 hijackers who hijacked four civilian aircraft, and 15 of these terrorists had entered the United States through normal non-immigrant visa channels (primarily B-1/B-2 tourist or business visas) in the years preceding the attack. If the U.S. government had tightened restrictions on the entry and exit of people from sensitive regions (such as strengthening visa screening for individuals from countries with known terrorist links, verifying the authenticity of travel purposes, and improving information sharing with foreign intelligence agencies) before the incident, such a catastrophic terrorist attack would have been much less likely to occur. This is precisely why the U.S. government significantly enhanced its visa screening procedures in the aftermath of the 9/11 incident—including introducing more strict, multi-layered background checks (such as checking against terrorist watchlists maintained by the FBI and DHS), extending visa review periods for high-risk applicants, and requiring biometric data (such as fingerprints and facial recognition) for all visa applicants—to prevent similar security lapses. Of course, the functions of travel visa measures in safeguarding national interests and international peace and security are not limited to the four aspects mentioned above; although the specific effects of cutting off human movement may vary depending on different national conditions (such as a country's border control capacity), regional contexts (such as whether the region is prone to conflict), and policy objectives (such as whether the goal is counter-terrorism or anti-crime), all these effects consistently revolve around the core, overarching goal of protecting the legitimate national interests of the implementing state and maintaining international peace and security. This makes travel visa measures a flexible, targeted, and important tool in the toolkit of modern international relations and global security governance, particularly in an era marked by transnational threats and interconnected risks.

National interests and international peace and security serve as crucial "safety valves" for the economic development of "Global South" countries—these two pillars underpin the stability, resilience, and long-term sustainability of all development initiatives in the region, from infrastructure projects to cross-border trade partnerships. Without the effective protection of national interests (including territorial sovereignty and resource security) or a stable environment of international peace and security free from conflicts and transnational threats, the "Global South" cooperation initiative, which aims to promote collective development, mutual benefit, and shared prosperity, would lack a solid, reliable foundation and be unable to achieve long-term sustainability. As the fundamental, non-negotiable interests of each sovereign nation, national interests enable "Global South" countries to implement win-win cooperation policies from a strategic global perspective: by taking the important interests of relevant partner countries as the starting point, combining them with their own actual national conditions (such as economic structure, resource endowments, and development stages), these countries can first achieve internal security and social stability—an essential, prerequisite foundation for any form of economic development—and then further advance the sound, orderly development of economic and trade exchanges among regional state alliances. In this context, it is widely recognized among international policy circles that the rational, proportionate adoption of travel visa measures will exert an irreplaceable positive impact on safeguarding the national interests of "Global South" countries and maintaining international peace and security. By virtue of their inherent flexibility in regulating cross-border human mobility, travel visa measures can effectively screen out potential security risks (such as individuals linked to terrorism, transnational crime, or other malicious activities) to protect the internal stability of each "Global South" country, while also facilitating the smooth, legal flow of personnel needed for legitimate economic and trade cooperation, cultural exchanges, and technical collaboration—striking a critical balance between security and development that is vital for the success of the "Global South" initiative. This dual, complementary role not only reinforces the "safety valve" function of national interests and international peace and security but also provides practical, actionable support for the sustainable advancement of the "Global South" cooperation agenda, making travel visa measures a key, indispensable auxiliary tool for the region's collective development.

3.2 Impact of Travel Visa Measures on the Security Interests of the Global South

If the maintenance of national interest is the basic interest, then the national security interest is the key to the stability of national sovereignty. As the "Global South" policy involves different countries, need to face the most important security interests is how to solve the occurrence of terrorist activities. Travel visa measures can effectively avoid the emergence of this risk, especially its pre-emptive function, it is a convenient way to prevent the development of trade and economic activities that threaten the "Global South". Here's how it would work:

As a significant and persistent obstacle to the peace and security of the international community, terrorism has long stood as the primary target of the United

Nations and all its member states in their collective efforts to uphold global stability. The word "Terror" originates from a Latin term that carries the meanings of "to frighten," "to fear," or "to alarm," tracing its linguistic roots to expressions of intense emotional and societal unease. As far back as the year 105 BC, the term "CIMBRICUS" was employed to describe a state of widespread panic and emergency that gripped the Roman people when soldiers of the Cimbri tribe arrived in Rome, triggering profound fear and chaos among the city's inhabitants. This historical precedent of linking collective fear to a threatening force was later invoked by the Jacobins during the French Revolution (1789–1799), who established a new "Terror regime" as their form of government— a system explicitly designed to purify the revolutionary cause by advancing the principles of democracy and popular rule [2], all while rooting out those deemed enemies of the revolution. After the Jacobins lost their hold on power, the word "Terrorist" became an overused label in political discourse, and the oppression and violence associated with those labeled as terrorists transformed the term into a feared tool of state control and repression. From that point onward, terrorism took on certain negative connotations, yet the term itself did not gain widespread circulation or recognition beyond limited political and regional contexts. It was not until the late nineteenth century, specifically after Sergey Nechayev openly described himself as a "Terrorist" and founded the Russian terrorist group known as The People's Revenge in 1869, that terrorism reemerged in public consciousness—this time as a tactic associated with revolutionary groups whose main purpose was to attract more members to their cause through violent struggle against the oppressive Tsarist rule of Russia. During that era, terrorism was generally perceived as a more familiar form of anti-government activity, closely tied to movements seeking to overthrow established political authorities. But in modern times, the meaning of "Terrorism" has shifted: it usually refers to acts in which private groups carry out the killing of innocent people, often staging such violence in a way that creates a media spectacle to amplify their impact and spread fear. Some scholars argue that terrorism constitutes a deliberate policy focused on terrorizing populations and instilling widespread fear as a means to achieve specific ends. More generally, it is understood as a distinct type of act, which can be further subdivided into three key categories: the first category encompasses acts aimed at creating a pervasive climate of overwhelming terror within a society; the second category includes acts driven by the goal of achieving an ideological objective, whether political, religious, or social; and the third category involves acts that deliberately target non-combatants or show a reckless disregard for the safety of non-combatants. Additionally, some definitions of terrorism also incorporate elements such as illegal acts, the use of violence, or the employment of unconventional warfare tactics that fall outside the norms of traditional armed conflict [3]. At present, the international community is in a state of constant change and development, with geopolitical dynamics, societal values, and security threats evolving rapidly—and because of these complexities, there remains no universal consensus on the precise definition of terrorism. The United Nations, as the leading global intergovernmental organization, and its diverse member states each apply different criteria when defining terrorism, reflecting their unique national interests, legal systems, and political perspectives. When it comes to the definition of terrorism in the United States, such definitions can be traced back to the United States Code, which contains two distinct and formally codified definitions. For instance, Section 18 of the United States Code—the section that governs criminal acts and criminal proceedings—defines international terrorism in the following way: [4] the term "International terrorism" means an activity that involves an act of violence or an act that endangers human life, where these acts either violate the criminal law of the United States or the criminal law of any other country, or would constitute a criminal offense if committed within the jurisdiction of the United States or the jurisdiction of any other country; the main purpose of such activities is to intimidate or coerce civilian populations, to influence government policy through intimidation or coercion, and the main acts involved are those intended to influence government decision-making by means of mass destruction, assassination, or kidnapping; furthermore, such activities occur primarily outside the territorial jurisdiction of the United States, or they transcend national borders in terms of the means used to carry them out, the people intended to be intimidated or coerced, or the place where the perpetrator operates or seeks asylum after committing the act. In contrast, Section 22 of the United States Code defines terrorism as follows: The term "Terrorism" refers to premeditated, politically motivated acts of violence that are committed by subnational organizations or secret agents and are directed against non-combatant targets [5]. Under United States law, the legal understanding of terrorism is explicitly divided into two categories: domestic terrorism and foreign (or international) terrorism. Although the content covered by the definition of international terrorism is more specific and detailed, encompassing cross-border elements and particular tactics, the scope of application of the broader term "terrorism" is wider than that of "international terrorism," as it includes both domestic and international acts that meet its criteria.

The European Union defines terrorism in the following manner: terrorist offences refer to a set of specifically listed criminal offences, primarily consisting of serious crimes that inflict harm on individuals and property; due to the inherent nature or contextual background of these offences, they have the potential to cause severe damage to a sovereign state or an international organization, and their core purposes include three key aspects: first, to seriously intimidate the general population and create a climate of fear among ordinary people; second, to unduly draw the attention of a government or an international organization to actions they have taken or failed to take, thereby pressuring these entities to change their policies or behaviors; third, to seriously damage or even destroy the fundamental political, constitutional, economic, or social structure of a state or an international organization, undermining the foundational systems that sustain their operation [6]. Although this definition of terrorism makes it relatively easier in practical operations to distinguish the specific scope of what constitutes a terrorist offence, and in terms of clarity, its content is more straightforward and understandable compared to the definitions outlined in U.S. law, the comprehensiveness of this EU definition still has gaps that need to be supplemented and improved to cover more complex scenarios of terrorist activities. At present, among the various definitions of terrorism put forward by different international bodies and countries, the definition proposed by the United Nations is generally considered to be more comprehensive in scope and more operable in practical application. Specifically, in the document titled "Measures to Eliminate International Terrorism," which was officially adopted by the UN General Assembly through its Resolution 49/60 on December 9, 1994, there is a clear provision that describes terrorism as a criminal act; this act is committed with the intent—or with the purpose of inciting—a state of terror among the general public, a specific group of people, or particular individuals, and it is driven by political motives; crucially, the provision emphasizes that such a criminal act cannot be justified under any circumstances, and no considerations of a political, philosophical, ideological, racial, ethnic, religious, or any other nature can be invoked as grounds to justify its commission. Starting from the year 2000, the United Nations began the process of formulating a Comprehensive Convention on International Terrorism, and during this process, the definition of terrorism has been a key issue placed on the negotiation table for discussion among member states; the draft definition proposed during these negotiations is as follows: 1. An offence as defined by this convention shall be deemed to have been committed by any person who, in any manner whatsoever, unlawfully and intentionally causes one of the following consequences: (a) the death of any person or serious bodily injury to any person; (b) or serious damage to public property or private property, including damage to public places, state facilities, government buildings, public transportation systems, critical infrastructure, or the natural environment; (c) economic loss that causes or is likely to cause significant damage to the property, premises, facilities, or systems mentioned in paragraph 1(b) of this article; and a key prerequisite for classifying such an act as an offence under this convention is that, based on the nature of the act itself or the specific context in which it is committed, the purpose of the act is to intimidate a population or to compel a government or an international organization to take a particular action or to refrain from taking a particular action [7]. While this draft definition does embody the specific ways and means through which terrorist acts are typically committed, it fails to fully cover the new types of terrorist acts that have emerged and evolved in the subsequent years, leaving gaps in addressing emerging threats. Subsequently, the United Nations Security Council, through its Resolution 1566 (2004), put forward a new definition of terrorism: it defines terrorism as criminal acts that are committed with the intention of causing death, inflicting serious bodily injury, or taking hostages—including acts directed against civilians—and the aim of these criminal acts is to incite a state of terror among the general public, a specific group of people, or particular individuals, to intimidate a population, or to compel governments or international organizations to take a particular action or to refrain from taking a particular action. A few months after the adoption of this resolution, in March 2005, a panel established by the United Nations once again provided a description of terrorism, defining it as any act that "is intended to cause the death of civilians or non-combatants or to inflict serious bodily injury on civilians or non-combatants, and the aim of such an act is to intimidate a population or to compel governments or international organizations to take a particular action or to refrain from taking a particular action." [8].

From the perspective of major international organizations (such as the United Nations, NATO, and the African Union) and individual sovereign countries, the concept of terrorism has undergone an evolving process from being concrete to becoming abstract, and the main driver behind this evolution lies in the dynamic, adaptive nature of terrorism itself: as terrorism continues to develop in form and scope, new types of terrorist acts (such as cyber-terrorism and lone-wolf attacks) constantly emerge, yet concrete definitions of terrorism often fail to keep pace with these new manifestations amid social and technological progress—additionally, the inherent lag of legal systems, including legislative and judicial processes, means that existing laws cannot promptly exert effective sanctions on these emerging terrorist acts. Therefore, by formulating abstract, principle-based definitions of the terrorism concept, we can more effectively punish and curb new forms of terrorism, as abstract definitions possess greater adaptability to cover evolving threats that concrete, scenario-specific ones struggle to encompass. From the perspective of the definition outlined in United Nations Security Council Resolution 1566 (2004)—a legally binding document under international law—it is not difficult to observe that terrorist acts have gradually become a key target of travel visa measures, and this connection is mainly reflected in the following three aspects: first, there is alignment in the suppression of relevant subjects: the purpose of terrorist acts, as defined in the resolution, is "to incite a state of terror among the general public, a group of persons or specific individuals," and the specificity of the subjects targeted by such acts (whether the general public, specific groups, or particular individuals) is consistent with the scope of subjects restricted by travel visa measures—travel visa measures, in their classification of restricted entities, can also distinguish between ordinary citizens, specific groups (such as extremist organizations), and specific individuals (such as key terrorist operatives), with their sanction targets also being clearly specific, making them highly compatible with addressing the subject-related characteristics of terrorism. Second, there is synergy in the containment of methods: the core way terrorism operates is to incite a state of terror among people, and any act where an individual illegally or deliberately damages public or private property, or causes harm to others' person or property through any means (including violence, threats, or sabotage), may be associated with terrorist acts—ultimately, such acts result in substantial harm to individuals or severe damage to public and private property; travel visa measures, precisely by imposing entry and exit restrictions, visa bans, and similar administrative measures to deny freedom of movement to groups or individuals with potential terrorist tendencies, serve to prevent acts that could cause harm to others' person or property or damage to public and private property, thereby aligning with the need to contain terrorist methods. Third, there is consistency in the containment of consequences: the end result of terrorism is to achieve political objectives (such as overthrowing governments) or undermine a country's national stability and social order, and in contemporary times, terrorism also exhibits a clear trend of cross-border and cross-regional spread; travel visa measures, by fundamentally blocking cross-border and cross-regional mobility of potential terrorist actors, play a direct role in restoring and maintaining national security and stability, and this restrictive effect on mobility also generates a strong deterrent impact on terrorist acts, effectively curbing their cross-border proliferation and mitigating the severe consequences they pose to national and regional order.

In practical application, travel visa measures continue to play a crucial role in deterring terrorism, with their anti-terrorist value having gained explicit legal recognition in key international and national contexts. A notable example of this legal validation is seen in the United States: when former President Trump issued an executive order titled "Protecting the Nation from Foreign Terrorist Attacks"—which aimed to restrict travel to the U.S. from specific countries deemed high-risk for terrorism—the U.S. Supreme Court ultimately upheld the legality of this order. Though the implementation period of this particular executive order was not lengthy, this short-lived application process marked a significant turning point: it became the starting point for travel visa measures to be independently implemented for the realization of their anti-terrorist functional value, rather than merely serving as a supporting tool alongside other policies. Prior to the issuance of this executive order, the anti-terrorist function of travel visa measures had long remained in a phase where they were applied by the international community in conjunction with other types of sanctions, lacking independent recognition as a standalone anti-terrorist tool. One such early case of coordinated application is the sanctions imposed on Sudan by the United Nations Security Council in 1996 under the framework of Resolution 1054 (1996) [9]: these sanctions not only included restrictions on Sudan's economic activities (such as limiting its access to international financial markets) but also explicitly imposed entry or transit restrictions on Sudan's key government officials and members of its armed forces who were suspected of links to terrorist activities. Additionally, the resolution further called on all United Nations member states to actively provide assistance in curbing the spread of terrorist activities within Sudan's borders [10]. Among these measures, the restrictions on the entry into or transit through other countries of Sudan's key individuals directly fall under the scope of travel visa measures, as their core mechanism is to cut off the cross-border movement of persons associated with terrorism. Beyond multilateral sanctions led by international organizations, travel restrictions also continue to play a major role in countering terrorist activities within the context of unilateral economic sanctions, with the 2011 Syrian crisis serving as a prominent instance. During this period, the European Union imposed targeted sanctions on Syria's President Bashar al-Assad, accusing him of being involved in "acts of terrorism"; these sanctions included a ban on Assad entering any EU member state and the freezing of his overseas assets. Subsequently, the EU further expanded the scope of its sanctions list: it added 22 Syrian individuals to the blacklist on the grounds of their alleged "human rights violations" and included 8 Syrian companies for their "financial support to the Syrian regime." Concurrently, the EU issued a prohibition stating that no EU member state could issue visas to the aforementioned 22 individuals, while also mandating the freezing of all assets held by the 8 listed companies within European territories—once again, the visa ban component of these sanctions clearly demonstrates the application of travel visa measures in countering terrorism and related destabilizing activities [11].

In the implementation of targeted sanctions aimed at countering terrorism, the case that most vividly reflects the function of curbing terrorist acts is the issuance of the U.S. executive order—specifically Executive Order 13769 (2017), later revised as Executive Order 13780 (2017)—focused on "protecting the nation from terrorist attacks by foreigners." The core thrust of this legally binding executive order is to prevent individuals posing potential terrorist dangers from entering the United States by imposing strict, risk-based visa restrictions on citizens of several countries (initially seven, later adjusted to five) formally identified by U.S. security agencies as having a high risk of terrorist activity or inadequate security cooperation. While such mobility restriction measures run counter to the right to freedom of movement enshrined in international law—a fundamental human right explicitly recognized in key documents like the Universal Declaration of Human Rights (Article 13) and the International Covenant on Civil and Political Rights (Article 12)—they nonetheless play an important, often contested role in deterring the occurrence of terrorist activities within U.S. borders, with this deterrent effect manifesting in three distinct, actionable key ways. First, travel visa measures directly cut off the cross-border flow of personnel that is critical to the planning, coordination, and execution of terrorist operations. The premise of carrying out a large-scale or organized terrorist act typically involves reaching a collective consensus among operatives: this could mean the establishment of a cohesive terrorist organization (such as al-Qaeda or ISIS cells) or the alignment of opinions and objectives among the main actors who intend to commit the terrorist act. In the process of forming such a consensus, recruiting and organizing members, or coordinating logistical and tactical plans, the free movement of personnel across national borders is inevitably required—whether to meet in person, train together, or position operatives in the target country. Without the ability to move freely across borders, the terrorist group cannot complete the implementation of its consensus-driven decisions, whether that involves gathering key operatives in a staging area, transporting weapons or explosive materials, or coordinating on-the-ground actions with local sympathizers. On the other hand, the restrictive measures imposed by travel visa policies—such as outright visa denials, heightened security screening for high-risk applicants, or outright entry bans for citizens of designated countries—can just delay or even prevent the formation of such terrorist agreements in the first place, effectively curbing the evolution of terrorist plots from their very source by disrupting the essential personnel mobility that underpins their operational capacity. Second, travel visa restrictions significantly raise the time, financial, and logistical cost of traveling to the target country (the country the terrorists intend to attack), creating a practical, multi-layered barrier to their operations. The implementation of terrorist activities usually targets a specific country or region, and the common strategic purposes of such acts include disrupting the target country's social stability, destroying its public order, and sowing widespread psychological panic and fear among its civilian population. To achieve these goals, terrorists must first gain legal or illegal access to the target country—and fundamentally restricting this free access through visa policies is a key, proactive way to prevent terrorist acts from being carried out. Travel visa measures achieve this by increasing the number and stringency of restrictions on visa issuance: for example, by extending the standard review period from weeks to months, requiring more detailed background checks (including verification of employment, travel history, and social connections), or limiting the types of visas available to short-term, single-entry only. From the perspective of time cost alone, these measures can curb or delay the implementation of terrorist acts—each additional step in the visa application and review process adds to the time terrorists need to reach the target country, giving domestic and international security agencies (such as the FBI, DHS, or Interpol) more time to detect and investigate potential threats through intelligence sharing and surveillance, and ultimately creating opportunities to fundamentally prohibit the implementation of terrorist plans before they can be executed. Finally, the blacklisting mechanism closely associated with travel visa measures enhances deterrence and monitoring capabilities by including specific high-risk groups (such as designated terrorist organizations), affiliated entities, or individuals with elevated risk factors (such as those with links to extremist networks) into real-time, cross-border regulatory blacklists—including the U.S. Terrorist Screening Database (TSDB) and the UN Security Council's ISIL (Da'esh) and al-Qaeda Sanctions List. Once placed on these legally enforceable blacklists, the movements of these entities or individuals are closely tracked and restricted by border control authorities worldwide: they may be denied visas outright by all UN member states, subjected to additional, rigorous screening at airports and border crossings (including body searches and luggage inspections), or have their travel records monitored across multiple countries through Interpol notices. This level of constant oversight not only allows security authorities to effectively cut off the planning of terrorist activities—by preventing key operatives from moving internationally to coordinate plans or transfer funds—but also ensures that terrorism does not occur in an unknown or unguarded state. By maintaining constant awareness of the movements of high-risk individuals and groups, security agencies can proactively deploy resources to respond to potential threats (such as increasing patrols at key locations or conducting pre-emptive raids), better minimizing the probability and overall risk of terrorist acts being carried out within the target country.

The above content has explained the travel visa measures for curbing terrorism from both theoretical perspectives (such as alignment with counter-terrorism objectives) and practical cases (like U.S. executive orders), and these measures are mainly implemented by imposing visa restrictions on personnel groups from specific countries with potential terrorist risks and on individuals affiliated with specific hazardous organizations (such as designated terrorist networks), all with the clear aim of avoiding the risk of these high-risk individuals entering the territory of other countries to carry out malicious acts. At the current stage, the complexity of cross-border personnel mobility has become particularly prominent in the context of globalization: the continuous advancement of transportation technology (including air travel and cross-border land routes) has made long-distance travel faster and more convenient, while the differences in travel policy services (such as visa processing efficiency) and border management standards (such as document verification rigor) between different countries have further increased the uncertainty of mobility, and these factors together have greatly elevated the risks associated with cross-border personnel movement—including the risk of terrorists exploiting loose mobility channels to carry out cross-border attacks. Therefore, it is essential for the international community, especially regional alliances, to formulate and implement targeted, risk-based precautionary measures to prevent potential terrorist acts from undermining the peaceful interaction and cooperative relations between countries. For "Global South" countries, which are actively advancing the practice of the community with a shared future for mankind concept in areas like infrastructure connectivity and trade integration, this concept has effectively enhanced the level of economic and trade exchanges between friendly neighboring countries in the region, promoting mutual development and win-win cooperation in sectors such as agriculture, manufacturing, and tourism; however, on the other hand, we must also remain alert to the potential dangers hidden behind the increased personnel and trade flows—especially the risk of terrorists taking advantage of the frequent exchanges (such as tourist arrivals or business trips) to infiltrate target countries or carry out destructive activities. This makes the focus on "stemming dangers before they arise" through proactive security measures particularly critical, and in this context, travel visa measures play an irreplaceable important role: by conducting strict, multi-layered screening of relevant personnel from target countries or specific groups of incoming individuals (including background checks and intent verification), we can accurately identify and exclude those with certain security risks (such as individuals with terrorist ties, criminal records, or suspicious travel intentions), thereby avoiding irreparable losses (such as loss of life or economic damage) that may occur after risks materialize. Similarly, among the countries covered by the "Global South" cooperation policy— which emphasizes mutual benefit in trade and investment—building a security barrier centered on travel visa measures can better protect the transaction security in the process of "Global South" economic and trade development: for example, by screening out individuals or entities that have a history of breaking trade agreements (such as non-payment of dues), engaging in fraudulent activities (such as counterfeit goods trade), or posing transaction risks (such as links to illegal financial networks), we can effectively safeguard the integrity of cross-border trade transactions, reduce the occurrence of trade disputes and economic losses (for both exporters and importers), and ultimately create a stable, secure, and trustworthy internal and external environment for business exchanges and cooperation among "Global South" countries.

3.3 The Impact of Travel Visa Measures on the Economic Development of the Global South

When it comes to the relationship between travel visa measures and economic development, the tourism services sector is the most relevant. In addition to the tourism service industry, we are easy to ignore the convenience effect of the visa.

This kind of convenience effect can go beyond the travel service industry and affect the economic and trade exchanges of other industries. The specific aspects can be discussed as follows:

First, the impact of travel visa measures on the economic development of the "Global South" can be highlighted as the effect of achieving efficient movement of people. The foregoing discussion of the development and characteristics of travel visa measures also distinguishes between different types of visas. Among them, business visa, study visa and visit visa is outside the tourist visa to achieve the best types. The above three types of visas can still bring good economic benefits to the relevant countries. Imagine if facilitation measures for business visas were agreed in the countries covered by the "Global South" policy, such as a modest increase in the visa approval process for business negotiations, it would attract more people to invest, start businesses, and do business. The expansion of similar travel visa measures will significantly increase the degree of economic development linkages between countries of the "Global South", we should quickly achieve policy communication, facility connectivity, unimpeded trade, financial integration and people-to-people communication, and strengthen the trust between countries in the process of regional coordinated development.

Second, the tourist visa measures will also attract more countries to participate in the "Global South" policy promotion process. This, too, is easy to understand. If countries in the "Global South" feel the benefits of the travel visa measures, it will spread the good news, let more people know about the "Global South" policy and be willing to take advantage of the facilitation of travel visas by joining the initiative. Policy engagement between countries of the "Global South" is itself a desire to diversify economic development models, adhere to the concept of openness and inclusiveness, and if the travel visa measures are well utilized, so will let more countries choose to join them, become the economic and trade exchanges in the process of the beneficiary countries.

To wrap up, travel visa measures also serve as a robust diplomatic restriction tool, capable of fostering effective checks and balances between nations—this means they can be leveraged to implement targeted countermeasures against countries that are unfriendly in economic and trade interactions, particularly those with hegemonic tendencies that seek to dominate or disrupt global economic order. The very essence of sustainable economic development lies in the formation of mutually beneficial, win-win two-way positive interactions between countries, where each party stands to gain from cooperation and shared growth. However, in reality, some countries prioritize their own interests by obstructing the economic development of others—such actions not only harm the direct interests of the affected nations but also disrupt the stability of the global market economy in the long run, undermining the foundation of fair and equitable international trade. The implementation of the "Global South" policy is precisely an effort to break this negative, hegemony-driven model that distorts global economic development; it advocates for a diversified development path, replacing the exclusive economic development mode in which a handful of countries monopolize discourse power and impose their rules on others. Therefore, from a long-term perspective, the "Global South" initiative holds unlimited potential and represents a correct direction for global economic development: it strengthens friendly relations between neighboring countries through equal cooperation, provides a practical pathway to boost economic growth for developing nations, and further facilitates the advancement of transnational economic development models that prioritize inclusivity and shared benefits. On the whole, by safeguarding security, promoting orderly exchanges, and enabling diplomatic countermeasures against unfriendly forces, travel visa measures exert a direct and long-lasting positive impact on the economic development of "Global South" countries, acting as a practical safeguard for the region's collective growth agenda.

The positive and defensive restrictive effects exerted by travel visa measures on the tourism service industry and other sectors critical to economic development stand as important manifestations of their role in supporting the economic progress of "Global South" countries. To fully grasp how these measures shape economic dynamics, we need to further examine their economic restrictive effects—particularly the targeted economic restrictions they enable, which are implemented with clear strategic objectives. The first key objective of such targeted economic restrictions is to serve a punitive purpose, and a prominent example of this is the travel restrictions imposed on Qatar by four Arab countries in mid-2017. For Qatar, tourism had long been identified as one of its five core priority sectors for economic diversification; the country was actively pursuing the development of business and leisure tourism as a key economic transformation strategy, with the explicit aim of reducing its heavy, single reliance on oil and gas revenues and building a more resilient, multi-sector economy. In response to Qatar (over allegations of supporting terrorism), one of the core strategies adopted by the four Arab countries was to impose no-fly restrictions and other travel-related bans, which were designed to minimize the inflow of people into Qatar and geographically isolate the country from the outside world—directly targeting its tourism-driven diversification efforts. The implementation of these travel visa and mobility restrictions inflicted tangible damage on Qatar's ongoing economic transformation: its tourism industry, in particular, bore the brunt of these punitive measures, suffering significant setbacks. According to estimates, approximately 1 million tourists visited Qatar in the first half of 2018—a figure that represented a one-third decrease compared to the same period before the sanctions took effect. Concurrently, hotel occupancy rates in Qatar also declined, falling slightly to 60 percent in the first half of 2018 when compared to the pre-sanction period. These concrete economic losses not only vividly illustrate the severe impact that the targeted economic restrictive effects of travel visa measures can have on a specific industry (in this case, Qatar's tourism sector) but also underscore the resolve of the four Arab countries to push back against Qatar over the alleged support for terrorism—using travel-related restrictions as a direct, impactful tool to advance their punitive goals.

Secondly, with a certain corrective purposes. This corrective purpose can be seen as a continuation of the effect of the warning purpose, that is, when the warning effect fails to achieve the purpose of the sanctions, it will correct its adverse effects from restricting the economic development of the target country. For example, when the United States imposed sanctions on Iran, initially in 2011, it believed that Iran had begun to seek nuclear technology in order to manufacture and acquire nuclear weapons, and handed them over to Turkey, Egypt and other allies, while it may pose a certain threat to the security of the United States, Iran denies the accusation that it is seeking nuclear technology, it has also explained its involvement in all international resolutions on the non-proliferation of nuclear weapons and the prohibition of weapons of mass destruction, responses that have failed to prevent the imposition of sanctions, the United States has joined the European Union and Canada in imposing travel restrictions on Iran [12]. And to prohibit the free movement of government officials involved, at a time when the travel restrictions are more of a warning function, and the countries implementing the travel restrictions mentioned above have not clarified the details of their implementation, the main hope is that the Iranian nuclear issue can be resolved through agreement. The warning effect also had the desired effect, in July 2015, the signing of the Iran nuclear agreement, the United states-led allies announced the suspension and lifting of economic sanctions [13]. Then, in 2018, the Trump administration began imposing the toughest sanctions on Iran when it obtained information that Iran was violating the nuclear deal by secretly developing uranium enrichment and starting production of ballistic missiles, chief among them is a demand that other countries stop importing Iranian oil, cut off trade with Iran and reduce the number of visas to the country [14]. These measures have directly led to a serious economic downturn in Iran, and the visa restrictions have also had a major impact on Iran's tourism industry, iran's planned economic transition from a single oil export to a diversified tourism and services sector has been put on hold as the country looks for other ways to revive its economy. However, the second sanction imposed by the United States is more of a purpose to correct Iran's policy behavior, which is mainly manifested in the following points: one is to directly withdraw from the Iran nuclear agreement, and then implement a comprehensive economic blockade. The second is to ask the Allies to impose an oil embargo on Iran, which directly cuts off Iran's economic lifeline. Third, the imposition of sanctions on the assets of key Iranian officials and oil company entities, as well as the imposition of travel restrictions and asset freezes on the visa ban on travel to Iran, cutting off the right to free movement, this has fundamentally affected Iran's economic development. In the face of multiple pressures, Iran can only make the decision to compromise, but this kind of severe sanctions more lead to Iran's national life is difficult.

Finally, targeted economic restrictions facilitated by travel visa measures also serve a specific purpose of cooperation—this form of cooperation is primarily oriented toward supporting United Nations sanctions, with other countries providing collaborative efforts and assistance to enforce such sanctions. Some scholars also refer to these coordinated actions as "parallel sanctions," which typically encompass two main forms: first, a combination of United Nations sanctions and unilateral sanctions imposed by individual countries; and second, sanctions jointly implemented by the United Nations alongside regional organizations such as the European Union or the African Union, as well as unilateral sanctions imposed by individual states, groups of states, the European Union, or any other regional bodies [15]. When the United Nations formally imposes travel restrictions on a country, it inherently signifies that the sanctioned state has engaged in actions that violate international law rules, and such actions may even pose consequences that threaten international peace and security—making the collaborative enforcement of these restrictions a critical part of upholding global order. A typical case that illustrates this cooperative purpose remains tied to the Iranian nuclear issue: back in 2002, when the United Nations uncovered Iran's secret nuclear facilities and its nuclear-related ballistic missile program, it promptly initiated the imposition of a series of targeted sanctions on Iran. Over the three-year period from 2006 to 2008, these United Nations sanctions included several key measures against Iran: the freezing of personal financial assets belonging to Iran's key government officials, strict restrictions on Iran's arms sales and international financial transactions, and limitations on the transfer of assets used for both civilian and military purposes. Importantly, these United Nations sanctions also received strong echoes and support from the United States and the European Union, which joined in by imposing additional economic restrictions on Iran through the implementation of parallel sanctions. For instance, in 2008, the United States introduced specific measures as part of its parallel sanctions: it prohibited U.S. banks from acting as intermediaries to help Iran obtain international funds, banned all trade activities related to petrochemical products with Iran, and imposed restrictions on travel to Iran for certain individuals. Meanwhile, the European Union, starting from 2010, implemented an oil embargo against Iran, froze the financial assets of Iran's central bank, and imposed restrictions on both the assets and visa applications of specific Iranian individuals.[1] The visa restrictions introduced by the United States and the European Union, in essence, represented a targeted effort to impact Iran's tourism economy, as they directly reduced the inflow of international tourists and disrupted Iran's tourism-related economic activities. While these coordinated measures effectively sent a clear signal of firm opposition to Iran's nuclear program, their most significant role was to demonstrate the strong support and active cooperation of the United States and the European Union for United Nations sanctions—additionally, they also highlighted that these three key international actors (the United Nations, the U.S., and the EU) maintained a high level of consistency in their stance toward addressing the Iranian nuclear issue, thereby strengthening the overall impact of the sanctions regime.

The effects of the aforementioned economic restrictions linked to travel visa measures have been thoroughly analyzed starting from real-world, practical cases (such as sanctions on tourism-dependent nations), and the resulting conclusion is remarkably clear: in those countries where economic development is primarily driven and sustained by the tourism service industry (including small island nations and cultural heritage-rich states), the impact of travel visa measures is not only highly significant but may even directly touch upon and influence the personal interests of the country's ordinary citizens—such as their income from tourism-related

[1] Seyfi, S., & Hall, C. M. (Eds.), Tourism in Iran: Challenges, development and issues. Abingdon: Routledge.2018. (Timeline of main international sanctions against Iran).

jobs. The travel restrictions imposed on ordinary citizens are intentionally designed to exert a certain targeted, proportional impact on the target country's economic development, and such restrictions mainly cover key areas including cross-border work opportunities (for tourism and hospitality employees), international travel for leisure (by foreign tourists), overseas study pursuits (by students in tourism management programs), and family visit trips (by diaspora communities). Restrictions implemented in these critical domains will inevitably cast a negative shadow over the target country's economic growth trajectory; specifically, placing limitations on the free movement of ordinary citizens will unavoidably lead to a substantial and noticeable reduction in the number of people entering the target country (including tourists, workers, and students), which in turn makes the tourism industry the first and most severely affected sector. This direct blow to the tourism industry will then quickly extend to and disrupt the broader service and consumption industries—sectors that are closely intertwined with tourism, such as restaurants, hotels, and souvenir retail—thereby causing serious and tangible losses to the target country's tourism-related economic revenue, which often constitutes a vital, revenue-generating part of its overall economic structure. Furthermore, restrictions on cross-border work, overseas study, and family visits will also exert varying degrees of indirect impact on the target country's local economy: for instance, fewer international workers may lead to labor shortages in certain service sectors (like hotel housekeeping or tour guiding), reduced numbers of international students can affect the education industry's income (from tuition and accommodation fees), and fewer family visitors may decrease spending in retail and hospitality (on groceries, dining, and local transportation). Once these restrictions are formally put into implementation through administrative and legal procedures, the target country's service industry will bear the brunt of the impact as the first affected sector, and this negative influence will subsequently spread outward to other crucial fields such as domestic consumption (by reducing household disposable income) and national taxation (by lowering tourism-related tax revenues). Although the magnitude of the effect on these latter fields is not as immediate or intense as that on the tourism industry, it will still gradually accumulate over months or years and form an indirect "butterfly effect"—where a small initial change (the visa restrictions) triggers a chain of events that ultimately has far-reaching, long-term consequences for the entire national economy, including slower GDP growth and higher unemployment.

Restrictions targeting specific groups, by contrast, are primarily directed at individuals who hold the potential to engage in terrorist activities (such as extremist operatives), pose a threat to the national interests of the country that initiates the sanctions (including economic or territorial interests), or endanger the overall peace and security of the international community (like those linked to transnational crime). These specific groups are often already under strict regulatory oversight or included in official blacklists maintained by relevant international bodies or individual sovereign countries—such as the well-known "Stop Lists" overseen by the U.S. Office of Foreign Sanctions Control (OFAC), the restrictive "Blacklists" established by the European Union (EU) to curb security threats (pursuant to EU Council Regulations), and the comprehensive sanctions blacklists issued by the United

Nations Security Council (UNSC) to address global security concerns (under Chapter VII of the UN Charter). While the exact individuals or entities included in these lists cannot always be precisely and exhaustively defined due to the dynamic, evolving nature of security threats (such as the emergence of new extremist groups), any person or group that is determined through intelligence verification to be related to activities that threaten international peace and security will be promptly included in the scope of restrictions imposed on specific groups, ensuring that potential risks are closely monitored and controlled through cross-border information sharing.

It is undeniable that as a unique and special policy measure within the broader framework of "Global South" national cooperation policies (focused on mutual development), the full range of roles and potential of travel visa measures still remains to be further explored and unlocked through ongoing practical application (such as pilot programs for visa facilitation). Even when considering only their current applications, however, travel visa measures have proven capable of effectively facilitating the smooth flow of people in the field of economic and trade exchanges between countries along the "Global South" initiative—streamlining cross-border interactions that are essential for business cooperation (such as trade fairs and investment negotiations). Additionally, these measures can clearly and reasonably differentiate visa processing procedures for different groups of people, such as business travelers (with expedited business visa channels), tourists (with simplified tourist visa requirements), and students (with study visa support services), ensuring that each group receives appropriate and efficient service while maintaining necessary security checks (including background screenings). In terms of safeguarding regional and international peace and security, travel visa measures also play a crucial role in enabling better pre-screening of individuals who may pose potential dangers—identifying and preventing high-risk individuals (such as those on terrorist watchlists) from entering, thereby significantly improving the overall security of commercial and trade exchanges and creating a more stable environment for economic cooperation. More importantly, as a practical and operational carrier of economic and trade policies under the guiding concept of the community with a shared future for mankind, travel visa measures can be effectively implemented by countries along the "Global South" through the establishment of specialized, streamlined visa processing and approval procedures tailored to the needs of cross-border economic and cultural exchanges (such as joint visa application centers). These specialized procedures can actively attract more people from around the world to travel to these "Global South" countries for purposes such as international trade negotiations (between enterprises), leisure tourism (to cultural or natural attractions), academic study (at local universities), and cultural exchanges (such as art exhibitions)—all of which are activities that directly contribute to boosting the countries' economic development by increasing revenue (from tourism and trade), creating jobs (in service and hospitality sectors), and promoting knowledge sharing (in technology and education). At the same time, by leveraging the facilitation policies inherent in travel visa measures (such as visa waivers for frequent travelers), "Global South" countries can encourage and involve more nations to participate in the implementation of economic policy initiatives among "Global South" states (such as regional free trade agreements), fostering greater cooperation and solidarity within the region. In the long run, this increased cooperation and streamlined people-to-people exchanges will not only drive the economic growth of individual "Global South" countries (by expanding market access) but also have a positive and effective impact on promoting the diversification of the global economy—reducing reliance on a small number of dominant economies (such as the U.S. or EU) and creating a more balanced, inclusive, and resilient global economic system that aligns with the interests of developing nations.

References

1. White House (n.d.) Executive Order—Protecting the Nation from Terrorist Attacks by Foreign Nationals [Section 2, Policy]
2. During the French Revolution, the Jacobins invoked this precedent when imposing a reign of terror in a region. After the Jacobins lost power, the term "terrorist" became one that was abused
3. Kunwar Gopal (2019) Definition of terrorism and its typology. Parisheelan XV(1):540, ISSN 0974-7222
4. United States Code (n.d.) 18 U.S.C. § 2331(1) [Definition of International Terrorism]. Retrieved from http://www.law.cornell.edu/uscode/18/usc_sec_18_00002331.000-html
5. Gaswaga D (2013) The definition of terrorism. Int J Ethical Leadership 2:Article 15, 141, p 146
6. In Art. 1 of the Framework Decision on Combating Terrorism (2002)
7. United Nations General Assembly, Report of the Ad Hoc Committee, sixth session, (January 28–February 1, 2002), Annex II, art. 2.1
8. Deen T (2005) Politics: UN Member States Struggle to Define Terrorism. IPS, 2005, July 25
9. United Nations Security Council Resolution 1054 (1996), adopted on April 26, 1996. http://www.un.org
10. Felbermayr G, Kirilakha A, Syropoulos C, Yalcin E, Yotov YV (2020) The Global Sanctions Data Base, School of Economics Working Paper Series 2020-2. LeBow College of Business, Drexel University. (Table B.1: Different Types of Sanctions. Historical Examples)
11. Moret ES (2015) Humanitarian impacts of economic sanctions on Iran and Syria. Eur Secur 24(1):120–140
12. Irfan N, Nawaz M, Jamil S (2021) US economic sanctions: a controversial foreign policy tool in international politics. Glob Econ Rev VI(I):152–165
13. Seyfi S, Hall CM (eds) (2018) Tourism in Iran: challenges, development and issues. Routledge, Abingdon
14. Gilsinan K (2019) A boom time for U.S. sanctions. Retrieved from www.theatlantic.com/politics/archive/2019/05/why-united-states-uses-sanctions-so-much/588625/
15. Subedi SP (2021) Unilateral sanctions in international law. Hart Publishing, Oxford/New York, an imprint of Bloomsbury Publishing

Chapter 4
"The Global South" and the Coordinated Development of Cultural Heritage

The in-depth promotion and systematic implementation of the "Global South" National Policy Initiative, through the formulation and implementation of a series of targeted favorable policies (such as preferential trade tariffs and joint infrastructure investment plans), has significantly strengthened the strategic cooperative partnership between our country and neighboring countries in key areas such as cross-border economy and trade (including goods and service exchanges), regional transportation systems (such as cross-border railways and highways), and large-scale infrastructure construction (like energy pipelines and port facilities). In addition, culture is undoubtedly another pivotal spiritual core of the "Global South" initiative and also serves as the key foothold for the "Global South" national policy to advance the integration of non-governmental cultural exchanges (such as folk art exhibitions and cultural festivals). The prosperity and sustainable development of the cultural field can not only effectively promote the time-honored excellent culture of the Chinese nation to the international community (including traditional art, philosophy, and customs) but also attract more foreign citizens to proactively seek to understand the profound intrinsic spiritual value of Chinese culture. To achieve genuine cultural inclusion, we must rely on the two-way policy of "Bringing in" and "Going out"—a policy that requires concrete implementation (such as cultural exchange programs and artist residencies) rather than remaining a theoretical concept suspended in the air. Therefore, it is essential to utilize important external carriers in the cultural field. As a tangible and visible type of cultural expression, cultural heritage presents a rich variety of forms, such as the majestic Great Wall (a symbol of ancient defense), the solemn Temple of Heaven (a site of traditional ritual), and the grand Forbidden City (a former imperial palace)—all iconic historical buildings located in our country's capital, Beijing. These architectural treasures not only occupy an irreplaceable important position in the system of Chinese traditional culture but also serve as a critical channel for the world to gain insights into China's history and values. In 1972, the General Conference of the United Nations

X. Dong, J. Gu, *The Belt and Road Initiative and the Global South*, Energy, Climate Change & Sustainability in the Global South,
https://doi.org/10.1007/978-981-92-0144-0_4

Educational, Scientific and Cultural Organization (hereinafter referred to as "UNESCO") formally adopted the Convention concerning the Protection of the World Cultural and Natural Heritage at its seventeenth session; Article 1 of this convention explicitly classifies monuments, historical buildings, and cultural sites (including archaeological sites) into the category of cultural heritage and is open to all member states for signature, ratification, and accession in accordance with their domestic legal procedures. Since its entry into force in 1975, the convention has further formalized a set of standardized approaches to cultural heritage protection (such as heritage site registration and conservation funding mechanisms), with the aim of better respecting and supporting the diverse cultural content of all countries. Taking this convention as a key opportunity, many countries have initiated efforts to explore their unique types of cultural heritage and established corresponding legal and regulatory frameworks (such as heritage protection laws and oversight bodies) to protect them. Just as people naturally associate the pyramids with Egypt (a symbol of its ancient civilization), no country can exist without the long-term accumulation of its own culture—especially our country, which possesses a rich, diverse, and deeply rooted cultural heritage spanning thousands of years. Thus, the core question lies in how to effectively disseminate these different types of Chinese cultural heritage to various parts of the world, enabling an increasing number of people globally to know, truly understand, and sincerely love China. This constitutes the ultimate mission and fundamental goal of the coordinated development of the "Global South" initiative and cultural heritage promotion.

4.1 An Overview of Cultural Heritage

As a product of history, cultural heritage is an important way for mankind to understand the events of the past. Culture itself is too all-encompassing to exhaust all its subsets, and what can express culture externally or in some way fix it and perpetuate it deserves a special name. Before the establishment of the United Nations Educational, scientific and cultural organization, the world was full of cultural objects scattered around the world. With the continuous improvement of human cognition, began to realize the need to preserve the many activities, objects, buildings, rituals, and crafts of great artistic value in the past, in order to inherit as the common heritage wealth of all mankind. Cultural Heritage is also taking this opportunity to begin to be known to more people.

4.1.1 The Definition of Cultural Heritage

UNESCO, the United Nations Educational, Scientific and Cultural Organization, operates as a specialized intergovernmental agency under the United Nations system, specifically tasked with the systematic management of global cultural heritage (including tangible and intangible forms) and the supervision of all relevant administrative, protective, and promotional matters (such as heritage site monitoring and capacity-building for member states). It formally adopted the Convention for the Safeguarding of the World Cultural and Natural Heritage in 1972 to address tangible heritage preservation (like historical buildings and archaeological sites), and later, in 2003, enacted the Convention for the Safeguarding of the Intangible Cultural Heritage—with Article 2 of this latter convention providing a precise, operational definition of intangible cultural heritage (covering practices, expressions, and knowledge systems). The establishment of the intangible cultural heritage concept has been instrumental in granting scattered, region-specific cultural elements—such as indigenous languages (like Inuktitut), traditional artistic forms (such as Chinese paper-cutting), and community celebratory activities (like India's Holi)—a formal, internationally recognized framework and sustainable space for intergenerational inheritance (through documentation and transmission programs). The Convention for the Safeguarding of the Intangible Cultural Heritage introduces a clear, standardized classification of contemporary intangible cultural heritage into five distinct, non-overlapping categories: first, oral traditions and expressions, which explicitly include language as the fundamental medium for transmitting intangible cultural heritage; second, performing arts that encompass diverse forms like music (such as African drumming), dance (like ballet folklórico), and theater (such as Noh); third, social practices, ritual ceremonies, and festive events that reflect the communal identity and lifestyle of a group (like Japan's tea ceremonies); fourth, traditional knowledge and practices concerning nature and the universe, rooted in long-standing ecological wisdom (such as Indigenous land management); fifth, traditional craftsmanship techniques that require hands-on skill and generational transmission (like Italian leatherworking). Unlike the 1975-enforced convention (focused on tangible heritage protection and site conservation), the 2003 convention is exclusively dedicated to the safeguarding of intangible cultural heritage (emphasizing living traditions). In contrast, the Convention for the Protection of the World Cultural and Natural Heritage—initially promulgated by UNESCO in 1972—primarily governs explicit, physically tangible cultural contents, including historical sites with archaeological significance (like Machu Picchu), architectural complexes of artistic value (like the Taj Mahal), and ancient ruins of civilizational importance (like Pompeii). The substantive scopes of these two conventions are distinctly different, leading some scholars to term culturally significant elements with physical external manifestations as "tangible cultural heritage"; to systematically integrate and standardize the differentiation criteria for various cultural heritage types, the elements defined in the Convention for the Safeguarding of the Intangible Cultural Heritage—those lacking concrete physical characteristics (such as traditions or skills)—are formally classified as "intangible cultural heritage." The visual and experiential perceptual orientations of cultural heritage audiences serve as the core differentiating factors for this classification: the visual group takes visible cultural landscapes (like heritage buildings) as the central basis for value judgment, recognizing and appraising genuine cultural heritage through a "what you see is what you get" (WYSIWYG) approach, and such groups typically form immediate, intuitive judgments about the presented cultural heritage based on its physical form (like architectural style or material). The experiential group, by contrast, does not prioritize visual appreciation as the core of value judgment; instead, it perceives and internalizes the spiritual value impact brought by cultural heritage through active participation in the dynamic processes of cultural heritage (such as rituals, craftsmanship practices, or festive celebrations). Therefore, tangible cultural heritage, also referred to as material cultural heritage (hereinafter abbreviated as "material cultural heritage"), mainly shapes the value judgments of the visual group, while the value judgments at the spiritual level—derived from the experiential group's participation—serve as a supplementary dimension (enhancing emotional connection). For example, the landscape of China's Great Wall, with its lofty, magnificent, and historically resonant scenes (spanning mountain ranges), delivers a highly intuitive visual impact to the visual group; this powerful visual shock further attracts people from all over the world to visit the Great Wall for in-person experiential engagement (like hiking its sections). What becomes evident from this example is the clear prioritization of visual perception over experiential engagement in the context of material cultural heritage. On the contrary, intangible cultural heritage (hereinafter abbreviated as "intangible cultural heritage") primarily embodies a value judgment logic where experiential engagement takes precedence over visual perception. For instance, in China's Spring Festival customs, the lively, warm, and culturally rich atmosphere of this tradition requires individuals to participate directly—through practices like family gatherings (for reunion dinners), red envelope exchanges (conveying good wishes), or temple fairs (enjoying folk performances)—to obtain a profound spiritual value judgment; this spiritual understanding then forms the basis for developing visual value judgment standards (such as recognizing Spring Festival decorations like red lanterns or dragon dances), and ultimately, the goal of fully understanding the Spring Festival as a representative form of Chinese intangible cultural heritage is achieved. The differences in the visual and experiential value criteria among different groups arise from individual variations shaped by diverse growth environments (urban vs. rural), distinct ways of thinking (collectivist vs. individualist), and varying educational levels (formal vs. traditional); this phenomenon not only helps us clarify the underlying origin of the classification system for tangible cultural heritage and intangible cultural heritage but also enables us to better distinguish the different sequential changes (i.e., which perception comes first) between these two types of heritage.

4.1.2 The Characteristics of Cultural Heritage

Two different classifications of cultural heritage are important factors to clarify its characteristics. The definitions of tangible and intangible cultural heritage established by the United Nations Educational, scientific and cultural organization (UNESCO) from the evaluation criteria of different periods actually contain internal explanations, combining the content and classification of cultural heritage, the characteristics of cultural heritage can be discussed as follows:

a. Cultural Heritage is Historic

As the irreplaceable "witness" to the long history of the Earth and human civilization, one of the most important and inherent features of cultural heritage is its profound historicity—this characteristic anchors cultural heritage in specific time periods (ranging from ancient civilizations to modern eras), making it a living, tangible record of human development spanning millennia. By its very nature, heritage serves as a form of inheritance for humanity: it may manifest as the continuation of material wealth (such as artifacts and structures), carrying the tangible traces of past societies' production modes and lifestyles, or as the transmission of spiritual wealth, preserving the values, beliefs, and wisdom of earlier generations that shape cultural identities. The United Nations Educational, Scientific and Cultural Organization (UNESCO), pursuant to its mandate under the Convention for the Protection of the World Cultural and Natural Heritage (1972), has categorized material cultural heritage into three distinct and well-defined types: the first is movable material cultural heritage, which includes items such as ancient paintings (like China's Silk Road murals), intricate sculptures (such as Greece's marble statues), historical coins (bearing royal emblems or trade symbols), and precious manuscripts (including medieval religious texts)—objects that can be physically relocated while retaining their cultural significance and historical context; the second is immovable material cultural heritage, encompassing structures like monumental buildings (such as France's Eiffel Tower), ancient archaeological sites (like Iraq's Babylon), and historical complexes (such as India's Taj Mahal Complex) that are permanently tied to specific geographic locations and reflect local architectural traditions; the third is underwater material cultural heritage, consisting of relics such as sunken ships (carrying trade goods from colonial eras), underwater ruins of ancient settlements (like Egypt's submerged Heracleion), and submerged cities that lie beneath aquatic surfaces (oceans, lakes, or rivers). All three categories fall under the umbrella of visible cultural heritage, and these tangible heritage assets are inherently products of specific historical eras, each bearing the unique 印记 (imprint) of the time in which they were created—including technological levels, aesthetic preferences, and social structures. A classic example is Egypt's pyramid complexes (dating back to the Old Kingdom, around 2600–2500 BCE), which are thousands of years old: these magnificent structures not only witnessed the rise of one of the world's earliest cradles of civilization (the Nile Valley civilization) but also showcase the extraordinary sophistication of ancient Egyptian architectural and engineering techniques (such as precision stone-cutting and structural load calculation), captivating the attention of countless scholars, historians, and visitors from around the globe. When comparing underwater cultural heritage with its land-based counterpart, land cultural heritage holds a certain advantage in terms of sheer quantity, as many historical civilizations (such as the Roman Empire and the Han Dynasty) primarily developed and left their marks on terrestrial landscapes. However, in terms of the unique value and significance of cultural heritage, underwater cultural heritage often stands out for its ability to reveal unexplored and overlooked historical clues—clues that may be lost or obscured on land due to natural erosion or human activities (like urban construction). For instance, the discovery of underwater porcelain artifacts (such as China's Song Dynasty celadon) and sunken merchant ships (from the Maritime Silk Road) provides an accurate and detailed reflection of the trade patterns (routes connecting East Asia to Southeast Asia), economic activities (commodity exchange volumes), and technological capabilities (shipbuilding and ceramic craftsmanship) of a specific historical period, offering insights that written records (which may be incomplete or biased) alone may not fully capture. A typical and highly representative example of this is the historical event of the seven maritime voyages to the Western Oceans during China's Ming Dynasty (led by Admiral Zheng He between 1405 and 1433). As techniques for excavating underwater cultural relics have become increasingly advanced and mature (including the use of remote-operated vehicles and underwater mapping technology), the exquisite porcelain (blue-and-white porcelain from Jingdezhen), high-quality tea (Longjing and Tieguanyin), and fine knitting products (silk tapestries) that Zheng He's fleets carried to Western regions (such as Southeast Asia, South Asia, and East Africa) during these seven voyages have all been recovered during the salvage of sunken ships from that era (such as the "Nanhai No. 1" shipwreck). These artifacts not only verify the historical accounts recorded in Ming Dynasty official documents (like the Ming Shilu) but also vividly reflect the comprehensive panorama of commercial and trade exchanges between China and other countries at that time—including the types of goods traded, transaction scales, and cultural interactions. Underwater cultural heritage primarily owes its formation to two major historical opportunities or circumstances: the first stems from the influence of natural factors, such as severe floods (caused by climate change or river course shifts) that submerged entire cultural heritage sites, and in some cases, even entire city-states (like Italy's Baiae), preserving them beneath water over centuries in an oxygen-poor environment that slows degradation; the second is linked to the emergence of the Age of Discovery (15th to 17th centuries), a period that saw a dramatic increase in maritime trade activities (between Europe, Asia, and the Americas)—and with this increase came heightened risks. Many merchant ships of this era were forced to sink to the ocean floor due to a variety of hazards, including devastating natural disasters at sea (such as storms, tsunamis, and hurricanes), accidental ship collisions (due to poor navigation tools), and threats from piracy (targeting valuable cargo), all of which left behind a rich legacy of underwater cultural heritage.

The historicity of cultural heritage embodied in the aforementioned events can also be systematically summarized in the following two key aspects: first, cultural heritage serves as a tangible and credible representation of the economic development level during a specific historical period. Different categories of cultural relics, each carrying the unique mark of their era (such as material composition and craftsmanship), distinctly reflect varying degrees of economic advancement—for instance, the differences in weaponry used across time, such as the crude yet functional stone weapons (hand axes and spears) of the Stone Age versus the more sophisticated metal weaponry (bronze swords and iron spears) of the Cold Weapon

Age, as clearly observed in the remains of ancient buildings (fortresses) and archaeological sites (battlefields), directly illustrate the gradual evolution of productivity (from stone tool making to metal smelting), resource utilization (from stone extraction to mineral mining), and overall economic capacity (from subsistence economies to surplus-producing economies) across different historical stages. Second, cultural heritage vividly captures and conveys the local conditions, folk customs, and social norms of a particular period. A typical example lies in the diverse cultural relics unearthed from the Tang Dynasty (618–907 CE), including delicate pottery figurines (of court ladies and scholars), vivid mural paintings (from the Mogao Grottoes), and intricate stone sculptures (of Buddhist deities): these artifacts prominently highlight the distinctive cultural trait of the Tang Dynasty where plumpness was widely regarded as a standard of beauty for women—a reflection of the era's material abundance. Beyond merely depicting this unique aesthetic preference, these exquisitely crafted objects also offer a profound glimpse into the broader social landscape of the Tang Dynasty—they not only portray a vivid scene of the Tang people living in peace, contentment, and freedom from worries about food and clothing (evidenced by the variety of leisure activities depicted) but also allow people to infer, through these tangible cultural carriers, the grand picture of the Tang Dynasty's strong national power (reflected in its vast territory and international influence), the simple and honest character of its people (shown in daily-life scenes), and the harmonious and stable state of the entire nation (evidenced by the absence of war-related damage in many relics).

Thirdly, it can illustrate the current situation of national governance in a certain period. For example, the Great Wall of China, initially constructed during the Qin Dynasty (221–207 BCE) and expanded in subsequent dynasties, was built to resist the invasion of northern ethnic minorities (such as the Xiongnu). Its purpose was to send warning messages to vassals and military outposts via beacon fires (lighting bonfires on watchtowers to signal threats). Although this large-scale military defense project was built to resist the invasion of foreign enemies, it failed to stabilize the unity of the Qin dynasty—due in part to the heavy tax and labor burdens it imposed on the people, which contributed to social unrest. On the other hand, the construction of the Yuanmingyuan (Garden of Perfect Brightness) and the Summer Palace (Yiheyuan) in the late Qing Dynasty (1636–1912) reflects the decline of the country during that period. Although the Yuanmingyuan was burned down by Anglo-French forces during the Second Opium War (1860), the construction cost—including massive manpower (craftsmen and laborers), material resources (rare woods and stones), and financial resources (state treasury funds)—exceeded the Qing dynasty's annual investment in key sectors (such as military and agriculture) over many years. The construction of the Yuanmingyuan is an important symbol of the gap between the late Qing government (which prioritized imperial luxury) and Western countries (which focused on industrialization and military modernization). Amidst the song and dance of imperial leisure, the Qing government failed to recognize the looming threat of Western powers, eventually ushering in the "war of ships and guns" (the Opium Wars) and leading to its demise. In addition to the Yuanmingyuan, the Summer Palace and other imperial gardens (such as the Chengde Mountain Resort) all illustrate the state of national governance in that historical period—reflecting the ruling class's detachment from public needs and its inability to adapt to global changes.

b. Cultural Heritage Is Representative

Cultural heritage embodies specific events passed down from the past, and if we examine cultural heritage itself closely—whether movable, immovable, or underwater—each piece is accompanied by a unique, specific story that contextualizes its existence, including the circumstances of its creation, use, and preservation. This inherent connection between heritage and narrative can be clearly illustrated by analyzing different categories of cultural heritage, as each type carries distinct historical context that aligns with international standards for heritage documentation (such as UNESCO's Heritage Inventory Guidelines). From the perspective of material cultural heritage, movable artifacts such as sculptures (like Greece's Venus de Milo) and paintings (such as the Renaissance's Mona Lisa) not only stand as testaments to the superb sculptural and artistic skills of bygone eras but also serve as authentic products of their specific historical periods, bearing the distinct marks of the society that created them—including social structures, aesthetic trends, and technological capabilities. Immovable heritage, including monuments (such as the Washington Monument) and archaeological sites (like Mexico's Teotihuacan), similarly reflects the architectural and construction techniques prevalent during the dynasty or civilization that built them, offering insights into the era's engineering capabilities (such as load-bearing design) and aesthetic preferences (such as decorative styles). Even underwater cultural heritage, hidden beneath aquatic surfaces (oceans, lakes, or rivers), can bear witness to important events that unfolded in the past between humans and the water bodies they relied on—such as ancient maritime trade journeys (along the Maritime Silk Road) or historical water-related disasters (like floods that submerged settlements)—with relics preserved in an oxygen-poor environment that maintains their historical integrity. Therefore, material cultural heritage can represent at least three distinct types of historical events. The first is the political patterns of the past: unearthed ancient currencies, for instance, vividly reflect the shifts in political structures (such as centralization or feudalism) across successive dynasties, as currency systems are often tied to state authority. A prime example is the Qin Dynasty's (221–207 BCE) unification of the currency system—only after this landmark political reform, which centralized economic power under the imperial government, was the "Ban Liang Coin" (Half-Two Coin), a round copper coin with a square hole, uniformly adopted across the unified nation. This currency unification not only consolidated the Qin Dynasty's centralized authority by standardizing a key economic tool (eliminating regional currency chaos) but also promoted overall economic development and significantly enhanced the convenience of economic and trade exchanges among different regions of the empire (from the Yellow River Basin to the Yangtze River Basin). From the Qin Dynasty onward, each subsequent dynasty—such as the Han (202 BCE–220 CE) with its "Wu Zhu Coin" and the Tang (618–907 CE) with its "Kai Yuan Tong Bao"—adopted unique currencies as the official medium for national economic and trade transactions, and these unearthed coins serve as the most tangible and credible evidence of these historical political and economic policies, verified through archaeological dating and historical 文献 (texts). Archaeological sites further exemplify this category: the Terracotta Warriors unearthed from the Mausoleum of Qin Shi Huang in Xi'an, Shaanxi Province, for example, provide a vivid, lifelike representation of the formidable military prowess of the Qin Dynasty—with thousands of life-sized soldiers, horses, and weapons—reflecting the dynasty's political emphasis on military strength (to maintain unification) and its ability to mobilize massive resources (manpower, materials, and funds) for state-level projects. The second type of historical event represented by material cultural heritage is the religious ethics of the past. Artifacts like sculptures (of deities) and paintings (of religious scenes), crafted with meticulous skill by master craftsmen, often carry distinct religious undertones that reflect the spiritual beliefs of the era. Take China's Longmen Grottoes (located in Luoyang, Henan) and Yungang Grottoes (in Datong, Shanxi) as examples: these magnificent cultural relics, carved into limestone cliffs, emerged during periods of prolonged social turmoil (the Northern Wei Dynasty, 386–534 CE), yet they stand as unparalleled artistic treasures of Buddhist art. Beyond showcasing the extraordinary sculptural and painting skills of China during the Northern and Southern Dynasties (a period preceding the Five Dynasties and Ten Kingdoms), these grottoes—adorned with works infused with Buddhist religious meaning (such as statues of Buddha, Bodhisattvas, and arhats)—also served as vessels for people to pray for the country's peaceful development, in the hope of alleviating the suffering and loss of life caused by ongoing wars and social instability. Moreover, aside from the Buddhist visual art represented by these grottoes, material cultural heritage also includes manuscripts (such as Taoist scriptures on silk) and paintings (of Confucian sages) related to Taoism and Confucianism—two other major ideological systems in ancient China. Particularly significant are the important theoretical works passed down since the Spring and Autumn and Warring States periods (770–221 BCE), a time that saw the emergence of a group of renowned historical figures—such as Confucius (representing Confucianism, advocating benevolence and ritual), Laozi (founder of Taoism, emphasizing harmony with nature), and Han Feizi (a leading Legalist thinker, focusing on law and authority)—who stood as representatives of different philosophical schools. Their ideas, preserved through written works (such as Confucius' Analects and Laozi's Tao Te Ching) and related cultural artifacts (like stone inscriptions of Confucian classics), continue to exert a profound influence on later generations, shaping ethical and social norms even today. The third type of historical event captured by material cultural heritage is the true portrayal of daily life in the past. History, much like time itself, fades away like distant stars, yet from artifacts such as ancient paintings (depicting daily scenes), manuscripts (including personal letters and household records), sculptures (of ordinary people), and monuments (commemorating folk events), we can reconstruct detailed, vivid insights into past daily life: the diets of ordinary people (evidenced by food residues in ancient pottery), the languages they spoke (reflected in written scripts on bamboo slips), the etiquettes they followed (shown in mural paintings of social gatherings), and the customs they practiced (such as wedding or funeral rituals depicted in sculptures). These details highlight the irreplaceable importance of material heritage as a window into the lived experiences of our ancestors, complementing written historical records that often focus on elites. Additionally, the classic works passed down through material heritage—such as the Four Books (including The Great Learning and The Doctrine of the Mean) and Five Classics (such as The Book of Songs and The Spring and Autumn Annals), core texts of traditional Chinese culture—can still be found in our modern learning materials (such as history and literature curricula). The knowledge systems we follow today also draw on scholarly efforts to explore the profound meanings embedded in these classical manuscripts (through philological research and cultural interpretation), linking the daily lives, intellectual traditions, and value systems of the past to the present.

c. Cultural Heritage Is Inherited

Compared with the other two characteristics, inheritance stands out as a pivotal embodiment of cultural heritage at the spiritual level, carrying the core of a culture's essence across generations. When examining the entire developmental trajectory of cultural heritage—whether it be tangible cultural heritage with physical forms or intangible cultural heritage rooted in practices and traditions—inheritance has consistently remained an inherent and distinctive attribute of cultural heritage. The inheritance of cultural heritage manifests as the intersection and continuous extension of time and space: it bridges the past and present, connects diverse regions, and ensures that the accumulated wisdom of earlier civilizations is not lost to history. It is precisely based on this intergenerational inheritance of cultural heritage that humanity can trace the track of historical development, draw lessons from the experiences of predecessors, and choose a rational and sustainable path of development, enabling us to thrive and live better within the Earth's ecosystem amid the vastness of the galaxy.

In comparison, intangible cultural heritage exhibits more prominent and distinct inheritance characteristics due to its unique types and forms of existence—characteristics that are deeply tied to human interaction and experiential learning. As we have discussed earlier, the classification of material cultural heritage and intangible cultural heritage highlights their inherent differences: while material cultural heritage does possess a certain degree of inheritance, its 传承 (inheritance) is more inclined to be visible and object-based. For instance, manuscripts, as a form of material cultural heritage, preserve content through written records, and this recorded information undoubtedly constitutes a form of heritage. However, this type of heritage is not exclusive to specific groups of people; there are no strict restrictions on who can access or inherit the knowledge within, as the physical manuscript itself serves as a universal carrier. Among the five categories of intangible cultural heritage, only a few rely on manuscript records for preservation—such as some social practices and festival activities in the third category, certain knowledge and practices concerning nature and the universe in the fourth category, and part of the traditional handicraft techniques in the fifth category. Most other forms of intangible cultural heritage cannot be simply or fully recorded through material carriers alone. Therefore, from the perspective of how inheritance is manifested and realized, the oral traditions and expressions, as well as the performing arts, within intangible cultural heritage, must be acquired, mastered, and passed down through traditional experiential learning and hands-on acquisition. This direct, interactive experience is not just a method but an essential carrier of their inheritance: without the sharing of practical experience from inheritors to learners, and without the learners' personal acquisition of skills and insights, these oral traditions and performing arts would lose their critical channels of transmission, gradually fading into obscurity. At present, there are numerous intangible cultural heritage items scattered across the globe, and among them, those that rely on experiential inheritance are particularly vulnerable. With the rapid development of the times and the profound changes in social lifestyles, many of these intangible cultural heritage items have lost their original foundation for inheritance. This is especially true for some skills handed down from remote areas or technologies that are relatively distant from modern life—such as Fujian puppetry, which requires meticulous manual manipulation and a deep understanding of traditional storytelling, and Chinese wooden movable type printing, a technique that demands precise craftsmanship and adherence to ancient procedures. These intangible cultural heritage items not only hold significant historical value (recording the development of traditional technologies and arts)、cultural value (embodying the unique cultural concepts and aesthetic pursuits of a nation) and artistic value (showcasing the superb creative skills of predecessors) but also stand as precious cultural treasures of the Chinese nation. However, due to a variety of reasons—including the lack of young inheritors, the impact of modern technologies on traditional practices, and the diminishing social contexts where these heritage items were once applied—they are now facing inheritance crises of varying degrees. As a result, these vulnerable intangible cultural heritage items have been formally listed as key protection objects, with targeted measures implemented to safeguard their survival and ensure their continued transmission to future generations

Combined with the above argumentation, we can systematically summarize the main manifestations of the inheritance of cultural heritage as follows: first, cultural heritage must rely on specific subjects for its inheritance and transmission. The so-called "specific subjects" essentially refer to individuals or groups who hold a genuine interest in cultural heritage and take the initiative to join the ranks of heritage inheritors and protectors. As the United Nations Educational, Scientific and Cultural Organization (UNESCO) classifies cultural heritage into various types and catalogues, the vast majority of these heritage items—whether tangible or intangible—require the continuous condensation and transmission of human wisdom to sustain their existence. Even the Great Pyramids of Egypt, magnificent structures built thousands of years ago, stand as enduring testaments to the extraordinary wisdom of humanity that transcended the technical limitations of their era; their preservation and the understanding of their historical significance today still depend on the efforts of modern scholars, archaeologists, and cultural workers as inheritance subjects. Looking to the future, a large number of protected objects within the broader scope of cultural heritage will face the looming risk of disappearance. This threat is particularly acute for artistic forms and traditional craftsmanship in the field of intangible cultural heritage, as many of these practices rely on direct human interaction and experiential learning, making them highly vulnerable to the loss of inheritors and the erosion of traditional contexts. In response, countries around the world have been actively advocating for the protection of these endangered skills, and the most crucial part of these protection efforts lies in encouraging more interested groups to join the ranks of inheritors: guiding them from initially recognizing the value of cultural heritage, to accepting and engaging in systematic learning of heritage-related knowledge and skills, and ultimately taking themselves as the core carriers to fulfill the mission of inheriting cultural heritage. Second, cultural heritage needs to be inherited through specific and targeted channels. The inherent diversity of cultural heritage—encompassing differences in form, content, and origin—determines that its geographical distribution and transmission paths also vary significantly, and these unique paths serve as the media for the inheritance of cultural heritage. For instance, numerous ancient ruins preserved throughout history are often located in areas that were strategically chosen in their respective eras: places with convenient transportation networks to facilitate communication and trade, favorable natural environments suitable for human habitation, and certain military strategic layouts to ensure security. After enduring the erosion of time and the changes of dynasties, these once-thriving human settlements have naturally evolved into monuments, archaeological sites, and other forms of tangible cultural heritage, with their geographical locations themselves becoming a fixed channel for inheriting the historical context and spatial memory of the heritage. Beyond these site-specific heritage items, other types of cultural heritage also rely on distinct transmission channels. For example, some performing arts, such as traditional stunts and ritual ceremonies, cannot be fully preserved or passed down through written records or material carriers alone; instead, they depend on "oral instruction and hands-on demonstration"—a direct, face-to-face teaching method where inheritors impart skills and insights to learners through verbal guidance and practical demonstration. There are also special traditional skills that follow strict family inheritance rules, passed down only within blood relatives and not disclosed to outsiders. These specific inheritance channels not only reflect the great importance that people in ancient times attached to certain core skills but also highlight the practical value of these skills: the scarcity resulting from restricted transmission meant that those who inherited and mastered these skills could gain a stable means of survival and social status in society. Therefore, these special inheritance channels endow the corresponding cultural heritage projects with unique and high social value, making them not only cultural symbols but also carriers of historical social structures and livelihood models. In essence, the inheritance of cultural heritage is a core attribute that ensures its continuity across generations; it not only bears witness to the glory and brilliance of cultural heritage in different historical periods but also serves as a solemn reminder for us today to attach greater importance to cultural heritage—as an irreplaceable treasure shared by all humanity—and to take active actions to protect and pass it on to future generations. The combination process of "Global South" initiative and cultural heritage is also a practical path to better play the role of cultural heritage characteristics. From the attribute of cultural heritage, we can see the spiritual treasure and material representation of the whole world history. Through the implementation of the "Global South" initiative, we can have more opportunities and channels to learn about the excellent cultural "Genes" of other countries. While learning from the excellent cultural achievements of other countries, it can also better integrate with our country, and jointly exert the influence and effect of cultural heritage.

4.2 The Impact and Effects of Cultural Heritage

Through the interpretation of the connotation and characteristics of cultural heritage, we can see that cultural heritage is not a single content. It has a wide range of heritage types and a long time and space continuity, all of these will have an important impact on the internal force of cultural heritage. At present, all parts of the world are actively seeking the comprehensive protection of cultural heritage based on the convention implemented by the United Nations Educational, scientific and cultural organization, with a view to "Archiving" the excellent cultural "Genes" of the region. We can also learn that cultural heritage is not simply limited to the classification of diversity, which has an important internal driving force. From the perspective of economics, scholar Marilena VECCO has summarized and refined the value theory as the internal driving force of cultural heritage, cultural heritage is divided into four parts: cultural values, economic values, communication values and ecological values. The classification of the above four kinds of values belongs to the macro division, and the four kinds of values can be divided into different types from the micro level. For example, cultural values include aesthetic value, artistic value, historical value, spiritual value, commemorative value and so on. Economic values are more of a result-oriented value, such as scientific value, social value, moral value and so on. Communication value focuses on the expression of realistic value in interpersonal communication, among which the use value, market value and tourism value are the most important manifestations. Ecological values emphasize the representation of values in a particular region, such as biodiversity, ecosystem uniqueness, etc. These micro values can expand the impact and effect of cultural heritage. From the perspective of the development of the Global South, the value impact and effect of cultural heritage is indeed very important, but it also needs its specific impact and effect. To this end, we can draw on the "Value theory" and combine the "Bring in" and "Go out" two-way development model in the "Global South" policy, the influence and effect of cultural heritage are classified into spiritual value, realistic value and social value according to the time axis of development process. The spiritual value represents the influence and effect of cultural heritage on human development. Realistic value is the actual influence and effect that cultural heritage can bring. Social value is mainly the evaluation of the possible impact and effect of cultural heritage in the future.

4.2.1 *Influence and Effect of Spiritual Value of Cultural Heritage*

As the primary evaluation standard of cultural heritage, spiritual value is an important value influence and effect accumulated over time, which can be divided into two different forms: broad sense and narrow sense. The so-called generalized spiritual value is a general term that includes all non-material values. In a narrow sense, spiritual value is a form of value with a certain guiding value or religious overtones. The spiritual value in a narrow sense is usually a kind of concrete expression. For example, some temple buildings, Buddhist caves or sacrificial halls in the past, etc. These cultural relics are the external manifestation of the power of faith. These buildings themselves are no different from other monuments, but they can produce a cohesive force of spiritual sustenance, the power of spiritual values is thus realized. Therefore, the influence and effect of spiritual value in a narrow sense usually have a specific direction. The influence and effect of a specific direction generally acts on a specific matter, which can more intuitively produce influence and effect in a certain field, for example, the mentioned historical sites with different religious colors, from the time they were built, they represented areas of activity at particular religious sites, and their value was often attributed to the piety and number of their adherents. The influence and effect of this narrow spiritual value can release great potential in essence, but it loses the significance of further exploration because of its specific directivity. However, we can not deny the influence and effect of spiritual value in a narrow sense. On the contrary, spiritual values in a narrow sense are usually the basis of other values and the deep "Participants" precipitated by history.

Comparatively speaking, the generalized spiritual value inherent in cultural heritage exhibits distinct diversity and profound complexity—two core attributes that make it well worth in-depth exploration and discussion from a systematic, multidimensional perspective. According to the specific correspondence between spiritual value and different dimensions of human sensory perception, we can reasonably divide the scope of influence and effects of generalized spiritual value into the following two core aspects: First, visual aesthetic value constitutes a fundamental and pivotal manifestation of the influence and effects of generalized spiritual value. The diverse forms and specific types of cultural heritage that we directly perceive through visual intuition undergo complex cognitive processing in the human brain—including attention, interpretation, and emotional association—ultimately generating corresponding, personalized evaluation criteria for spiritual value. These criteria inevitably produce differentiated feedback due to inherent variations in individuals' conceptual frameworks, unique growth environments, gender differences, educational backgrounds, occupational types, and other subjective and objective factors. As a result, cultural heritage shaped by the dimension of visual aesthetic value will exert distinctly different influences and practical effects on various groups of people. For material cultural heritage, its visual impact varies significantly across different audiences: individuals with a solid background in history, for instance, will form updated and refined historical perceptions in their cognitive systems through visual engagement with scenes such as ancient monuments, well-preserved archaeological sites, and historical landscapes, and this influence of fresh historical perspectives will in turn give rise to diverse practical effects in academic, creative, and experiential fields. To elaborate, historians, by integrating feedback derived from these visual scenes with existing historical records, will compile systematic written manuscripts to conduct in-depth theoretical research on the contextual settings, construction backgrounds, and historical functions of such sites; designers, drawing inspiration from the spatial layout, structural aesthetics, and cultural connotations of these scenes, will develop distinctive design styles that blend traditional elements with modern aesthetics; and ordinary tourists will mentally contrast the unique spatial layouts and cultural atmospheres of these scenes with those of other tourist destinations, thereby identifying the exclusive cultural and experiential value of the specific site. Intangible cultural heritage, too, generates varied influences and effects related to visual aesthetic value. Taking a handwritten manuscript of a classic work as an example, the subjective judgments of different reader groups—such as scholars, students, and general readers—lead to noticeably divergent output effects: after the manuscript (including its calligraphy style, marginal notes, and content layout) is visually processed and cognitively fed back to the brain, readers' outputs (e.g., academic reviews, reading reflections, or public evaluations) often differ significantly based on their personal knowledge reserves, value orientations, and reading purposes, ultimately resulting in mixed, multi-faceted evaluations of the work. In essence, visual aesthetic value primarily presents a clear phenomenon of differentiation, which originates directly from the inherent differences between individual visual subjects and their cognitive contexts. Second, tactile symbolic value serves as a crucial and irreplaceable support for the influence and effects of generalized spiritual value. Although generalized spiritual value, by its nature, belongs to an intangible form of value evaluation that exists in the cognitive and emotional realms, its practical mode of action still requires reliance on tangible external carriers; otherwise, it would remain abstract and disconnected from real-life experiences like a castle in the air, unable to exert substantive, sustained influence on individuals and society. The core function of tactile symbolic value lies in effectively bridging the gap between intangible spiritual value and tangible external material forms, transforming abstract spiritual connotations into perceivable, interactive tactile experiences. We generally recognize that cultural heritage typically manifests itself within specific, fixed contextual scenarios—such as historical sites, cultural ceremonies, or traditional craft workshops—and in this process, our spiritual attachment and emotional identification with cultural heritage are often initially acquired through intuitive visual means. However, human memory, constrained by psychological and temporal factors, tends to grow increasingly vague and fragmented over time, gradually creating a sense of alienation and distance between cultural heritage and its associated spiritual values. The optimal solution to this issue is to enable people to perceive and connect with the spiritual value of cultural heritage at any time and in any context, and the emergence of creative products derived from cultural heritage—such as miniature replicas, cultural souvenirs, and functional craft derivatives—precisely addresses this alienation; these products also serve as the primary, most effective carriers of tactile symbolic value. Through these tangible creative products, we can systematically transfer and embed the spiritual value of the original cultural heritage (e.g., its historical significance, cultural connotations, and aesthetic charm) and further realize the transformation of tactile symbolic spiritual value via these visible, touchable, usable items. A typical example is China's Great Wall, one of the world's most renowned and iconic tourist attractions: it has engraved unique, profound spiritual values—including national pride, historical continuity, and architectural grandeur—in the hearts of millions globally, and the time-honored slogan "No man is a hero until he reaches the Great Wall" has deepened people's yearning and emotional identification with it. Nevertheless, the Great Wall, as a large-scale immovable cultural heritage, is geographically fixed, and most individuals lack the time, energy, or opportunity to visit it daily to sustain the spiritual sentiments it evokes. To compensate for this gradual fading of spiritual values, people can purchase Great Wall-related cultural heritage creative products (e.g., scaled-down models, printed artworks, or functional souvenirs), allowing them to touch, use, and appreciate the Great Wall's spiritual essence in daily life. In essence, tactile symbolic value acts as a necessary, effective supplement to visual aesthetic spiritual value; from this perspective, it not only extends the duration of people's emotional connection and cognitive memory of visual aesthetic value but also expands its reach to a broader, more diverse group (including those unable to visit heritage sites in person) and spans a longer timeline and wider spatial scope. Those influenced by tactile symbolic value can integrate cultural heritage's spiritual connotations into daily life, creative practices, or social interactions via these tactile objects, further sublimating the influence and cultural force of heritage.

These two types are common forms of spiritual value, and vision and touch are also the two most frequently used human senses. Although the value influence and effect of the two different senses are different, in essence, they both need to take the existing cultural heritage as the source of spiritual value, however, the experience brought by the two values is completely different in the level of spiritual value influence. This influence will change according to the cultural heritage directed by aesthetic value and symbolic value. Human thinking is complex and diverse, but many new things can be created based on the spiritual value feedback from this cultural heritage. Therefore, the most important embodiment of the spiritual value influence and effect of cultural heritage is creativity, which is also the internal source of power to promote the development of human society.

4.2.2 The Influence and Effect of the Realistic Value of Cultural Heritage

Realistic value is the important value of cultural heritage to promote social development. Whether the cultural heritage can effectively achieve the state of sustainability, the decisive factor lies in the realistic value evaluation system. The types represented by realistic value also show diversity. We explain its influence and effect from the economic market, architectural culture and tourism service represented by realistic value, this analysis helps to distinguish the different evaluation methods brought by real value more intuitively.

a. The Influence and Effect of Economic Market Value

Although cultural heritage is universally recognized as a project embodying the shared cultural characteristics of humanity, this unique cultural foundation also inherently carries certain market value that can be translated into tangible economic benefits. To clarify this relationship, we will conduct a specific analysis by distinguishing between the two primary categories of cultural heritage: tangible cultural heritage and intangible cultural heritage. The economic market value of tangible cultural heritage is typically relatively fixed, primarily due to the special constraints imposed by its inherent type—such as its immovability, uniqueness, or historical specificity. A representative example is the Forbidden City in Beijing, China: endowed with unparalleled historical and architectural charm, it attracts a massive influx of visitors to the areas surrounding it nearly every day. This constant concentration of people inadvertently lays a solid foundation for the emergence of a vibrant economic market, as dense human gatherings have long been recognized as the most favorable venues for commodity trading and commercial activities. For anyone who has the opportunity to visit the Forbidden City, it is easy to observe a wide array of shops—varying in size and offering diverse forms of goods—operating in the vicinity; these shops, leveraging the steady flow of tourists, often achieve considerable profitability. This phenomenon directly reflects the tangible economic market value generated by tangible cultural heritage. Intangible cultural heritage, too, possesses significant economic market value, with many of its forms—such as renowned historical manuscripts, traditional currency-making techniques, distinctive local food craftsmanship, and time-honored artisanal skills—capable of being practically applied to increase economic income for individuals and communities. Take the traditional production process of Shaoxing rice wine, which has been officially included in the intangible cultural heritage list of Zhejiang Province, China: by adhering to this age-old, refined processing and production technology, Shaoxing rice wine has won widespread favor among consumers both domestically and internationally, thereby securing a stable and competitive position in the global wine industry's economic market. Similar cases of intangible cultural heritage driving market value can be found in the tea industry, such as Hangzhou's West Lake Longjing tea, Xinyang Maojian tea, and Yunnan Pu'er tea. Although these tea-making traditions have not yet been formally included in the World Cultural Heritage List, they have achieved high visibility and reputation in their respective industrial fields. More importantly, they have effectively driven the development of related upstream and downstream processing markets—including tea planting, harvesting, processing, packaging, and sales—gradually forming relatively complete industrial chains. These mature chains, in turn, strongly promote the prosperity and sustainable development of the local and even national economic market.

Through the above argument, we can be summarized as follows, that is, the economic market value of cultural heritage and the effects of diversity and significance. The diversity of cultural heritage can be seen from both horizontal and vertical aspects: from the perspective of the horizontal field of the market, it can achieve the effect of the industry community, that is, to form an aggregation effect in the value field created by the same cultural heritage, to fully protect and utilize the cultural heritage, such as relying on the commercial and trade markets formed around the palace museum, while generating economic benefits, it also virtually makes more people aware of the history of the Palace Museum, and consciously join the ranks of the protection of this cultural heritage. From the perspective of the vertical field of the market, cultural heritage can improve the upstream and downstream industrial chain, and can be combined with cultural heritage in all aspects of the market, such as the aforementioned Shaoxing rice wine, it can not only combine with the production technology, but also promote shaoxing rice wine at the sales end, so that more people can know the origin of Shaoxing rice wine and join the promotion and Protection Team of Shaoxing rice wine.

b. The Influence and Effect of Architectural Cultural Value

The value of architectural culture primarily originates from the category of material cultural heritage within the broader framework of cultural heritage. These monumental structures and archaeological sites exert a profound and far-reaching influence on the historical evolution of global architectural civilization, and the historical relics themselves stand as exquisitely crafted testaments to ancient wisdom. Take traditional Chinese garden design as a paradigmatic example: the spatial layout and drainage systems of these gardens exhibit extraordinary ingenuity—so much so that it is remarkable to observe how little standing water accumulates in a forest-style garden spanning a vast construction area. Additionally, certain ancient temples and residential buildings were constructed with meticulous consideration to avoid erosion by rainwater, a design choice that has enabled their preservation to the present day. Egypt's pyramids, widely renowned as among the world's greatest wonders, similarly embody this exceptional architectural value. Their construction entailed addressing a multitude of complex challenges: for instance, how to transport and position the colossal stone blocks, how to design the construction plan to ensure the long-term preservation of the tomb chambers, and how to select an optimal geographical location for the pyramids. Overcoming these challenges required humanity to mobilize enormous human, material, and financial resources, while integrating a diverse range of technical methods to complete such a grand and magnificent construction project. To this day, the pyramids continue to leave many archaeologists in awe, as they struggle to fathom how humans, thousands of years ago, could conceive and construct such an ingenious architectural form. Similar architectural cultural heritage, comparable in significance to the Egyptian pyramids, can be found in numerous other countries across the globe. Through these cultural heritage sites, we can not only directly perceive the wisdom and creativity of ancient civilizations but also trace the evolving history of global cultures. Therefore, we can explore the influence and effects of architectural cultural heritage from two key perspectives. From the standpoint of architecture's intrinsic value, its influence and effects primarily lie in providing a reference standard for the advancement of contemporary architectural techniques. Ancient architecture was typically designed in adherence to principles of aesthetics, practicality, and habitability—principles that have exerted a profound impact on the fundamental types of modern architecture and continue to guide its detailed classification. For example, the layout of modern high-rise buildings is primarily based on the criteria of practicality and habitability, ensuring functionality and comfort for occupants. In contrast, aesthetic value in modern architecture is most prominently reflected in the layout of public park facilities and landscape design, where traditional aesthetic concepts are adapted to contemporary needs. From the perspective of cultural heritage's essential attributes, architectural cultural heritage serves as a reflection of the dominant direction and trends of a society's culture during a specific historical period. Taking ancient temples and Buddhist grottoes as examples, these structures fully demonstrate that during the Wei, Jin, Southern, and Northern Dynasties, religious Buddhism was venerated by individuals across the social spectrum—from emperors to ordinary commoners. During the Tang and Song Dynasties, a wealth of intangible cultural heritage works, with poetry as a representative form, were continuously created and circulated. A large number of these literary works were cited and inscribed on architectural structures (such as stone tablets or building facades), a practice that not only attests to the prosperity of the Tang and Song Dynasties—where the state thrived and the people lived in stability—but also indicates that the number of talented individuals and cultural creators during this period had increased significantly compared to previous eras.

It can be seen that the influence and effect of architectural cultural value can more intuitively reflect the main theme of history in a certain period, and restore and retain modern life through the current situation of People's life in this period. In the past, some excellent traditional culture needs to be inherited by future generations, so it is necessary to completely restore the scenes at that time, such as the architectural scenes needed for the recording of film and television plays. The repair and maintenance of the scenic spot, the sale of the antique Tang suit and so on, in fact, all reflect the influence of the past architectural cultural value on modern life.

c. The Impact and Effect of Tourism Service Value

As the concrete bearing core of the realistic value of cultural heritage, tourism service is obviously different from other values, the reasonable utilization, protection and promotion of cultural heritage all need the help of tourism service value. The influence and effect of tourism service value can be discussed from three aspects: firstly, tourism service can attract more people to pay attention to cultural heritage. The protection of cultural heritage is an important issue in the world. How to make the endangered cultural heritage return to the public's vision is also the direction of the current efforts of all countries. Cultural heritage is often a symbol of the national spirit, which needs to be passed down from generation to generation to ensure that the country's cultural heritage remains unchanged. Today, the biggest problem facing cultural heritage is the lack of outreach. The root cause is that there is too little coverage, so that many younger generations do not know enough about the content of cultural heritage, therefore, the corresponding promotion work can not be carried out. The value of tourism services can just solve the problem of insufficient promotion and publicity. Through the value output of tourism services, cultural heritage can cross the ocean and have in-depth dialogue with distant groups, this can effectively solve the problem of group coverage. Generally speaking, cultural heritage represents the spirit of a country. If the spirit of the country wants to continue, it is necessary to let the people have a deeper understanding of their cultural heritage and do a good job in publicity. Tourism service itself is a kind of dynamic propaganda measure, which can break the deadlock of subject scarcity and let more people participate in the "Journey" of becoming familiar with cultural heritage. Second, tourism services can strengthen the maintenance and repair of cultural heritage. Cultural Heritage itself has a certain degree of vulnerability, in the process of the passage of time in urgent need of repair and protection, how to support the corresponding cultural heritage to be properly maintained requires two conditions: one is to have a fixed repair and maintenance funds. Second, through the acquisition of visibility so that more people understand the cultural heritage, and then consciously join the ranks of the maintenance of cultural heritage. Of these two conditions, the supply of funds is very important, and the tourism service can provide corresponding maintenance funds on a sustainable basis. The second condition can also play a role in promoting cultural heritage by making it more widely known, indirectly, it helps raise money for renovations. Finally, tourism services can drive the development of areas related to cultural heritage. The scope of cultural heritage needs to be certified by the relevant organizations in order to be eligible, and these certification procedures ensure that cultural heritage is in a state of scarcity, and therefore, taking cultural heritage as the center can derive the development of many related fields, such as the construction of transportation facilities, the development and utilization of resources, etc., which can well form the advantages of location tourism around cultural heritage. Tourism services can be more convenient to introduce the cultural heritage to the public, attracting them to visit the experience. These groups have also become the main object of tourism services. In order to better serve the relevant groups, the surrounding cultural heritage will also have a related industrial agglomeration effect. The direct impact and effect of the above two-way symbiotic tourism service value is that the cultural heritage and its surrounding areas have been well utilized and developed.

The impact and effect of tourism service value is very significant. The most important thing is to have a positive impact on the daily maintenance and management of cultural heritage, and also play a corresponding role in promoting cultural heritage. At present, cultural heritage is in urgent need of proper protection, otherwise it will face the risk of being destroyed or disappeared. The value of tourism services can fundamentally solve the problem that the channels for publicizing cultural heritage are blocked, the utilization and management from the perspective of cultural heritage protection will help to achieve the purpose of sustainable utilization.

4.2.3 The Influence and Effect of Cultural Heritage on Social Value

The social value of cultural heritage is mainly from the perspective of public interest, reflected in the social effects of cultural value. The social value of cultural heritage involves a wide range of content, and its impact and effect is also far-reaching. Therefore, we can mainly demonstrate the impact and effect of the social value of cultural heritage from two aspects. On the one hand, cultural heritage can promote interpersonal communication, through the two-way cycle of domestic and international exchanges to provide a platform for the "Global South" policy and programs. On the other hand, cultural heritage can also provide certain educational value. Through the promotion of the social value of cultural heritage, more people can have a more comprehensive understanding of the evolution history of human civilization, educational value can also be combined with inheritance to enhance the utilization and protection of cultural heritage, thus creating a favorable environment for social development.

a. The Influence and Effect of the Exchange Value of Cultural Heritage

The exchange value of cultural heritage can be systematically analyzed from three interrelated perspectives: the individual level, the group level, and the societal level. First, from an individual perspective, interpersonal communication often achieves emotional resonance through shared interest in a common topic, and cultural heritage precisely provides such a topic to facilitate meaningful interaction between individuals. In the process of communicating about cultural heritage—whether discussing its historical connotations, aesthetic characteristics, or protection challenges—individuals can gain corresponding inspiration, broaden their cognitive horizons, and even jointly propose scientific and reasonable plans for the rational utilization and targeted protection of cultural heritage. This kind of communication not only strengthens interpersonal connections but also transforms individual insights into collective wisdom for heritage preservation. Second, from a group perspective, cultural heritage has the capacity to unite relevant groups into cohesive organizations with clear goals. For instance, handicrafts endowed with intangible cultural heritage attributes—such as traditional weaving techniques, hand-carving crafts, and ancient pottery-making skills—can serve as a unifying core, enabling practitioners, enthusiasts, and inheritors to form organizations like inheritance associations, craft guilds, or protection alliances. Similarly, numerous religious associations and folk cultural groups are established on the basis of material cultural heritage sites such as temples, ancestral halls, or historical religious complexes; these organizations take the protection of such heritage sites as their mission and develop into influential civil society entities dedicated to safeguarding both the tangible sites and their associated intangible cultural practices. Finally, from a societal perspective, the exchange value of cultural heritage transcends not only geographical boundaries between different regions and countries but also professional boundaries across various industries. The cross-regional and cross-national dimension of this exchange is primarily reflected in collaborative efforts among countries where specific cultural heritage is located, with protection as the core intention. Countries in the region of a given cultural heritage often reach consensus on its preservation and management through mutual consultations and agreements; a typical example is the International Charter for the Conservation and Restoration of Monuments and Sites (commonly known as the Venice Charter), which entered into force in 1964. This convention, specifically aimed at the protection of heritage buildings and historic sites, plays an irreplaceable role in promoting cross-regional and cross-national exchange, cooperation, and standardized protection of material cultural heritage among the participating regions and countries. Beyond geographical scope, cultural heritage also generates significant exchange value across different industrial fields, with such exchanges differentiated by the type of cultural heritage. Material cultural heritage mainly drives exchange and cooperation in fields such as archaeology, cultural tourism, and architectural design: particularly when a new material cultural heritage site is discovered (e.g., an ancient ruin or a historical building), experts from multiple authoritative fields—including archaeologists, historians, architectural conservationists, and cultural heritage managers—convene to conduct joint research, discuss protection strategies, and share professional insights. For example, the protection and study of the Sanxingdui Ruins (a major archaeological site in Sichuan, China) and the murals of the Mogao Grottoes (a world heritage site in Gansu, China) both involve in-depth cross-industry exchanges and collaborative efforts. In contrast, intangible cultural heritage primarily fosters in-depth exchanges in fields such as traditional handicraft manufacturing, cultural and creative industries, and media and communication; the core purpose of these exchanges is to explore effective ways to maintain the continuous inheritance of intangible cultural heritage, such as promoting the integration of traditional crafts with modern design or using media platforms to disseminate intangible heritage practices. In essence, societal exchange is a direct and intuitive manifestation of the social value of cultural heritage. It is through such cross-boundary, cross-industry, and cross-group exchange that cultural heritage gains broader recognition, attracts more social forces—including governments, enterprises, non-profit organizations, and the general public—to participate in its support and protection, and ultimately achieves sustainable development in the context of global cultural interaction.

b. The Influence and Effect of the Educational Value of Cultural Heritage

The educational value of cultural heritage stands as another pivotal manifestation of its social value, and by starting from the distinct dimensions of educational backgrounds—family education, school education, and social education—we can comprehensively explore the specific impacts and practical effects of this educational value. From the perspective of family education, cultural heritage serves as a unique and profound educational resource that enables family education to place greater emphasis on shaping the individual's thinking concepts and cognitive frameworks. When family education is effectively integrated with cultural heritage, it can at least achieve two significant effects: On one hand, the children receiving this education can broaden their cognitive horizons through understanding the evolution of history—by appreciating tangible cultural heritage such as ancient buildings and historical monuments, they can quickly grasp the historical logic and contextual significance behind these historical sites; by learning about intangible cultural heritage including classic literary works, traditional handicrafts, and age-old cultural customs, they can recognize the differences between contemporary culture and historical culture, thereby developing a dialectical thinking perspective that allows them to view cultural continuity and change rationally. On the other hand, such family education can help the educated group understand the diversity and complexity of the world at an earlier stage, fostering their ability to discern right from wrong, respect cultural differences, and form a sound sense of judgment. From the perspective of school education, cultural heritage exerts a positive influence on the development of systematic and rigorous thinking consciousness among the educated group—two core thinking abilities that school education aims to cultivate. Systematic thinking, as a primary goal of school education, requires the educated group to avoid viewing things and understanding the world in an isolated or fragmented manner; cultural heritage, in turn, possesses an inherent systematic value connotation: its diverse and complex types (spanning tangible and intangible forms) rely on the participation of different social groups, integrate varied value concepts, and ultimately converge into representative works of cultural value. This systematic nature of cultural heritage can be well integrated with school education, serving as a concrete teaching resource to demonstrate the interconnectedness of cultural elements and historical contexts. Rigorous thinking, meanwhile, focuses on enabling the educated group to establish logical and objective evaluation criteria; cultural heritage encompasses numerous historical artifacts and sites that reflect dynastic changes, many of which bear traces of the ruling class in different periods—such as the construction of Qin Shihuang's Mausoleum in China and the Egyptian Pyramids. While these magnificent structures are admired by later generations for their architectural grandeur, they also subtly reflect the characteristics of class differentiation in ancient societies, as the construction of such grand tombs often involved the exploitation of ordinary people. History exists in an objective form, and school education seeks to help the educated understand this objective nature of cultural heritage, guiding them to go beyond surface phenomena and explore the inherent attributes and historical implications of heritage. From the perspective of social education, cultural heritage enables the educated groups to comprehend the operational rules and interpersonal dynamics of society. We can regard cultural heritage as a vivid representation of historical scenes, and social education can leverage the reproduction of these cultural heritage scenes to allow the educated group to experience the division of different social roles, deeply understand the logic of social operation, and learn to handle various interpersonal and social relationships in real-life contexts. Another positive local impact and effect of social education lies in its ability to arouse greater interest among young people in engaging with cultural heritage—for instance, by attracting young people through modern, interactive venues that simulate historical scenes, such as VR (virtual reality) cultural heritage exhibition halls and immersive role-playing sites; additionally, social education can realize the educational value of cultural heritage through role-playing games, such as integrating general knowledge about cultural heritage into tabletop card games or embedding cultural heritage clues into the characters and plots of scripted games. The integration of these innovative elements with cultural heritage not only generates new and effective publicity and promotion effects for heritage dissemination but also plays a positive guiding role in learning at the social group's educational level, making cultural heritage education more engaging, accessible, and resonant with contemporary young people.

Although the spiritual, practical and social values of cultural heritage do not represent the full scope of its influence and effects, but we can use these values to dig out the advantages of combining cultural heritage with the "Global South", and use these advantages to cooperate deeply with countries along the route. Culture is a national invisible industry, but also reflects the spirit of the country, the customs of the intuitive mirror. Only a deep understanding of the impact and effect of cultural heritage value can better coordinate with the "Global South" initiative.

4.3 Trends in the Coordinated Development of the Global South and Cultural Heritage

The proposal and practical advancement of the "Global South" initiative are essentially centered on pursuing shared economic prosperity and social development with neighboring countries; guided by this core goal, countries along the routes of the "Global South" initiative will engage in extensive cooperation and in-depth exchanges with China. Beyond the traditional "Silk Road Economic Belt," the "21st-Century Maritime Silk Road"—as a crucial transportation hub linking China with Southeast Asian nations and other regional partners—will also play an indispensable role in facilitating this collaborative development. The development trajectories of China and its neighboring countries are inherently intertwined and mutually influential: through the north-south connectivity routes under the initiative, China can more actively and effectively participate in global development dynamics, while the international community can gain a deeper and more comprehensive understanding of China. Ultimately, this mutual engagement and trust-building will contribute to the realization of the "Community with a Shared Future for Mankind" concept. As a vital carrier for fostering people-to-people bonds within the framework of the Global South initiative, cultural heritage must maintain consistent coordination with the initiative's goals and directions at all stages; only by doing so can it fully serve the broad range of countries and communities covered by the Global South initiative. We can specifically explore the synergy between cultural heritage and the Global South initiative by integrating the inherent characteristics of cultural heritage and its far-reaching impacts, focusing on two interrelated dimensions: cultural heritage output and cultural heritage input. Cultural heritage output is an active effort rooted in the context of China's "culture going out" strategy. It primarily leverages the platform of the Global South initiative to promote

China's outstanding traditional and contemporary cultural achievements to other countries in the Global South, enabling more nations and peoples to gain an in-depth understanding of China's cultural connotations, historical traditions, and development concepts. In contrast, cultural heritage input refers to the process of integrating the excellent cultural elements of other countries covered by the Global South initiative with China's own cultural context, absorbing valuable foreign cultural experiences, and promoting the localized development and innovative adaptation of these imported cultural resources within China. Among these two dimensions, cultural heritage output serves as the primary approach to enhancing synergy. As one of the four cradles of ancient civilization, China boasts a vast repository of exceptional cultural achievements—spanning tangible heritage such as historical monuments and traditional crafts, and intangible heritage including folk arts and cultural practices. If these rich cultural resources can be tailored to align with the unique local conditions, customs, and cultural backgrounds of countries along the Global South routes, they will significantly contribute to the improvement of the political mutual trust, economic cooperation mechanisms, and cultural exchange ecosystems of these countries, laying a solid foundation for long-term, win-win collaboration.

4.3.1 The Trend of Coordinated Development in the Context of Cultural Export

Under the background of cultural output, the trend of coordinated development between the Global South Initiative and cultural heritage is mainly manifested in the following key aspects: First, cultural heritage can serve as a solid value foundation for the implementation of the Global South Initiative. The value of cultural heritage possesses inherent universality, encompassing and embodying multiple dimensions such as spiritual value, realistic value, and social value. Therefore, when positioned as the value foundation for advancing the Global South Initiative, cultural heritage can be leveraged to promote China's outstanding culture through these diverse value dimensions, enabling more people overseas to gain a comprehensive, in-depth understanding of China's development history and cultural connotations. From the perspective of spiritual value, China can showcase its historical cultural heritage as representative carriers to the countries covered by the Global South strategy. For instance, by organizing traveling exhibitions in international cultural venues, China can display representative cultural relics such as traditional paintings, exquisite porcelain, and intricate handicrafts to other countries. This not only allows more nations to recognize the unique spiritual value embedded in China's cultural heritage but also, by virtue of this spiritual value, conveys China's outstanding cultural qualities that have endured since ancient times—such as diligence, friendship and mutual assistance, and the pursuit of love and equality. Additionally, through the dissemination of items that embody China's outstanding spiritual values, foreign groups can be closely connected via visual and tactile engagement (e.g., observing the details of cultural relics or touching cultural and creative replicas), thereby sparking their interest in these cultural heritages and fostering a deeper emotional connection. From the perspective of realistic value, the output of cultural heritage can directly generate tangible economic benefits. Taking the cultural and creative industry as a typical example: cultural and creative products that reflect the distinct characteristics of various cultural heritages, after being exported to other countries through the platform of the Global South Initiative, will quickly enter the trading markets of these nations. Owing to their exquisite craftsmanship and unique cultural novelty, these products are likely to gain favor in foreign markets. This form of foreign trade not only brings economic returns to cultural and creative enterprises but also serves as a medium to convey China's representative cultural heritage to a broader range of countries. For example, refrigerator stickers featuring designs of the Great Wall of China, though affordable, can evoke in citizens of importing countries an association with the magnificent scenery of the Great Wall and even inspire their desire to travel to China to visit this heritage site in person. In essence, this entire process relies on the realistic value of cultural heritage, forming a linked development model between the Global South Initiative and cultural heritage. From the perspective of social value, communication constitutes an indispensable link in the process of cultural output. To translate the concept of people-to-people integration under the Global South Initiative into practice, it is necessary to use communication as a "bridge" to deeply connect the cultural sentiments between China and other countries. Currently, China has signed cultural cooperation agreements with over 60 countries along the Global South routes, and mutual hosting of cultural festivals and art festivals has become a shared consensus among these partners. During the organization of these cultural events, China can further export its excellent culture to countries along the routes, deepening the friendship and mutual assistance between Chinese society and non-governmental groups in partner countries. Furthermore, China has implemented a series of facilitation measures, such as providing visa-free access policies for citizens of some Global South countries and supporting Chinese citizens to travel to these countries for academic research, study, and business activities. These measures not only enhance people-to-people exchanges but also exert a positive impact on the export of Chinese culture, strengthening the social value-driven coordination between the Global South Initiative and cultural heritage.

Second, the Global South Initiative can better facilitate the sustainable development of cultural heritage, and sustainability itself serves as a core driving force for the intergenerational inheritance of cultural heritage. As a key channel for China to showcase its friendly international image, the Global South Initiative—against the backdrop of cultural export—plays a pivotal role in addressing the challenge of unsustainable development that cultural heritage faces. Through the platform of the Global South Initiative, cultural heritage can be promoted to organizations, groups, and individuals across different regions of the world, effectively overcoming the shortcomings of cultural heritage discontinuity or "fault lines" that may arise due to limited dissemination, lack of inheritors, or insufficient attention. Countries along the Global South routes, influenced by China's cultural export efforts, have begun to proactively engage with Chinese culture—with a particular focus on certain types of intangible cultural heritage, such as traditional handicrafts and performing arts. These categories of intangible heritage not only embody unique cultural spirits and historical connotations but also spark global interest in learning and preserving such heritage, especially in the case of performing arts and handicrafts that require hands-on practice and experiential learning. Since the advancement of the Global South Initiative, an increasing number of foreign groups have started to explore and learn about China's distinctive intangible cultural heritage items, including traditional wine-making techniques, crosstalk (a form of Chinese comedic performance), and traditional martial arts. Even some endangered skills, which were once at risk of being lost, have gained a new chance for inheritance as the Global South cooperation deepens, thanks to the enhanced cross-border exchanges and collaborative protection efforts fostered by the initiative. The emergence of these phenomena not only provides new opportunities for the sustainable development of China's cultural heritage but also offers inspiration to other countries worldwide that face similar obstacles in ensuring the sustainability of their own cultural heritage. These countries are more likely to join the cultural cooperation agreements and organizations under the Global South framework, thereby enabling their own cultural heritage to access platforms for exchange, protection, and inheritance, and thus gaining opportunities for sustainable development. The sustainable development of cultural heritage is an essential carrier of human civilization; if its sustainability cannot be guaranteed, the "kindling" of human civilization—passed down through generations—will gradually dim. The cultural export driven by the Global South Initiative has reignited this "flame" of human civilization, allowing it to be passed on continuously once again. It is believed that in the course of future development, more countries will join hands under the Global South framework to strengthen cooperation in cultural heritage protection and inheritance, collectively ensuring the sustainable development of global cultural heritage.

Third, the "Global South" will deepen cooperation in the protection and use of cultural heritage. Under the background of cultural export, China and the countries along the "Global South" will further strengthen cooperation in various fields, which will form a series of programs in the cultural field. As an important part of cultural export, the protection and utilization of cultural heritage have experience and enlightenment in practice in many countries. Before the implementation of the "Global South" strategy, the level of exchanges and cooperation between countries was not deep, and further cooperation in the field of cultural heritage could not be generated between them. However, with the deepening of the "Global South", the synergy between it and cultural heritage will be mainly reflected in how to strengthen the use and protection of cultural heritage, these new trends will continue to have a positive impact, especially on the restoration and protection of cultural heritage. Countries can learn from each other's experience. The restoration of cultural heritage will have different restoration problems due to differences in geographical location, climate conditions, construction time and so on. At this time, international cooperation and exchange are very important. Some cultural heritage sites are located at the borders of countries, which can also lead to management difficulties.

Using the "Global South" to break down communication barriers between countries will solve the management dilemma, it will help countries reach a consensus on the protection and utilization of cultural heritage as soon as possible.

4.3.2 The Trend of Coordinated Development in the Context of Cultural Input

Under the background of cultural input, the collaborative development trend between the Global South Initiative and cultural heritage is mainly manifested in the following aspects: First, the Global South Initiative can leverage cultural heritage to drive the rapid development of the tourism service industry. The connection between cultural heritage and the tourism service industry is inherently strong; beyond the influence of tourism service value within the scope of realistic value, under the context of cultural input, the role of cultural heritage in boosting tourism service value becomes particularly prominent. Relying on its unique cultural advantages, China can attract a large number of visitors from countries along the Global South routes to travel within its borders, while also effectively promoting some of its well-known cultural heritage sites to these countries. These foreign tourists, taking advantage of the convenience policies under the Global South Initiative (such as visa facilitation and travel support), can visit locations where tangible cultural heritage is situated, fully immersing themselves in local customs and traditions during their trips. In the course of their travels, they will learn about the historical stories, cultural connotations, and symbolic meanings behind these cultural heritage sites, and later share these experiences with others upon returning to their home countries, thereby acting as informal promoters of China's cultural heritage. This process not only achieves a positive and interactive publicity effect—where tourists become "cultural messengers" to spread awareness of China's cultural heritage—but also brings a continuous flow of visitors to China's domestic tourism market, injecting sustained vitality into the industry. With the support of these favorable factors, the tourism service industry will witness rapid development: it will gradually drive the optimization and upgrading of tourism product quality (such as the development of cultural heritage-themed tour routes) and service standards (such as multilingual interpretation services and improved visitor facilities), ultimately realizing a major transformation of the domestic tourism service market toward higher quality and greater diversity. As a unique and core object of tourism services, cultural heritage will see its internationalization trend gradually gain an important position with the deepening practice of the Global South Initiative. Under the context of cultural input, constructing international cultural heritage tourism destinations—sites that attract global visitors with their distinctive cultural value and well-developed supporting services—has become another key task for the future development of China's tourism service industry. The internationalization of cultural heritage tourism will not only directly promote the rapid and high-quality development of the tourism service industry but also bring about implicit internal effects: cultural heritage itself will receive wider attention globally in the long run. This increased attention will enhance the status and influence of China's cultural heritage on the international stage, attract more international resources for its protection and inheritance, and further advance the achievement of its sustainable development goals. In this way, the Global South Initiative, cultural heritage, and the tourism service industry form a mutually reinforcing collaborative relationship, driving common development in both cultural exchange and economic growth.

Second, the Global South Initiative will further reinforce the profound international educational significance embedded in cultural heritage. Under the background of cultural input, cultural heritage, beyond its role in supporting family education, school education, and social education, will further fulfill the purpose of promoting an international educational concept that transcends national boundaries. Compared with these three more localized forms of education, international education driven by cultural heritage exhibits a far broader reach, and its audience naturally presents a cross-national development trend—encompassing individuals from diverse cultural backgrounds, age groups, and professional fields across the Global South countries. Most notably, this international education will generate targeted educational differences tailored to the unique cultural contexts, cognitive characteristics, and developmental needs of different groups in various countries, ensuring that the educational content resonates with local audiences. The distinct advantage of this form of international education lies in its ability to enable more people in countries along the Global South routes to witness the remarkable integration of diverse cultural elements within China and observe how these cultures coexist harmoniously while preserving their respective uniqueness. This firsthand observation and understanding will gradually foster a sense of identity with China's cultural diversity and spark a genuine interest in China and its rich cultural heritage. The core value of cultural input, in this context, lies in guiding more countries to gradually form a positive and comprehensive impression of China through a three-step process: first, gaining a basic understanding of China's historical development, social system, and cultural background; second, deepening their knowledge of Chinese customs, traditions, and daily practices; and finally, developing a sincere identification with China's core values such as harmony, mutual respect, and win-win cooperation. The significance of this international education is mainly reflected in two key aspects: on one hand, international education serves as a bridge to bring China's cultural heritage to a wider range of countries, allowing these nations to recognize and appreciate the important cultural qualities embodied in China's heritage—such as tolerance toward cultural differences, modesty in interpersonal interactions, benevolence as a guiding principle, friendliness in international exchanges, and diligence as a national virtue—and enabling these positive qualities to exert a constructive and positive impact on their own social development and cultural progress. On the other hand, international education can leverage the platform and convenience provided by the Global South Initiative to facilitate more foreign individuals to travel to China with greater ease, enabling them to personally explore the unique and profound charm of China's cultural heritage; during their appreciation of cultural heritage sites, these visitors can engage in in-depth interactions with local customs, traditions, and communities, and gradually develop an emotional identification with China's excellent cultural values. This not only showcases the inherent allure of cultural heritage but also embodies the strong spiritual concepts and valuable value orientations that are deeply rooted in cultural heritage and have sustained Chinese civilization for millennia.

Third, the digital connection between the Global South Initiative and cultural heritage has been significantly strengthened, marking a new era of cross-border heritage collaboration driven by technological innovation. The rapid development of the global digital industry in recent decades has fundamentally transformed traditional modes of information communication, cultural dissemination, and interpersonal interaction, and it has also played an increasingly prominent and positive role in addressing the challenges of cultural heritage protection and intergenerational inheritance—particularly for heritage at risk of damage or loss. In the context of cultural input, China can proactively engage in collaborative efforts with countries along the Global South routes to integrate their respective innovative digital technologies into the practical work of cultural heritage protection, creating a synergy that combines diverse technological strengths for a common goal. For instance, advanced digital scene reconstruction technology can be applied to tangible cultural heritage, such as ancient buildings, archaeological sites, and historical monuments, breaking through the inherent limitation of their immovability and realizing a transformative shift from "fixed existence" to "mobile accessibility"—allowing people around the world to experience these heritage sites through virtual means without geographical constraints. Additionally, China can collaborate with Global South partners to integrate emerging blockchain technologies into cultural heritage dissemination, enabling the display of specific cultural heritage items in secure, transparent, and interactive virtual network environments; this approach allows more individuals, regardless of their location, to gain an intuitive, detailed, and immersive understanding of cultural heritage through web-based browsing, virtual reality (VR) devices, or other digital platforms. A typical application of this is the establishment of digital cultural heritage museums on the internet, where cultural heritage can be presented in a variety of innovative forms—including 3D models, interactive exhibitions, and audio-visual narratives—that transcend the limitations of physical museum spaces. Digital technology not only serves as a powerful tool for publicizing and popularizing cultural heritage but also plays a crucial role in mitigating the vulnerability of cultural heritage to natural erosion, human damage, or accidental loss. For example, the murals in cultural heritage sites such as the Dunhuang Mogao Grottoes and Yungang Grottoes, which are precious examples of ancient art, are inherently prone to gradual deterioration and disappearance over time due to factors like changes in temperature, humidity, and air quality. By applying sophisticated digital scanning and restoration technology to these endangered murals, we can achieve a 100% restoration of their original clarity, color, and detail, and permanently preserve these digital replicas in cyberspace—making them accessible to more global groups for appreciation, research, and learning. This not only effectively safeguards against the risk of irreversible loss of cultural heritage but also opens up new opportunities for the global promotion and dissemination of cultural heritage. On one hand, through the framework of the Global South Initiative, China can introduce advanced digital technologies developed by partner countries, integrating them with its own cultural heritage resources to enhance the efficiency and effectiveness of heritage protection and dissemination. On the other hand, China can also strengthen the localization adaptation and innovation of imported digital technologies through in-depth technological learning, joint research, and independent research and development—ensuring that these technologies are better suited to the unique characteristics of China's cultural heritage. Once these localized digital technologies reach maturity, China can further promote the export of digital cultural heritage products and services to Global South countries, thereby maintaining a two-way, efficient, and circular development trend of cultural heritage exchange between China and the international community, and ultimately elevating the global influence and sustainable development of cultural heritage to new heights.

Regardless of the background of cultural output or cultural input, the protection and utilization of cultural heritage can not be separated from publicity and promotion, so as to maintain the state of sustainable development. As an important platform for cooperation and exchange between China and other countries, the global south needs to strengthen the breadth and depth of cooperation and exchange through economic and trade exchanges, infrastructure construction and financial policy support. However, these cooperation exchanges must also be based on the common understanding of the concept, cultural exchanges will certainly play a key role in them. Cultural exchange can go beyond national boundaries and realize the common identity and feelings of the peoples along the "Global South" at the ideological level. Therefore, an important factor of the "Global South" is to achieve the exchange of cultural ideas, and in this process, cultural heritage as an important part of the world's recognition, it will represent cultural ideas and become a hub for maintaining deep ties between countries, and will also become an important "Witness" in the implementation of the "Global South" strategy. We hope that with the further implementation of the "Global South", the concept of "A community of shared future for mankind" will find its value in more countries. We also believe that cultural heritage, as an integral part of the Global South, will enable people from more countries to work with the Chinese people to realize cultural unity and prosperity.

Chapter 5
The Global South and Carbon Neutrality

The "Global South" is not a purely geographical concept, but a term derived from political economy and international relations to describe a group of countries with similar historical experiences and development aspirations. It broadly encompasses the vast majority of developing countries in Asia, Africa, Latin and the Pacific, and its core features include a shared colonial history, a relatively marginalized position in the global political and economic system, and the quest for a more just and equitable international governance order. With the rise of emerging economies, the influence of the "Global South" has increased significantly, and north-south conflicts are emerging in international environmental law, particularly on climate change. Hurrall points out, the pattern of world political inequality is reflected in the following aspects in the environmental field: 1) historical inequality in the use of resources has brought difficulties to developing countries in balancing their own development and sustainable growth. 2) the impact of globalization on the world is not uniform. There are differences in the ability of countries and communities to cope with and adapt to environmental change. Some local environmental problems have expanded to the global scale, which has a more serious impact on developing countries. 3) national strength affects the setting of environmental political agenda. The international community is more likely to pay attention to the ecological and environmental issues that the northern countries are concerned about and ignore the ecological and environmental issues that are important to the southern countries [1]. At the intersection of Economics, trade and the environment, the "Global South" is increasingly an issue that can not be ignored. In his research on international environmental law and Southern countries, Alam discusses international environmental law and international trade law from the perspective of developing countries, and points out that non-tariff barriers to trade in developed countries set unreasonable barriers to developing countries [2].

In the climate negotiations, China's status as a developing country is being questioned and demands for China to take on more responsibilities are growing. Alam

X. Dong, J. Gu, *The Belt and Road Initiative and the Global South*, Energy, Climate Change & Sustainability in the Global South,
https://doi.org/10.1007/978-981-92-0144-0_5

and Atapattu argue that China's identity straddles the developed and developing worlds, in some cases copying the trade and investment patterns of the developed world, while remaining a "Developing country". Cullet, Susskind and Ali point out that China's development challenges the principle of differential treatment and "Common but differentiated responsibilities." Differential treatment needs to change to suit emerging economies such as China and BASIC countries [3]. China is still a developing country, but with a strong economy and the largest total carbon emissions, positioning China in climate negotiations is more difficult. However, some Western scholars are biased in their criticism of China. Although China is the largest emitter of greenhouse gases, its per capita emissions are much lower than those of the United States and Europe, and a considerable proportion of its products are sold overseas, they are consumed in Europe and the United States. In his analysis of China's environmental problems, Japanese scholar Shinichi Takemura pointed out that "It is the whole world that is polluting China" and that industrial transfer from developed countries has not reduced total carbon dioxide emissions, they are shifting the environmental burden to developing countries, such as China [4]. As a responsible country, China has carried out a series of legislative, judicial and law enforcement practices in the field of carbon neutrality. The purpose of this paper is to introduce the legal practice of carbon neutrality in China and discuss the legal structure of carbon neutrality in China.

Article 2 of the Paris Agreement aims to "Limit the increase in global average temperature to no more than 2 °C above pre-industrial levels and strive to limit the increase to no more than 1.5 °C above pre-industrial levels", article 4 states that "In order to achieve the long-term temperature goal set out in article 2, parties aim to achieve global peaking of greenhouse gas emissions as soon as possible… … To achieve a balance between anthropogenic emissions by sources and removals by sinks of greenhouse gases in the second half of this century on the basis of equity" [5]. This goal sets out a vision of "Peak carbon, carbon neutrality" and forms the basis for a number of countries, including China, to commit to carbon neutrality in their ndcs.

At the UN General Assembly in September 2020, China set a "Carbon peaking" target for 2030 and a "Carbon neutrality" target for 2060. In October 2021, China submitted to the UNFCCC secretariat the effectiveness of China's ndcs and new targets and measures, "By 2030, China's carbon dioxide emissions per unit of GDP will be 65% lower than in 2005, the proportion of non-fossil fuels in primary energy consumption will reach around 25%, forest stock will increase by 6 billion cubic metres, and the total installed capacity of wind and solar power will reach more than 1.2 billion kilowatts," the updated NDC said [6]. Since the "Double carbon" goal was proposed, legislation and judicial practices related to carbon neutrality have continued to emerge, policies have advanced rapidly, and a legal framework for carbon neutrality has initially taken shape. However, due to the lack of core special legislation that governs the whole system, the carbon neutrality rule of law structure is fragmented and flat. There are more policies than laws, and more local-level legislation than national-level legislation, legislative, judicial and law enforcement links are not smooth, resulting in structural imbalances. There is a lack of coordination between domestic sectoral laws, local legislation and between domestic and international law, and the country is faced with dual challenges at the national and international levels. To improve the legal structure of carbon neutrality, it is necessary to take the dynamic system theory as the methodology, the Green Low-carbon principle, the risk prevention principle, the proportion principle and the public participation principle as the basic principles, and the establishment of special legislation on carbon neutrality as the core, the concept of carbon neutrality is integrated in different sectoral laws to form a coordinated governance structure between central and local legislation, between sectoral laws, and between concluded international conventions and domestic laws.

5.1 Status and Challenges of the Rule of Law Architecture for Carbon Neutrality

5.1.1 The State of the Legal Architecture for Carbon Neutrality

The rule of law is the rule of law. The rule of law is the basic way of modern state governance, and the implementation of the rule of law is the inherent requirement of the modernization of state governance [7]. The structure of the rule of law refers to the dynamic structure formed between laws in the process of governing the country according to law, including the relationship and hierarchy between the main regulatory objects of law and law. In order to analyze the legal structure of carbon neutrality, we should start with the legal provisions of each level and the relationship between laws, and analyze from the three elements of legislation, judicature and law enforcement.

a. Carbon Neutrality Legislation

(1) Constitution

As the fundamental law of the country, although the constitution, which occupies the highest position in the legal hierarchy, has no direct provisions related to carbon neutrality, it contains content related to environmental protection. The 2018 amendment to the Constitution of the People's Republic of China added a "New development concept" that includes green development in the preamble, making "Ecological civilization" a fundamental task of the country, clearly building a "Beautiful China". The content of "Beautiful China" in the preamble of the Constitution and the legal system to protect "Double carbon" have formed a coincidence and coherence in the regulatory function [8]. The content of ecological civilization in the preamble of the constitution is also reflected in the principles and objectives of the separate laws. For example, article 1 of the forest law states: "This law is formulated in order to put into practice the concept that lucid waters and lush mountains are invaluable assets, to protect, cultivate and rationally utilize forest resources, to speed up the afforestation of the national territory, to ensure the ecological security of forests, to build an ecological civilization, and to achieve harmonious coexistence between man and nature." [9] The concept of building ecological civilization in the constitution should be incorporated into special laws on forest protection.

(2) Environmental protection law and air pollution prevention law

At present, there is no special carbon neutrality legislation in our country, but the concept of green and low-carbon runs through the environmental law, renewable energy law, Forest Law and other separate laws. The laws most closely related to carbon neutrality are the Environmental Protection Act, the Energy Conservation Act and the Renewable Energy Act. As a law that covers all branches of environmental protection, the environmental protection law first undertakes direct or indirect provisions related to carbon neutrality. The "Environment" protected in the environmental protection law is defined as "The totality of natural and artificially modified natural factors affecting the survival and development of mankind", the atmosphere, water, sea and land are all included. The changes that greenhouse gases are causing in the atmosphere and the effects of climate change on water, oceans, forests and wildlife fall into this category. Article 6 of the environmental protection law stipulates that "Citizens should enhance their awareness of environmental protection, adopt a low-carbon and frugal lifestyle, and consciously fulfill their obligations to protect the environment." [10]. This is the clearest expression of low-carbon. In terms of cleaner production, the environmental protection law also has corresponding provisions. Article 40 of the Environmental Protection Law encourages cleaner production and resource recycling. To promote the production and use of clean energy, enterprises are required to give priority to the use of clean energy and adopt processes with high resource utilization and low pollutant emissions to reduce the generation of pollutants.

The air pollution prevention and control law is also the main content of the legislation related to carbon neutrality. Article 1(2) of the air pollution prevention and control law states that "Air pollutants and greenhouse gases shall be subject to coordinated control". This means that the obligation to control greenhouse gases and reduce emissions shall be subject to the air pollution prevention and control law. In practice, some cases related to climate change are indeed based on the Air Pollution Prevention and Control Act. For example, the Supreme People's court has issued "Dual-carbon" cases, deqing County People's Procuratorate v. Deqing thermal insulation material company air pollution liability dispute civil public interest litigation case as the first civil public interest litigation case of ozone depleting substances (ODS) air pollution liability, among them, a thermal insulation material company in Deqing, which uses CFC-13 to produce, was ordered to pay compensation for ecological damage [11].

(3) Energy law

Adjusting the energy mix is an important way to achieve the "Dual carbon" goal. Therefore, energy law plays an important role in carbon neutrality legislation, justice and law enforcement. Article 7 of the energy conservation law states that, "The state implements industrial policies conducive to energy conservation and environmental protection, and restricts the development of high-energy-consuming and high-pollution industries and the development of energy-saving and environment-friendly industries… … The state encourages and supports the development and use of new and renewable sources of energy." [12] The Renewable Energy Act provides a stronger legal boost to clean energy The Renewable Energy Act begins with a clear legislative goal, to "Promote the development and utilization of renewable energy, increase energy supply, improve the energy structure, ensure energy security, protect the environment, and achieve sustainable economic and social development.". Encouragement and support for non-fossil fuels clearly support the achievement of carbon neutrality.

(4) Natural Resource Conservation Law

Climate change is also covered in natural resource conservation laws. Forest, grassland, wetland and other ecosystems have the functions of carbon sequestration, soil and water conservation, and climate regulation, which play an important role in climate change mitigation and adaptation. Article 28 of the forest law stipulates that "The state shall strengthen the protection of forest resources and give full play to the multiple functions of forests in conserving water and soil, regulating the climate, improving the environment, maintaining biodiversity and providing forest products", similar language is used in Article 3 of the wetland protection law and in the grassland law. Article 35 of the law also calls for "Enhancing the ecological and carbon sink functions of wetlands". In addition, China's meteorological law, which was revised in 2016, includes "Rational development, utilization and protection of climate resources" as one of its legislative purposes, the subsequent several local legislations on the protection of climate resources are based on the meteorological law.

In the newly introduced ecological protection legislation, carbon neutrality has been well integrated and integrated. The Yellow River protection law provides for cleaner production, encourages a green and low-carbon lifestyle, and promotes the development of green credit, green bonds and green insurance, article 87 clearly stipulates that "The local people's governments above the county level in the Yellow River basin should promote the high-quality development of the manufacturing industry and the transformation of resource-based industries, and develop modern industries with distinctive advantages and clean and low-carbon energy according to local conditions… … and promote peak carbon and carbon neutrality." [13], the Yangtze River Protection law has a chapter on "Green Development", which promotes a green, low-carbon lifestyle and green consumption The Qinghai-tibet Plateau Ecological Protection Law, which also covers climate change, focuses more on carbon sinks and climate adaptation As the "Water Tower of China", the ecosystem of the qinghai-tibet plateau is obviously affected by climate change, and it is necessary to add adaptation to climate change in ecological protection The protection of the qinghai-tibet plateau, the carbon sink function of the ecosystem, and the impact of climate change are all written into the legislation For example, Article 8 of the law on ecological protection of the qinghai-tibet plateau stipulates: "The state encourages and supports scientific investigation and research on the qinghai-tibet plateau to strengthen climate change and biodiversity on the plateau." …… Research on major scientific and technological issues and construction of major scientific and technological infrastructure in the fields of monitoring, early warning and Prevention of natural disasters, development, utilization and protection of energy and climate resources, and ecosystem carbon sinks, to promote long-term research and to grasp the ecological background of the qinghai-tibet plateau and its changes", the development and utilization of energy and climate resources and carbon sinks are directly related to carbon neutrality [14]. Article 41 provides more explicitly for the monitoring and assessment of the impacts of climate change and for strengthening the monitoring and assessment of climate change and its combined effects, particular reference is made to prediction systems for snow-covered mountains, glaciers, permafrost and the effects of natural disasters.

(5) Civil Code

The Civil Code indirectly provides legal support for carbon neutrality through provisions on environmental protection. For example, Article 9 of the civil code is known as the "Green Principle", which stipulates that "Civil subjects engaged in civil activities should be conducive to saving resources and protecting the ecological environment" [15]. The practice of the "Green principle" has already begun. According to this principle, in the dispute between Shanghai Qinju Industrial Co., Ltd. and Beijing Yuner Computing Technology Co., Ltd. over the entrustment contract, according to the "Green principle" in the civil code, the court determined that bitcoin mining consumes huge amounts of electricity and energy, which is not conducive to high-quality development, energy conservation and emission reduction, and the realization of the "Dual-carbon" goal, contrary to the "Green principle" in Article 9 of the Civil Code, it also does not meet the relevant policies, regulations and regulatory requirements for industrial restructuring, and violates public order and good customs, the contracts for bitcoin "Mining" and "Mining" are null and void. Litigation provisions on environmental torts provide a basis for litigation involving "Dual carbon" targets. The civil code stipulates the liability for environmental pollution and ecological damage in chapter 7 of the tort liability part, article 1232 of which stipulates punitive damages and increases the punishment for serious environmental pollution and ecological damage. Articles 1,234 and 1,235 define liability for environmental damage and the costs of restoration, and support environmental public interest litigation by providing that "Organs or organizations specified by the state or by law" have the right to claim compensation.

(6) Administrative regulations, departmental rules and local ordinance

In addition to the law, various administrative regulations, departmental regulations and local ordinances also play an important role in the dual-carbon target. Most of these laws and regulations are more detailed and specific than the law, covering specific measures such as information disclosure, carbon emissions trading and green finance.

Carbon trading is an important part of achieving the dual-carbon goal. With the establishment and expansion of the carbon emissions trading market, the demand for relevant laws and regulations has also increased. At the end of 2020, China introduced the "Measures for the administration of carbon emissions trading". The measures for the administration of carbon emissions trading put forward the establishment of a national carbon emissions trading market, defined key greenhouse gas emitters, and improved the system of emissions verification and quota payment, making the rapid development of the carbon trading market"Law-based". The national carbon market opened in July 2021. China's carbon market includes 2162 key emitters in the power generation sector, covering about 4.5 billion tons of carbon dioxide emissions, making it the world's largest carbon market [16]. Another important mechanism, the national voluntary greenhouse gas emissions trading market, has also continued to develop. The trading product of the voluntary emission reduction trading market is the national certified voluntary emission reduction (CCER), which is complementary to the carbon emission right trading market and constitutes the complete carbon trading system of our country [17]. In 2023, the Ministry of Ecology and environment revised the "Measures for the administration of greenhouse gas voluntary emission reduction trading" issued in 2012, stipulating the application, subject and subjective department of greenhouse gas voluntary emission reduction activities, the scope of sources of voluntary greenhouse gas emission reduction projects, and the process of project design, publicity and approval.

In terms of greenhouse gas emission information disclosure, in order to implement the "Carbon emission trading management measures (trial)", standardize the carbon emission accounting and reporting work of key emission units in the power generation industry, and improve the quality of carbon emission data, improving the long-term mechanism for data quality management in the national carbon emissions trading market, the Ministry of Ecology and environment (Mee) has developed the guidelines for accounting and reporting of greenhouse gas emissions by enterprises-power generation facilities (2021 revision)(draft for comment). Environmental disclosure laws for governments and companies are beginning to cover more carbon emissions. For example, on February 8, 2022, the administrative measures for the legal disclosure of environmental information by enterprises stated that enterprises are responsible for the legal disclosure of environmental information. Key polluters are required to disclose eight types of information, including carbon emissions. The Ministry of Ecology and Environment (Mee) issued guidelines on the format of corporate environmental information disclosure on 31 December 2021, which state: "Key emitters of greenhouse gases subject to the carbon emissions trading market quota management shall disclose information on their carbon emissions: (1) the actual annual carbon emissions and the actual emissions of the previous year; (2) the status of quota settlement; and (3) information on emission facilities and accounting methods in accordance with greenhouse gas emissions accounting and reporting standards or technical specifications.", the disclosure of carbon emission information is explained in detail, which promotes the establishment of carbon neutrality information disclosure system [18].

Local ordinance, departmental rules and regulations and regulatory documents are the main components of our current carbon neutrality legal structure. At present, there is no special legislation on climate change at the national level in our country, but there are many practices of special legislation on climate change and carbon neutrality in local regulations and ordinances. In 2010, Qinghai province promulgated the "Measures of Qinghai province to deal with climate change", which is the first local ordinance of our country to deal with climate change. Shanxi province has also formulated the "Measures of Shanxi province on coping with climate change".

In view of the characteristics of Shanxi's Coal-rich Province, special provisions have been made to reduce energy waste in coal production and encourage clean production, support for renewable energy. Since the "Double carbon" target was proposed, the practice of local legislation focusing on carbon neutrality has deepened. The regulations of the Shenzhen Special Economic Zone on ecological and environmental protection, promulgated in 2021, contain a special chapter dealing with climate change, including "Carbon peak carbon neutrality" and "Carbon emissions trading" two sections around carbon reduction as an important goal content. "Tianjin's regulations on promoting peak carbon and carbon neutrality" is China's first "Dual-carbon" local law. It proposes to adjust the energy structure, promote a green transition, reduce carbon emissions and increase carbon sinks, and encourage technological innovation, it also includes drastic measures, including a clear target for carbon neutrality. Shijiazhuang, Nanchang and other cities have formulated special regulations to promote low-carbon development, and Shanghai, Guangdong and other cities have formulated local "Trial measures for carbon emission management." We will standardize the allocation, trading and payment of carbon emission quotas and the monitoring, reporting, verification, verification, supervision and punishment of carbon emissions. These legislations can not only provide a reference for future carbon neutrality legislation at the national level, but also play a role in climate change litigation. Articles 2, 3 and 5 of the provisions of the Supreme People's court on the citation of laws, regulations and other normative legal documents in judgments provide that local ordinances may be directly cited in judgments. Local ordinances have played an important role in the "Dual-carbon" cases published by the Supreme People's court. In the case of Shenzhen Xiangfeng Container Company v. Shenzhen Development and Reform Commission, the People's Court of Futian District, Shenzhen City, Guangdong Province, repeatedly cited the regulations on the administration of carbon emissions in the Shenzhen Special Economic Zone, interim Measures for the administration of Shenzhen's carbon emissions trading, it is confirmed that the calculation formula of the government regulation "Interim measures for the administration of carbon emission trading in Shenzhen", which is based on the authorization provisions of the Shenzhen Special Economic Zone Regulations, does not violate the higher-level law. The practice of local legislation in climate change litigation has promoted the implementation of the "Double carbon" goal and responded to the rapid development of carbon-related trading [19].

b. Carbon Neutrality Justice

Since our country signed the Paris Agreement, carbon-related cases have risen sharply. The large number of carbon-related cases reflects the need to resolve carbon-related disputes, and promotes the improvement of judicial interpretation and guiding cases.

With the increase of carbon-related cases, climate change has begun to become an independent category of cases. In 2020, in the "Types of environmental and resource cases and statistical standards (trial)" issued by the Supreme People's Court, environmental and resource cases are divided into five types: environmental pollution prevention and control, ecological protection, resource development and utilization, climate change response, and ecological and environmental governance and services, a special category of climate change cases has been set up, highlighting the importance of climate change litigation.

The guidance of the Supreme People's court and others has played an important role in the conduct of climate change litigation. In its white paper on China's environmental and resource trials (2019), the Supreme People's Court made a separate section on "Handling climate change cases in accordance with the law", and put forward "Pay attention to the use of a variety of judicial means, promote the mitigation, adaptation to climate change two means of landing, promote the construction of national climate change response governance system". Article 15 of the opinions on strengthening and innovating environmental and resource trials in the new era to provide judicial services and guarantees for the modernization of harmonious coexistence between man and nature, issued by the Supreme People's Court in 2021, specifically addresses carbon neutrality-related justice, "To help achieve peak carbon and carbon neutrality. We should accurately grasp the economic, public and ecological attributes of carbon-related rights such as carbon emission rights, carbon sinks and carbon derivatives, and properly handle relevant civil disputes involving confirmation, trading, guarantee and enforcement according to law. We will support and supervise the efforts of administrative agencies to investigate and punish illegal acts such as false reporting, withholding greenhouse gas emissions reports and refusing to fulfill their greenhouse gas emissions reporting obligations. To hear cases of carbon-related public interest litigation and compensation for ecological and environmental damage brought by state organs or organizations as prescribed by law. … to adjudicate, in accordance with the law, all cases involving the illegal production and use of controlled ozone-depleting substances and environmental pollution, so as to contribute to the reduction of non-carbon dioxide greenhouse gas emissions and effectively respond to the global climate change crisis", comprehensive coverage of various forms of judicial cases to promote the "Dual carbon" goal [20].

In February 2023, the Supreme People's court issued the "Opinions of the Supreme People's court on the complete, accurate and comprehensive implementation of the new development concept and the provision of judicial services for actively and steadily promoting peak carbon and carbon neutrality", it is proposed to make a comprehensive green transformation to serve the economic and social development, ensure the in-depth adjustment of industrial structure, promote the construction of a clean, low-carbon, safe and efficient energy system, and promote the improvement of the carbon market trading mechanism, continue to deepen environmental judicial reform and innovation to provide judicial support for "Double carbon". At the same time as the guidelines were released, the Supreme People's Court also released a batch of 11 typical cases of judicial action to promote peak carbon and carbon neutrality, covering energy structure adjustment, carbon sink trading, forestry carbon sink, ODS emissions and many other aspects, including civil cases, criminal cases and administrative cases, civil cases include public interest litigation and ordinary civil litigation. Among them, the proportion of civil litigation is the highest, especially the contract dispute litigation, and the economic attributes of carbon emission rights have been greatly reflected. In climate change litigation, the risk of carbon emissions trading and carbon sink compensation issues occupy an important position.

Prosecutors also play a role in promoting carbon neutrality, especially in public interest litigation. In March 2023, the Supreme People's court and the Supreme People's Procuratorate issued an interpretation on several issues relating to the application of law in the handling of criminal cases involving environmental pollution, which specifies the criteria for determining whether the "Seriousness" of a case is caused by the deliberate provision of false documentation by staff of an intermediary organisation with responsibilities such as Environmental Impact Assessment, environmental monitoring, greenhouse gas emissions testing and the preparation or verification of emissions reports [21], this provides support for the trial of cases involving disputes over greenhouse gas emissions reports. In June 2023, the Supreme People's Procuratorate published a number of typical cases of prosecutors ensuring peak carbon neutrality. They include Administrative Public Interest Litigation, civil public interest litigation and criminal incidental civil public interest litigation [22].

c. Policies Related to Carbon Neutrality

Since the 12th five-year plan (2011–2020), the reduction of carbon dioxide emissions per unit of GDP has become one of the targets in the national economic and Social Development Plan. Both the 14th five-year plan (FYP) and the 2035 long-term target outline include a binding target of an 18% reduction in carbon dioxide emissions per unit of GDP by 2025 compared with 2020 levels. China's targets have been strengthened. As of the end of 2019, China had exceeded its 2020 climate targets ahead of schedule, according to a white paper on China's policies and actions on climate change. Compared with the NDC proposed by our country in 2015, the forest stock volume in the NDC target updated in 2020 is "6 billion cubic meters more than in 2005", this is an increase of 1.5 billion cubic metres over the forest stock proposed in 2015 [16]. In 2021, our country solemnly promised not to build new overseas coal power projects, reflecting the responsibility of a responsible power in global climate governance.

A "1 + N" policy system for peak carbon and carbon neutrality is under construction. The "1" of the "1 + N" policy system refers to the "Opinions on complete, accurate and comprehensive implementation of new development and the concept of achieving peak carbon neutrality" (hereinafter referred to as the "Opinions") and the "Action Plan for peak carbon by 2030" issued in 2021, "N" refers to a set of documents on policy measures and actions in key areas and sectors. "1" is the guiding ideology and top-level design for China to achieve peak carbon neutrality. It defines the timetable, roadmap and construction map for peak carbon neutrality [23]. The "1 + N" policy system has established a peak carbon and carbon neutrality policy system with clear objectives, rational division of labour, effective measures and orderly linkages, forming a good pattern of joint promotion by all parties.

"N" covers pollution control, green finance, energy, carbon emission rights and other aspects, from all areas of the social economy to achieve a comprehensive

"Double carbon" target requirements. In June 2022, the Ministry of Ecology and environment (Mee-RRB- and seven other departments jointly issued the implementation plan for pollution reduction and carbon reduction. The synergistic effect of pollution reduction and carbon reduction is an important way to achieve the goal of carbon peak carbon neutrality, which is conducive to mitigating carbon emissions from the source, coordinating the work of carbon peak carbon neutrality and ecological environment protection, enhancing the synergy between ecological and environmental policies and energy industrial policies. In the energy sector, the National Development and Reform Commission and other departments have issued the opinions of the National Development and Reform Commission and the National Energy Administration on improving the institutional mechanisms, policies and measures for the green and low-carbon energy transition, we will promote the establishment of a sound mechanism for promoting green energy consumption and a mechanism for developing and utilizing clean and low-carbon energy, and promote green and low-carbon transformation in the power, coal, clean energy and other fields. In the field of economy and trade, the state council has issued the "State Council's guidance on accelerating the establishment and improvement of an economic system for green, low-carbon and circular development," calling for accelerating the establishment and improvement of an economic system for green, low-carbon and circular development, from the aspects of industry, agriculture and service industry, logistics, consumption and energy system, urban environmental infrastructure construction, and transformation of scientific and technological achievements, the vision and related measures of building a green low-carbon economy system are fully demonstrated. In 2023, the National Standardization administration of China and other 11 departments issued guidelines for the development of a carbon neutrality standard system, we will promote the improvement of standards in such areas as carbon reduction and sequestration, carbon capture, utilization and storage, green finance, and carbon trading. In terms of green finance, the "Guidance on building a green financial system" issued in 2016 proposes the development of various carbon financial products. Promote the establishment of a unified national carbon emissions trading market and carbon pricing center with international influence. In 2021, the Green Finance Evaluation Plan for banking financial institutions issued by the People's Bank of China carried out a comprehensive evaluation of the green loans and green bonds of financial institutions and incorporated the results into the Central Bank's rating of financial institutions, integrating "Dual carbon" targets into the financial credit system. In the economy and trade, energy, finance, ecological and environmental protection and other aspects, "Double carbon" target has been a comprehensive integration and promotion.

d. Carbon-Neutral Enforcement

Due to the lack of special laws on carbon neutrality in our country, the law enforcement activities directly related to carbon neutrality are mainly carried out according to administrative regulations, departmental rules and local ordinances. The administrative measures for carbon emissions trading (trial) is the core content of law enforcement activities. Article 39 stipulates that key emitters shall be liable for falsifying or underreporting greenhouse gas emissions, or for refusing to fulfill their greenhouse gas emissions reporting obligations, article 40 stipulates the liability of key emitters for failing to pay their carbon allowances in full and on time. There have been a number of cases in which penalties based on these two types of liability have been imposed under the carbon emissions trading regulations (trial) or local regulations.

Before the implementation of the administrative measures for carbon emissions trading (trial), provinces or cities that had already made provisions for carbon trading in local legislation would be punished according to local legislation. For example, Shenzhen Huayuebao Battery Co., Ltd. was fined more than 470,000 yuan by the Shenzhen Bureau of Ecology and Environment for failing to meet its 2018 carbon emissions obligations, the size of the fine reflects the severity of the punishment [24]. After the implementation of the "Carbon emissions trading management measures (trial)", the punishment will be consistent with the provisions of the higher law. For example, an on-site investigation by the Department of Ecology and environment of Inner Mongolia found that the Baotou No. 1 thermal power plant had misrepresented its fuel use in its 2020 greenhouse gas emissions report, in violation of Article 25 of the regulations on carbon emissions trading. The Department of Ecology and environment of Inner Mongolia autonomous region found it "Serious" and fined it 30,000 yuan [25].

In the first cycle of the national carbon market, the completion of the payment of key emission quotas and the processing of information disclosure are also the focus of law enforcement activities. According to the administrative measures for carbon emissions trading (for trial implementation), the implementation cycle is one year at a time, and the provincial ecological and environmental authorities are required to verify the greenhouse gas emission reports of key emitters annually, make public the status of emissions payments [26]. Several provinces, including Guangdong, Shandong and Hubei, have published reports on their compliance with annual carbon quotas. As of December 31, 2021, the overall compliance rate was 99.5%. Among the 2011 key emission units that issued quotas, 1833 key emission units completed the payment of quotas in full and on time, and 178 key emission units partially completed the payment of quotas [27]. The majority of companies still abide by carbon-neutral laws and regulations and meet their obligations in a timely manner.

5.1.2 Challenges to the Current Legal Framework for Carbon Neutrality

The legal structure of carbon neutrality in our country shows the characteristics of flattening in the vertical dimension and fragmentation in the horizontal dimension, special legislation at the national level presents the phenomenon of policy, more local regulations than laws, and local legislation precedes central legislation. On the horizontal level, each department law develops and extends separately, and lacks overall coordination.

a. Flattening: Lack of Core Norms with Higher Hierarchy of Effectiveness

In the field of climate change, our country lacks special legislation and direct legislation at the national level. "Carbon emissions trading management measures" and other departmental regulations have a low level of effectiveness. The relevant provisions of carbon neutrality are mainly policies, and there is a lack of relevant laws. The lack of co-ordination at the national level hampers cross-regional industry co-operation and oversight under the dual-carbon target. The legal system on climate change has expanded horizontally but not vertically, presenting a loose and flat structure, there is an inverted development trend of climate change legislation from bottom to top, from part to whole, the upper and lower legal norms are disjointed, and there is no core norm to guide the whole carbon neutrality legal system [28].

In the case of carbon neutrality, this is reflected in the fact that existing policies are prior to laws and local legislation is prior to central legislation. There is no national carbon neutrality legislation in our country, but there are many local green and low-carbon legislations. In local legislation, there is also the phenomenon of municipal regulations pre-empting provincial regulations on carbon neutrality. For example, the Guangdong provincial environmental protection regulations lack provisions related to carbon neutrality, however, the "Regulations on ecological and environmental protection in Guangzhou" clearly stipulate that the municipal and district governments should formulate action plans for peak carbon emissions and take measures to promote peak carbon and carbon neutrality, to encourage openness of information on greenhouse gas emissions and a green, low-carbon lifestyle [29]. The regulations on climate change in Jiangxi province are mainly scattered in the regulations on the protection and utilization of climate resources in Jiangxi province, which stipulate climate adaptation rather than carbon neutrality, nanchang has regulations on the promotion of low-carbon development. Mechanisms closely related to carbon neutrality, such as green finance, carbon trading and greenhouse gas information disclosure, are often found in different local legislation rather than at the national level. This "Local-first" approach also shows that the legal framework for carbon neutrality is still developing, and that the basic principles, institutions and core concepts of carbon neutrality have yet to be clearly defined in national legislation. Although there are some indirect references to low-carbon life in environmental law and natural resources law or the emphasis on the protection of the environment, ecosystems or biodiversity as a whole, the concept of "Environmental protection" can also govern "Carbon neutrality". The lack of specific direct provisions still indicates the lack of carbon neutrality legislation.

Local practice is ahead of the law, and the phenomenon that local policies and legislation precede national legislation also restricts the development of local practice. For example, articles 12 and 13 of Tianjin's regulations on the promotion of peak carbon neutrality stipulate that "The city shall implement a carbon intensity and total amount control system in accordance with state regulations", "The city shall establish and improve a statistical accounting system for carbon emissions in accordance with state regulations.". If there is no unified legislation at the national level, the actual effect of the Tianjin regulations on promoting peak carbon neutrality will also be affected. A national standard governing the legal system of carbon neutrality is the proper meaning of improving the legal structure of carbon neutrality.

b. Fragmentation: There is a Lack of Co-ordination between Departmental Laws and Local Legislation

The provisions on carbon neutrality in the current law are scattered in the provisions related to carbon neutrality in the environmental protection law and the energy law, which are vague and general in language, and vary in legislative background and time, there is a lack of overall consideration of "Dual carbon" targets. In essence, these norms also fail to fully implement the value appeal and regulatory objectives of climate change response. The fragmentation of laws and regulations makes it difficult for a variety of systems to work together to mitigate climate change [30]. For example, the carbon sink function of forests, oceans and wetlands is very important for achieving carbon neutrality. In judicial practice, there have been a large number of cases exploring forest carbon sink compensation mechanisms, marine carbon sink compensation mechanism is also under exploration, "Forest Law" is still a lack of provisions for the protection of Forestry Carbon Sink. The Newly Revised Wetland Protection Law also lacks provisions on the carbon sink function of wetlands. The emphasis on carbon sinks is only on declarative words and lacks more specific measures.

In addition to environmental laws, civil and commercial laws also lack provisions related to carbon neutrality. The emergence of carbon trading disputes and CCER contract disputes has brought the need to regulate carbon neutrality in civil and commercial laws. However, there is still a disconnect between legislation and practice, and civil and commercial laws have few provisions directly related to carbon neutrality.

Not only between departmental laws, but also between local legislation. On the one hand, few provinces or cities have specific legislation on climate change. On the other hand, even if local legislation on climate change is in place, there are gaps in the content of specific legislation on carbon neutrality. "Carbon neutrality" is a relatively new concept, and early legislation on climate change failed to include elements closely related to carbon neutrality. For example, the Shanxi province measures for dealing with climate change were formulated in 2011, including mitigation and adaptation to climate change, control of greenhouse gases, etc., however, there is a lack of regulations on carbon market, carbon trading and other important means to achieve peak carbon and carbon neutrality, and the regulations on forestry carbon sink are insufficient. In some provinces, the goal of "Double carbon" is to encourage green and low-carbon development. There is a lack of specific regulations on pollution reduction and carbon sequestration.

In different places, the early local legislation and the recent local legislation are quite different in style and focus, lack of overall coordination, and fail to determine a more general model. For example, the Shanxi and Qinghai province measures for dealing with climate change, which were drawn up not long ago, are similar in style and are divided into two parts: climate mitigation and climate adaptation, carbon neutrality is rarely mentioned. In 2021, the regulations on the ecological and environmental protection of the Shenzhen Special Economic Zone set up a special chapter on climate change in the legislation on ecological and environmental protection. The chapter on climate change includes sections on "Carbon neutrality" and "Carbon emissions trading". It is clear that this climate change legislation focuses on reducing carbon emissions, this is quite different from Shanxi and Qinghai. As an administrative region under the jurisdiction of Guangdong Province, Guangzhou's Regulations on ecological and environmental protection deal with climate change in chapter 2, "Protection and optimization", but fail to form a specific chapter. The legislation on climate change in Jiangsu province can be found in the regulations of Jiangsu province on the protection, development and utilization of climate resources, and the upper-level law is the meteorological law, only declaratively encourage low carbon. Hubei province has also promulgated regulations on the protection, development and utilization of climate resources and interim measures for the administration and trading of carbon emission rights. Finally, there are regions with carbon neutrality legislation. For example, Tianjin has issued regulations on the promotion of peak carbon neutrality in Tianjin, and the situation in Shijiazhuang, Nanchang and other cities is similar, regulations of Shijiazhuang Municipality on the promotion of low-carbon development and regulations of Nanchang Municipality on the promotion of Low-carbon development were promulgated respectively, specifically promoting cleaner production and low-carbon consumption, carbon-related indicators will be incorporated into development planning and the government's statistical indicator system. Different provinces and cities have different forms and modes of carbon neutrality legislation, and the contents of the regulations are different, which makes the governance level of different regions quite different, and is not conducive to the unified promotion of carbon neutrality.

However, there is still an obvious imbalance in the local legislation. The system construction in the big cities in the eastern developed areas is more comprehensive, while the legislation in the Midwestern sectional figure skating championships is relatively less. For example, the Shenzhen Special Economic Zone has issued special local regulations and regulatory documents such as the Shenzhen municipal carbon emissions trading management measures, the Shenzhen Special Economic Zone Green Finance regulations, and the Shenzhen municipal carbon inclusive management measures, the "Regulations of Shenzhen Special Economic Zone on ecological environment protection" also involves "Double-carbon" related content, and establishes a relatively complete "Double-carbon" legal mechanism. Some Central and western provinces, such as Guangxi, Hainan, Heilongjiang and other provinces, have no "Dual-carbon" legislation. In the Midwestern sectional figure skating championships, the country's vast natural resources and fragile ecosystems will be affected by climate change.

c. Lack of Coordination Among Legislation, Judicature and Law Enforcement

Rule-of-law structures encompass the entire carbon-neutral governance process, including all elements of legislation, the judiciary and law enforcement and the relationships between them. They influence and support each other. In a carbon-neutral governance structure, coordination among the three is essential.

The lack of specific provisions at the legislative level will affect the judicial practice. In the process of achieving the goal of peak carbon and carbon neutrality, carbon trading, industrial restructuring, forest carbon sequestration and other issues will bring new disputes and new challenges to judicial practice. For example, there are many cases of forestry carbon sink compensation in practice, but the standard and calculation method of carbon sink compensation are not unified, and the system has not been established. For example, in the Chen Mouhua deforestation case in Longyan, Fujian, the trial court cooperated with the Xinluo District Forestry Bureau in Longyan City to explore a standardized measurement method for forest carbon sink losses, using norms and documents such as "Forest ecosystem service function assessment norms" and "Longyan City's work guidelines on judicial restoration of forest carbon sink compensation mechanisms in criminal cases (trial implementation)", it reflects the role of technical standards, local regulations and documents in promoting carbon sink compensation mechanism [19]. Although this practice can be described as local legislation playing a pilot role in carbon neutrality and cutting-edge areas, in the absence of uniform standards, compensation for forestry carbon sinks varies geographically in each case, this creates the possibility of "Different judgments in the same case", which is not conducive to improving the system.

The blank of legislation will also affect the law enforcement. Carbon neutrality laws are mostly encouraging and declarative, and lack provisions to establish legal liability, so administrative enforcement can not directly promote the dual-carbon goal. Law enforcement related to carbon neutrality only focuses on the synergy of pollution reduction and carbon reduction or the protection of ecosystems such as forests, grasslands and wetlands, indirectly involving carbon neutrality. In the areas where specific measures have been taken, the lack of legislation at the national level and the low legal hierarchy will also result in the lack of a basis for local law enforcement. The setting of administrative penalties in local regulations and ministerial rules is limited, and local regulatory documents can not set administrative penalties. Take the practice of the carbon inclusive system as an example, July 2015, the development and Reform Commission of Guangdong Province issued the implementation plan of Guangdong province's carbon GSP pilot work and the guide to the construction of Guangdong province's carbon GSP pilot, and proposed the construction of a carbon GSP platform. In April 2022, the Department of Ecology and environment of Guangdong Province issued the administrative measures for carbon inclusive trading in Guangdong Province, clarifying the management and trading of carbon inclusive. The cities of Guangzhou and Shenzhen have also developed their own management measures for inclusive carbon trading. Shanghai, Tianjin, Chengdu and Wuhan also have their own carbon-inclusive policies. However, there is no top-level design of carbon inclusion at the national level, and there is no mention of carbon inclusion in relevant laws. Most of the local pilot documents that have been issued are local government regulations or even policy documents in nature, which are relatively low in legal rank and difficult to stipulate the legal responsibility for violating the rules. However, the carbon GSP has produced some effects in practice. According to an announcement by the Guangdong Provincial Department of Ecology and Environment, the department has agreed to 1,046,100 tonnes of CO2 equivalent in carbon emissions reductions, including 932,000 tonnes of CO2 equivalent from forestry projects, accounting for 89%, cycling and distributed PV projects accounted for 53,800 and 58,200 tonnes of CO2 equivalent respectively, accounting for 5% and 6% respectively [31]. The development of practice and policy advocacy preceded the improvement of the legal mechanism, creating a large number of legal gaps in the field of peak carbon carbon neutrality. In the event of illegal issues or even disputes, the current mechanism lacks a response plan.

The differences and even conflicts between local legislations affect the effect of law enforcement. "If key emitters fail to fulfil their commitments in full and on time, they will be ordered to make up and submit quotas or certified emission reductions equal to their excess emissions within a time limit. If they fail to make up and submit quotas within a time limit, they will be forced to deduct the same amount of quota, and the shortfall will be directly deducted from their quota for the next year. They will be fined three times the average price of the quota for the six consecutive months preceding the month of implementation." [32]. However, the trial measures for the administration of carbon emissions in Shanghai stipulates that those who fail to fulfil their quota payment obligations shall be ordered to do so by the municipal development and Reform Department, and may be fined from 50,000 yuan to 100,000 yuan [33]. As a result, the amount of fines varies from region to region, which can lead to companies with low willingness to comply moving to the provinces with the most relaxed regulations, as well as creating difficulties for cross-provincial carbon trading. After the introduction of the administrative measures for carbon emissions trading (for trial implementation), Article 40 imposes a fine of at least 20,000 yuan and less than 30,000 yuan for failing to pay the carbon emission quota in full and on time, making the provisions more lenient than localities [34]. In order to be consistent with higher-level legislation, local regulations need to be revised.

The Lag of justice will reduce the power of law enforcement. For example, in foreign countries the practice of "Greenwashing" and lawsuits against data fraud is well established, but in China there are few such lawsuits. The Ministry of Ecology and environment (mee) has made public typical problems of fraudulent reporting by companies such as China Carbon Energy Investment Technology (Beijing) Co., Ltd. It will urge and guide local mee departments, further investigations will be carried out on the technical service agencies and related enterprises that have the above-mentioned problems [35]. At the same time, the all-china Environment Federation filed a civil public interest lawsuit against the company and related companies for falsifying and falsifying data on carbon emissions, this is the first time a public interest lawsuit has been brought in China over the falsification of carbon emissions data [36]. To realize the combination of justice and law enforcement and to promote the development of law enforcement with public interest litigation can strengthen the effect of law enforcement and arouse social concern.

d. Meeting the Challenges of New Technologies

In emerging and cross-cutting areas, such as the impact of artificial intelligence on carbon neutrality, the supply of rules remains a gap. Taking the impact of artificial intelligence on carbon neutrality as an example, artificial intelligence itself has become an important contributor to carbon emissions. Regulatory and technological advances, as well as improvements in energy efficiency, are crucial to slowing the rapidly rising energy consumption of data centres. The huge demand for computing power means an increase in energy consumption, but there is a lack of international and domestic legal regulations on the carbon footprint of artificial intelligence. The temperature control targets under the Paris Agreement continue to face challenges, with research pointing out that existing emission reduction measures are still insufficient to reverse the worsening trend of climate change and may drive the need to further strengthen nationally determined contributions. The IPCC's Sixth Assessment Report (AR6) states that existing mitigation measures are likely to exceed the 1.5 C target and make it more difficult to maintain the 2C target after 2030. Climate change is not just a matter of historical responsibility. It is also a matter of future development rights. Due to the consumption of resources and the pollution caused by them, the developing countries have more restrictions on the use of resources. According to the IEA's electricity 2024 report, 85% of the growth in electricity consumption by 2026 will come from economies outside the developed world, particularly China. The huge growth in electricity consumption corresponds to a rapid rise in carbon emissions, posing a challenge for emerging economies to develop artificial intelligence.

I. Environmental Justice Between North and South Countries as a Result of Emerging Technologies

At the international level, the impact of artificial intelligence on carbon neutrality may not only affect the direction of global climate negotiations but also give rise to prominent issues of environmental injustice. First, AI is likely to create the phenomenon of "Pollution havens". In today's global context, building data centres and computing infrastructure across national borders has become a common and widespread practice. Google, as a typical example, currently operates 21 large-scale data centres around the world, which are widely spread across Asia, the Americas and Europe. Back in 2024, Microsoft officially announced that it would invest a total of $2.2 billion in Malaysia over the next four years to construct cloud computing and AI computing infrastructure there. In the process of iterative development of artificial intelligence, developed countries are able to place power-hungry data centres in developing countries and regions—where carbon prices are relatively low and there is a lack of strict regulation on energy consumption—and let these regions bear the negative externalities of the environment; however, the core technology and frontier achievements derived from artificial intelligence development are exclusively enjoyed by developed countries and regions. Second, AI faces the risk of widening the "Digital divide" in the field of emissions reduction. Although artificial intelligence can play an important and even pivotal role in reducing carbon emissions, it may still pose prominent social equity issues in the specific fields of climate change and carbon reduction. Specifically, artificial intelligence may further expand existing climate inequities in the two key areas of climate change mitigation and adaptation, and may also exacerbate the already existing "Digital divide" when it comes to addressing climate change. The advanced artificial intelligence technology owned by developed countries could effectively help realize decarbonization in key industries such as oil, steel, power, transport and construction. For instance, in the construction industry, artificial intelligence can monitor the energy use of buildings in real time, automatically adjust lighting, air conditioning, and heating systems to minimize energy waste; in the transportation sector, it can improve route planning by optimizing relevant algorithms, thereby reducing carbon emissions. Meanwhile, AI data analytics can contribute to carbon emission reduction by optimizing the production and distribution of electricity and improving overall energy efficiency. Additionally, the in-depth analysis of data related to urban transportation, energy, water resources and other aspects can provide strong support for urban planning oriented towards green and low-carbon development. In sharp contrast, developing countries, particularly the least developed ones, lack such critical technology. It should be noted that the development and application of artificial intelligence technology require high levels of capital investment, advanced infrastructure support and a sufficient number of professional personnel; moreover, the consolidation of the dominant position of first-developed countries is often accompanied by a monopoly on key data and a certain degree of opacity in algorithms, which will further widen the digital divide between developing and developed countries. In the specific field of carbon pricing, the carbon emission algorithms assisted by artificial intelligence will bring more powerful information advantages to developed countries. Against this backdrop, some scholars have expressed their worries that with the gradual globalization of the carbon market, artificial intelligence may develop into a new form of colonization tool, thus providing new vitality for the plunder of capitalism in the global context.

II. Legislative Gaps for Emerging Technologies

In the context of applicable international conventions and domestic legal frameworks, there exists a noticeable gap in the regulation of emerging new technologies. Specifically, when it comes to climate change legislation and the legislation governing artificial intelligence, international conventions currently lack effective mechanisms to evaluate the multifaceted impact of artificial intelligence. The Paris Agreement, a cornerstone of global climate action, fails to adequately consider new technologies represented by artificial intelligence—it neither explicitly mentions the impact of artificial intelligence on climate change nor contains sufficient provisions targeting emerging technologies. While the Agreement does acknowledge the importance of technology for the implementation of mitigation and adaptation actions under its framework, this recognition is only reflected in Article 10, which outlines the technology transfer mechanism and requires parties to strengthen cooperative action on technology development and transfer. Although the Agreement proposes the establishment of a technical framework and the provision of support through financial means, it does not address specific incentives for emerging technologies (including artificial intelligence), nor does it tackle ethical risk issues or the potential negative environmental impacts associated with such technologies. The rules for the implementation of the Paris Agreement, adopted at the Katowice climate conference, have made certain improvements to the content of the technology framework; however, the scope of what constitutes "Technology" or "Climate technology" remains ambiguously defined. It is therefore unclear whether the widespread application of AI will qualify as "Climate technology" under these rules, and the risks posed by AI in the climate context are still not addressed. On the other hand, gaps also exist in international legislation specifically governing artificial intelligence, where "Soft Law" continues to occupy an important and dominant position. The 41st Session of the UNESCO General Conference considered and formally adopted the Recommendations on the Ethics of Artificial Intelligence, which contains three references to "Climate" and two references to "Carbon footprint". This Recommendation explicitly states that all actors involved in the entire life cycle of artificial intelligence systems "Must comply with applicable international law as well as domestic legislation, standards and practices", and further specifies that these actors "Should reduce the environmental impact of AI systems, including but not limited to the carbon footprint, to ensure that climate change and environmental risk factors are minimized". In the specific area of Environmental Impact Assessment, the proposal within the Recommendation clarifies that member states and business enterprises should assess both direct and indirect impacts on the environment, including those related to carbon footprints and energy consumption. This regulatory focus on carbon footprint to some extent fills the existing gap in regulating the impact of artificial intelligence on climate change. Nevertheless, due to the inherent nature of "Soft Law", the "Recommendation" itself lacks sufficient legal binding force to ensure universal compliance. The Framework Convention on Artificial Intelligence and Human Rights, Democracy and the Rule of Law, announced by the European Commission in May 2024, stands as the first legally binding international convention dedicated to the use of artificial intelligence systems. It emphasizes the importance of transparency and oversight mechanisms in the development and use of artificial intelligence, and mandates that parties take proactive measures to identify, assess, prevent and mitigate potential risks associated with AI. In its preamble, the Convention explicitly states that "Consideration of the broader risks and impacts associated with these technologies, including but not limited to human health and the environment, is encouraged" and establishes a comprehensive risk prevention mechanism for AI. That said, this convention primarily focuses on addressing the human rights risks of artificial intelligence—with particular emphasis on the protection of individual privacy and data—and rarely touches upon the specific environmental risks posed by artificial intelligence.

In domestic legislation, the specific issue of AI-related carbon emissions also remains largely unregulated. At present, dedicated legislation governing artificial intelligence in our country is still absent, yet the State Council's 2023 Annual Legislative Work Plan has clearly incorporated the formulation of an Artificial Intelligence Law into its legislative agenda. The Interim Measures for the

Management of Generative Artificial Intelligence Services formally came into effect in August 2023; these Measures cover key areas such as the management of artificial intelligence technology, the protection of personal information, and the encouragement of artificial intelligence technology development, but they do not address matters related to green low-carbon development and carbon emission reduction. In terms of guiding principles, Article 4 of the Measures stipulates that "The provision and use of generative artificial intelligence services shall abide by laws and administrative regulations, and respect social morality and ethics." The scope of this provision includes adherence to core socialist values, ensuring algorithm design avoids discrimination, respect for intellectual property rights, compliance with business ethics, and protection of personal information rights and interests—but it does not encompass requirements related to environmental ethics or green low-carbon practices. Additionally, there is no specific institutional framework within the Measures that pertains to ecological environment protection, leaving the part of environmental and social responsibility in the development of artificial intelligence still blank. With regard to the green and low-carbon development of artificial intelligence, the environmental and social responsibility of enterprises engaged in artificial intelligence development still awaits explicit regulatory provisions.

In the absence of targeted specific legislation, another approach to regulating the carbon emissions of artificial intelligence is to realize the green and low-carbon transformation of artificial intelligence through the provisions on corporate environmental and social responsibility or the promotion of "dual carbon" (carbon peaking and carbon neutrality) goals within the framework of environmental law. The provisions on corporate social responsibility in the newly revised Company Law can be found in Article 20, which states: "When a company engages in business activities, it shall fully take into account the interests of its employees, consumers, and other stakeholders, as well as social and public interests such as ecological and environmental protection, and undertake social responsibilities." This article also explicitly encourages companies to publish social responsibility reports. This provision aligns with the "green principle" enshrined in the Civil Code and explicitly incorporates environmental protection into the scope of corporate social responsibility. The 2018 revised Guidelines on the Governance of Listed Companies has established "green development" as one of the core development concepts for listed companies; Chapter 8 of the Guidelines is specifically dedicated to "Stakeholders, Environmental Protection, and Social Responsibility," requiring that "Listed companies shall actively practice the concept of green development, integrate the requirements of ecological and environmental protection into their development strategies and corporate governance processes, and actively participate in the construction of ecological civilization." The Carbon Peak Action Plan Before 2030 further proposes to guide enterprises to fulfill their social responsibilities and promote relevant listed companies and bond issuers to regularly disclose corporate carbon emission information in accordance with environmental information disclosure requirements and the law. However, the provisions on ecological and environmental liability in the Company Law remain insufficient, with gaps in institutional coordination—such as in the field of information disclosure. Notably, the requirement for publishing social responsibility reports is framed as an "encouragement," meaning it does not constitute a mandatory legal obligation. Furthermore, corporate social responsibility provisions have not yet incorporated content related to ethical issues specific to artificial intelligence. How to define the rights, obligations, and legal responsibilities of artificial intelligence in the context of corporate operations is an inevitable issue in the current and future reform of corporate law, and it is also an inherent requirement for constructing a modern, international, and high-quality corporate legal system.

Within the domains of environmental law and energy law, laws and regulations that promote the development of renewable energy provide crucial support for securing green power sources for artificial intelligence computing infrastructure. According to Article 7 of the Energy Conservation Law, "The State shall implement industrial policies that are conducive to energy conservation and environmental protection, restrict the development of high-energy-consuming and high-pollution industries, and promote the development of energy-saving and environment-friendly industries… The State shall encourage and support the development and utilization of new and renewable energy sources." The Renewable Energy Law offers an even stronger legal impetus for the development of clean energy; it opens with a clear statement of its legislative objectives, which are "to promote the development and utilization of renewable energy, increase energy supply, optimize the energy structure, ensure energy security, protect the environment, and realize the sustainable development of the economy and society."

Finally, the disclosure of carbon emission information and the improvement of carbon emission accounting methods are conducive to the disclosure of artificial intelligence carbon footprint. In terms of greenhouse gas emission information disclosure, in order to implement the "Carbon emissions trading management measures (trial)", standardize the carbon emission accounting and reporting work of key emission units in the power generation industry, and improve the quality of carbon emission data, improving the long-term mechanism for data quality management in the national carbon emissions trading market, the Ministry of Ecology and environment (Mee) has developed the guidelines for accounting and reporting of greenhouse gas emissions by enterprises-power generation facilities (2021 revision)(draft for comment). Environmental disclosure laws for governments and companies are beginning to cover more carbon emissions. Taking the "Administrative measures for the disclosure of enterprise environmental information according to law" as an example, the "Measures" point out that enterprises are the subject of responsibility for the disclosure of environmental information according to law. Key polluters are required to disclose eight types of information, including carbon emissions. The Ministry of Ecology and Environment (Mee) issued guidelines on the format of corporate environmental information disclosure on 31 December 2021, which state: "Key emitters of greenhouse gases subject to the carbon emissions trading market quota management shall disclose information on their carbon emissions: (1) the actual annual carbon emissions and the actual emissions of the previous year; (2) the status of quota settlement; and (3) information on emission facilities and accounting methods in accordance with greenhouse gas emissions accounting and reporting standards or technical specifications.", the disclosure of carbon emission information is explained in detail, which promotes the establishment of carbon neutrality information disclosure system. At the policy level, pilot projects have been carried out in Hebei, Jilin, Zhejiang, Shandong, Guangdong, Chongqing and Shaanxi to include carbon emissions in environmental impact assessment. However, the current pilot industry is limited to key industries such as power, steel, building materials, non-ferrous metals, petrochemicals and chemicals, but artificial intelligence and internet companies are not among the key industries. As for the impact of emerging technologies such as artificial intelligence, relevant laws and rcgulations still need to be improved.

5.2 The Transformation of the Carbon Neutrality Rule of Law Structure Under the Dynamic System Theory

5.2.1 Concepts and Advantages of Dynamic Systems Theory

a. The Emergence and Development of Dynamic System Theory

The dynamic system theory was first put forward by Austrian jurist Willberg, and was applied in European tort liability law. According to Wellberg's theory, the relationship between factors and effects is no longer "All or nothing" but "More or less" [37]. It does not have the character of "All or nothing" of the traditional legal elements, but has the characteristics of "Comparison", "Gradual change" and "Hierarchy", performance for "More or less", "... more... more", "More", "Less" and other forms. Welberg calls the different aspects that constitute liability for damage "Elements" or "Dynamic forces" [38]. In different cases, "Each case presents a particular picture that results from the particular combination and intensity of these forces". These forces are "The whole result of the interaction of mutable elements" on which responsibility is based.

Dynamic system theory has been applied in tort liability, contract law and other fields. The European principles of tort law adopts the legislative mode of dynamic system theory in the stipulation of negligence. After being introduced into our country, the dynamic system theory has been paid more attention to in the field of tort law and personality right law, and has been put into legal practice. Article 10 of the interpretation of the Supreme People's court on several issues concerning the determination of compensation liability for mental damage in civil tort does not adopt the theory of constitutive elements of traditional tort law, but applies the theory of dynamic system, and enumerates many factors to judge the amount of mental damage compensation. Article 998 of the Civil Code is also a typical example of the application of dynamic system theory. Article 998 of the Civil Code stipulates that, "The actor should bear the civil liability for violating the right of personality except the right of life, the right of body and the right of health, and should consider the factors such as the occupation, the scope of influence, the degree of fault of the actor and the victim, as well as the purpose, mode and consequence of the Act." [39]

These practices have laid the foundation for the application of dynamic system theory in our country's legislation, it also leads to the discussion of the application of dynamic system theory in other legislative fields. Compared with the field of civil law, there are few voices advocating the application of dynamic system theory in the field of environmental law, but some scholars advocate that dynamic system theory should be used as a methodology in the compilation of environmental law, dynamic system theory should also be adopted in the construction of environmental right and punitive damages for ecological environment damage [40].

b. The Advantages of Dynamic System Theory

The advantage of dynamic systems theory lies in its flexibility and ability to adapt to complex real-world conditions. Due to the complexity of the real society, it is difficult to deal with all the situations even if the legal provisions make fine provisions. Too specific provisions will make the provisions rigid and difficult to adapt to social development and changes, while too broad provisions will bring difficulties to the application of the law. In some cases, the isolated judgment of each constituent element is logically tenable, and it seems to have the convenience of judicial operation, but in essence, it may separate the internal relationship of the facts of the case, and make the result face the problem of justice [41].

The application of dynamic system theory can achieve a balance between flexibility and stability through the identification and arrangement of elements. By specifying the important factors that judges should consider in their decisions, legislators can achieve very specific regulatory purposes and can decisively limit the discretion of judges, it also makes the judge's discretion predictable, while taking into account the diversity of life facts in a controlled manner [42].

The dynamic system theory is also conducive to the stability and predictability of law. "Dynamic" does not mean that the judge's discretion is too large, resulting in uncertainty. On the contrary, the setting of various elements by dynamic system theory reduces the uncertainty of judgment. For issues with complex constitutive elements, courts need to take into account different factors when applying the rules. If the impact of the factors and weights to be considered is not clear, the standard of judgment still needs to be made by the court. The listing of relevant factors restricts the court to a greater extent, and thus more strictly limits the judge's discretion [43]. Of course, dynamic system theory is not the solution to all legal problems. The theory of dynamic systems provides only a "Limited" framework for criticism. As for the choice among various possible evaluations, it ultimately depends on the decision of the judge.

5.2.2 The Need to Transform the Rule of Law for Carbon Neutrality in the Face of Internal and External Challenges

a. Moving from Fragmentation to Systematization

The lack of legislation on carbon neutrality at the national level and the incoordination of"Dual carbon" content in departmental laws have led to a flat and fragmented legal structure for carbon neutrality, a clear hierarchy. The judiciary and law enforcement are constrained by the limited supply of rules, and their role is compromised. The existing scattered and weak legal norms to address climate change are difficult to meet the order expectations of carbon-neutral governance, whether it is the integrity of the external form or the coherence of the content, finally, the supply and demand of carbon neutrality rule of law fall into the pattern of structural imbalance [44]. To break this structural imbalance, we need to integrate the existing laws and regulations and realize the systematization of the rule of law structure.

The document calls for "A systematic approach" to work on "Carbon neutrality and peak carbon" [45], a clear legal framework for carbon neutrality is necessary to put this concept into practice. This systematization is first manifested in the coherence within the carbon neutrality rule of law system, that is, from special basic laws to administrative regulations, departmental rules and local regulations, there are corresponding rules at all levels of the legal system. Second, this systematization is also reflected in the coordination between the carbon-neutral rule of law system and other external sectoral legal systems. Legal norms are not isolated and closed "Islands", but are closely linked to other sectoral laws. From the upper level of environmental law departments, the concept of carbon neutrality needs to be integrated into many environmental legislation and judicial practices such as pollution prevention and ecological protection, promoting synergies between climate change and biodiversity and between pollution and carbon reduction. At the level of other legal sectors, the rule of law system for carbon neutrality echoes the trend of the "Green Civil Code", in which carbon trading rights and the nature of carbon emissions allowances, mortgages or pledges are registered, applicable property preservation aspects are linked to civil and commercial law. This requirement for internal and external coherence is not only the requirement for the normative nature of the legal system, but also the embodiment of the extensiveness and depth of carbon neutrality in the social and economic fields.

b. Shift from Executive-Led to Multi-Governance

In the current legal system of carbon neutrality, the government occupies a dominant position, the market and social forces are weak, and the participants are relatively single. In legislation, there are more policies than laws, and the rank of regulatory documents of carbon trading is low, which is not conducive to the improvement of the market. Judicially, the promotion of "Double Carbon" public interest litigation is dominated by the procuratorate, while the public interest litigation filed by social organizations is less. The Supreme People's Court has issued 11 cases of judicial action to promote "Dual-carbon" projects, with the Procuratorate bringing Civil Public Interest Litigation and criminal collateral civil public interest litigation accounting for four of them. There have been no cases of action by environmental groups [46]. The Procuratorate has the qualification to bring Civil Public Interest Litigation and administrative public interest litigation, and the way to participate in public interest litigation is wider. In the absence of special legislation on carbon neutrality at the national level, the exploration of subscribing carbon sinks to replace ecological environment damage restoration has been carried out by the judicial and procuratorial departments, resulting in many cases related to carbon sinks. While reflecting the innovation of the exploration, it also reflects the imbalance of the participants in the litigation. There is also a lack of social and market participation in the observance and implementation of legal rules. The carbon trading market still needs to be more active, and there is a lack of penalties for violations such as "Greenwashing".

Achieving Peak carbon and carbon neutrality is a broad and profound economic and social systemic change [47]. This change not only affects the legislative or judicial parts, but also affects all areas of society and all economic sectors. The requirement of systematic change has brought the need to change to the direction of diversified governance subjects. The rule of law structure of carbon neutrality needs to combine the power of government, market and society to realize public participation and multi-governance, so as to realize the systematic change of economy and society and promote the comprehensive green transformation of economic and social development.

c. From Separation of International and Domestic Governance to Integration of International and Domestic Governance

As a signatory to the Paris Agreement, our country has always been actively fulfilling its obligations to reduce emissions. However, the implementation of international conventions and the implementation of domestic legislation and policies are not connected in rules, and it is difficult to stipulate "International cooperation" at the local legislative level, which makes the integration of international and domestic climate governance difficult. International cooperation is an important part of the legal framework for carbon neutrality, according to the guidelines, which call for a "Two-wheel drive". The 20th party congress report also calls for "Active participation in global governance on climate change". Participating in global governance on climate change requires both international and domestic rule of law. Global issues require global governance, which is interlinked at both international and domestic levels. The interaction between international rule of law and domestic rule of law is the essence of global governance [48]. As the world undergoes unprecedented changes in a century, anti-globalization and unilateralism are on the rise, and climate change governance also faces challenges. Carbon neutrality has been used as a tool of trade protectionism in developed countries, and the climate issue has gradually spread to the political, diplomatic and security fields, climate governance is gradually deviating from the track of multilateral mechanism and the basic principle of "Common but differentiated responsibilities". The legal structure of carbon neutrality needs to respond not only to the domestic demand for green and low-carbon, but also to the pressure of international climate governance. On the one hand, it needs to respond to the commitments of the Paris Agreement and demonstrate the image of a responsible power, on the other hand, we should promote international cooperation with a sound rule system, enhance China's right to speak in global climate governance, and protect China's interests.

5.2.3 *The Basis for Introducing Dynamic System Theory into the Legal Structure of Carbon Neutrality*

a. Diversity in the Value of Carbon Neutrality

The aim and value of a legal system is pluralistic, so it is suitable for the legislation of dynamic system theory [41]. Wang Lei believes that in the case of "Strong value judgment" involving various interests, there is a sharp conflict between the certainty and appropriateness of the law. In order to pursue the appropriateness of the law or the stability of the value, need to sacrifice some certainty, or logical stability in order to pursue the stability of value, and this is the need to adopt dynamic systems theory [49]. In some cases, multiple, equally valid values may conflict because of the limited resources available, and the rigid way in which values are prioritized for the sake of certainty can lead to overly rigid legal systems, and even substantive injustice.

Carbon neutrality is an issue with multiple values, involving multiple complex and even conflicting interests. The goal of carbon neutrality contains environmental value, but also needs to take into account the socio-economic, sustainable development needs. The legislative purpose of carbon neutrality needs to consider different values equally, adopt methods to balance these values, and give a priority judgment under the conflict of values with the same legitimacy. This kind of value judgment needs to take into account different elements, and even varies from case to case. The guidelines include "Risk prevention" as one of their guiding principles, stressing "The need to balance pollution and carbon reduction with energy security, industrial chain and supply chain security, food security and the normal lives of the people" [45]. The "Opinions of the national development and Reform Commission and the National Energy Administration on improving the institutional mechanisms, policies and measures for the green and low-carbon transformation of energy" requires "Orderly promotion of the green and low-carbon transformation of energy on the premise of ensuring energy security" [50]. It can be seen that in the case of people's living needs, energy security, food security and other issues take precedence over Green Low-carbon. However, the "Ecological priority, green and low-carbon high-quality development path" also gives a higher weight to the ecological environment. Under which cases, which values should be given priority to be maintained needs to be judged by the method of dynamic system theory, and these values should be given different weights and balanced according to a certain proportion.

b. Complexity of Climate Change Attribution

The factors contributing to climate change-induced damage are so diverse that it is difficult to identify a single attribution. There is a long causal chain from the increase of carbon emissions to the change of climate patterns such as temperature and precipitation, the loss of ecosystem function or the loss of life and property caused by extreme weather, and there are difficulties in attribution. In addition, these elements work together to superimpose and influence each other. For example, under different uses, forests can be both a carbon sink and a carbon source. Despite the role of forests in absorbing and storing carbon dioxide, forest death and decomposition, forest fires, as well as man-made deforestation and unreasonable logging, and even the use and consumption of forest biomass products, and may release carbon stored in forests back into the atmosphere [51]. Damage to one element can have a "Game-changing" effect. There are also difficulties in determining the scale of liability and the parties responsible in climate change litigation. There are many subjects of carbon emissions and they affect the whole society. The subject of each responsibility is also difficult to determine because of the long causal chain. Dynamic system theory can absorb many different elements in the identification and relief of responsibility in legislation and judgment, and make a comprehensive and dynamic assessment according to their degree and relationship. Its "Dynamic" feature includes the study of the interaction between the various elements, to the greatest extent possible to deal with the interaction of many elements of the complex problem.

c. The Dynamics of Carbon Neutrality Development

The concept of "Carbon neutrality" is a new one. The goal itself and the means to achieve it are dynamic and will evolve with climate change. This dynamic can be seen in the following aspects:

First, climate change itself is a progressive and developing process, and the study of its causes and impacts carries with it scientific uncertainties. Some risks and damages can not be recognized with current technology, but they may emerge in the future and promote the establishment of new mechanisms. As in the AR6 Synthesis Report: Climate Change 2023, published by the Intergovernmental Panel on Climate Change (IPCC) in March 2023, the assessment of the role of human activity in global warming as "Established fact" and "Beyond doubt" was an escalation from previous assessments [52]. And in the previous five rounds of assessment reports, the role of human activities in global warming has been continuously clarified from "Likely" to "Very likely" to "Very likely." Judgments about cause and effect are in flux.

Second, as the science and technology of carbon sequestration and reduction continue to develop, the concept of carbon neutrality and the methods used to achieve it may change, and the law needs to retain certain openness and flexibility. The carbon inclusive system, green bonds and disclosure of corporate carbon emissions information are all emerging systems to promote peak carbon and carbon neutrality, and they are still in the process of being improved, new systems may be developed, designed and regulated by law. The application of dynamic system theory is conducive to retaining the flexibility of the whole governance structure and providing space for the emerging institutional design.

Finally, the concept of carbon neutrality is inseparable from the international climate negotiations, and is affected by the development of international climate change law. Carbon neutrality will be influenced by the global stocktaking of the Paris Agreement and the new commitments made at subsequent climate change conferences. For example, at the Glasgow Climate Conference, 22 countries including the United States, the United Kingdom and Japan signed the Clydebank Declaration on a green shipping corridor, commit to establish at least six "Green shipping corridors" globally by 2025 and decarbonise the shipping industry by 2050. If the shipping industry changes greatly under the new low-carbon commitments, it will also affect the development of our shipping industry. A series of commitments to stop deforestation, switch to clean energy and stop methane emissions will also have a full impact on the international environment for carbon neutrality. And the agreements or new commitments that our country has entered into will have a direct impact on the way in which the dual-carbon targets are reached and even on their content. This dynamic development will expand the number of elements to be considered, and the traditional "Element-effect" model is difficult to respond quickly.

5.2.4 The Application of Dynamic System Theory in the Legal Structure of Carbon Neutrality

a. Legislative Application

Dynamic systems theory can play a role in legislation. Chapter 7 of the Civil Code adopts the legislative model of dynamic system theory, and ecological environment tort can also be applied. Article 1231 stipulates: "Where two or more tortfeasors pollute the environment and damage the ecology, the extent of their liability shall be determined by factors such as the type, concentration and discharge of pollutants, the manner, scope and degree of damage to the ecology, and the effect of their actions on the consequences of the damage." [53]. This provision could be applied to torts related to the dual-carbon target, improving the proportional distribution of torts against multiple parties.

The characteristics of dynamic system theory, which considers many factors, provide a path to explain the more abstract concepts such as "Reasonable", "Necessary" and "Serious consequences". The elements that lead to this state may be set out in the legislation, taking into account different factors, and it is expressed that the judge may evaluate these elements according to different weights. Relief methods can also List A number of factors to consider, such as ecological restoration of different ways, forestry carbon sequestration purchase, ecological compensation and so on. The Five-Sphere Integrated Plan (encompassing economic, political, cultural, social and ecological progress) proposed in the Report to the 18th National Congress of the Communist Party of China, and the "Two Mountains" Theory (the concept that "lucid waters and lush mountains are invaluable assets") put forward by General Secretary Xi Jinping, both embody the balance and unity of different values. As a methodological tool, the Dynamic Systems Theory can be applied to the principles and objectives of carbon peaking and carbon neutrality legislation. It selects different values—such as economic development, green and low-carbon development, coordinated domestic and international efforts, and risk prevention—as core elements, and formulates specific provisions in the legislation to ensure the realization of these elements. Principle-based provisions, meanwhile, serve as a demonstrative basic evaluation to restrict the weight and proportion of each element. For example, Article 3 of the Law on the Ecological Protection of the Qinghai-Xizang Plateau requires that "ecological protection shall be given top priority, and natural restoration shall be the primary approach" [54]. This provision assigns greater weight to ecological protection, which is also reflected in the specific legislative contents of subsequent chapters. In future specialized legislation on carbon peaking and carbon neutrality, provisions elaborating on principles and objectives may specify elements with certain priority to guide the entire legislation. A case in point is the Action Plan for Carbon Peaking Before 2030, which puts forward the principle of "prioritizing conservation".

b. Judicial Applications

The dynamic system theory has already had certain influence in the judicial domain, in aspects and so on causality judgment, loss amount determination can be applied. In 2023, several provisions of the Supreme People's Court on civil litigation evidence of ecological environment tort adopted the method of dynamic system theory in many articles. For example, article 5 judges the relationship between the defendant's behavior and the damage, "The evidence submitted by the parties, combined with the pollution of the environment, the behavior of ecological damage, the nature of pollutants, the type of environmental media, the characteristics of ecological factors, time sequence, spatial distance and other factors" are used as the basis for comprehensive judgment of relevance [55].

The determination of the amount of loss is also the case where the dynamic system theory can play a role. There are some uncertainties in the assessment of the damage of ecosystem services, and the difficulty of restoration is related to the specific conditions of the ecosystem, which is difficult to be stipulated in one way in the provisions. The application of dynamic system theory can combine various factors that lead to ecological damage and the factors that determine the cost of restoration, and comprehensively evaluate the loss amount. The calculation of this amount can include the calculation of punitive damages, the calculation of the cost of ecological environment restoration, the assessment of the loss caused by ecological damage, etc. Take punitive damages as an example, according to the interpretation of the Supreme People's court on the application of punitive damages to cases of ecological environment infringement, the amount of punitive damages "Shall take into account the degree of malice of the infringer, the severity of the consequences of the infringement, the interests of the infringer due to environmental pollution and ecological damage, or the restoration measures taken by the infringer and their effects" [56]. Due to the highly subjective nature of punitive damages for ecological environment damage, it is difficult to establish a unified and accurate calculation standard, which determines the control of judicial discretion through the construction of rigid rules for multiple identification in a concrete way, it is not realistic to realize the stability of the law [40]. Too low amount may hinder the function of punitive damages as punishment and deterrence, while too high amount may bring heavy economic burden to infringers, and even reduce the effect of actual performance. The application of dynamic system theory can measure the weight and priority of different elements by clarifying the core content of each element, to find the best balance between economic, social development and environmental protection by focusing on the interaction and coordination of the various elements.

Article 31 of the provisions of the Supreme People's Court on evidence in civil litigation concerning ecological environment infringement stipulates that "In civil public interest litigation cases concerning ecological environment protection, the facts of damage are established, but the amount of the cost of restoration of the ecological environment, the loss of service function caused by the loss of the ecological environment from the damage to the completion of the restoration, and the loss caused by the permanent damage to the ecological environment function are difficult to determine. The People's court may, in light of the ascertained facts of the case such as the pollution of the environment and the scope and extent of the damage to the ecology, take into account such factors as the scarcity of the ecological environment and its elements, the difficulty of restoring the ecological environment, the operating costs of pollution prevention and control equipment, the interests gained by the defendant as a result of the infringement, and the degree of fault, and may refer to the opinions of the departments responsible for the supervision and management of the protection of environmental resources, etc., to make a reasonable determination", while giving judges some discretion, it also guarantees the flexibility to discuss the loss of ecosystem services and the cost of restoration in individual cases. These provisions have important implications for dual-carbon litigation. The identification standards of compensation related to carbon sink are different, the cost is high, and the identification and evaluation are difficult. However, it is very important to confirm the loss of ecological service function and the value of carbon sink. Clearly defining the discretion method of the dynamic system and listing the different elements for reference can increase the transparency of the case judgment standard and promote the development of carbon sink related compensation and compensation methods.

5.3 Global South, Carbon Neutrality and Green Bonds

5.3.1 Basic Principles for Transforming the Legal Framework for Carbon Neutrality

I. Green Low-carbon principle: the basic principle of carbon neutrality legal structure

The Green Low-carbon principle aims to regulate the value orientation of the legal structure of carbon neutrality. "Green and low-carbon" is often used in parallel in policy documents, such as the State Council's guidance on accelerating the establishment and improvement of a green and low-carbon circular economic system, and "Opinion" that "Unswervingly take the ecological priority, green and low-carbon high-quality development path. Therefore, "Green and low-carbon" has the conditions for an independent value. "Low-carbon" sets out a vision for achieving the "Dual-carbon" goal, and "Green" echoes the green principles of the Civil Code.

The "Green principle" has been stipulated for the first time in the Civil Code, which reflects the response of the civil code to the protection of the ecological environment. The essence of "Green principle" is to establish a communication mechanism for the coordination of individual economic interests and ecological public interests in the civil code, and to become a bridge between environmental law and civil law. It is not only the basic principle of the civil code, but also runs through the parts of the real right part, the contract part and the tort liability part of the Civil Code, combined with the specific rules guiding civil activities, the concept of environmental protection is deeply integrated into the civil law. The function of value judgment and value balance of green principle has been summarized by many scholars. Lu Zhongmei believes that the green principle contains the functions of coordinating economic development and environmental protection, establishing the value of ecological security, coordinating transaction security and ecological security, and coordinating intra-generational equity and inter-generational equity [57].

The introduction of "Green Principles" into the legal structure of carbon neutrality is not only the need of green development, but also the need to link up environmental law with civil law. Carbon-neutral rule-of-law structures need to be coherent internally as well as externally with other legal sectors. The civil and commercial activities such as Green Finance and green investment involved in "Double carbon" are closely related to the civil law department and regulated by the "Green principle" of the civil code. In the design of carbon neutrality rule of law structure, it is also necessary to embed the "Green principle" to achieve the coordination between environmental law and civil law.

II. The precautionary principle: the safety guarantee of the carbon neutrality legal structure

The precautionary principle in environmental law refers to the prediction, analysis and prevention of the deterioration of environmental quality or environmental damage caused by the development and utilization of the environment, in order to avoid and eliminate the possible environmental damage [58]. Article 5 of the environmental protection law stipulates: "Environmental Protection shall adhere to the principles of giving priority to protection, giving priority to prevention, comprehensive treatment, public participation and responsibility for damage." The precautionary principle is one of the basic principles of environmental law [59]. The precautionary principle is set out in Article 15 of the Rio Declaration and the UNFCCC also includes risk prevention as one of its basic principles, it was emphasized that "Where there is a threat of serious or irreversible damage, the absence of complete scientific certainty should not be used as a reason for postponing the adoption of such measures" [60]. The regulations of environmental assessment system and the contents of environmental health monitoring in the environmental protection law reflect that the legislation in the field of ecological environment in our country has developed from the principle of prevention to the principle of risk prevention [61], and the degree of attention to risk has increased. "Opinion" pointed out that we should adhere to the "National co-ordination, saving priority, two-wheel drive, internal and external unimpeded, risk prevention" principle, which "Risk prevention" reflects the need for risk prevention.

Taking risk prevention as the basic principle of building the rule of law for carbon neutrality is not only conducive to the convergence of domestic law and international law, but also to the need to deal with scientific uncertainty. The impacts of climate change on the socio-economic and natural environment are still scientifically uncertain and may change with changes in the level of prediction and science and technology. However, using this uncertainty as an excuse to block energy-saving and emissions-reduction measures could pose significant environmental risks. At the same time, risk prevention can not only be applied to the legislative field, but also can promote preventive environmental public interest litigation in the judicial field. The practice of cases such as the Green Peacock case and the five small leaf maple case has explored the development of preventive environmental public interest litigation, but the preventive environmental public interest litigation system itself is still in the ascendant, more support is needed, both in theory and in practice. The incorporation and application of the precautionary principle in the carbon neutrality rule of law structure will help to achieve the convergence from legislation to judicature, safeguard the environment with preventive public interest litigation, and help to achieve the goal of "Double carbon".

III. The principle of proportionality: an integrated approach to carbon-neutral rule of law structures

As a constitutional principle in many countries, the principle of proportionality has been applied in administrative law enforcement and legislation. It can act in the legislative, executive and judicial fields, and plays an important role in the balance of values. The principle of proportionality includes three elements: appropriateness, necessity and narrow proportionality. Appropriateness refers to the appropriateness between the end and the means. The principle of necessity is also known as the principle of minimum damage, which means that the measures taken are necessary to achieve the end, and the restriction and damage to people's rights are controlled to a minimum. In a narrow sense, the principle of proportionality is also called the principle of balance. Its core concept is the balance of value, which is carried out in the context of value conflict, and the damaged value is controlled to a minimum as far as possible.

The principle of proportionality is the core value in the field of constitution and administrative law, and has been applied in many countries. The principle of proportionality is embodied in the charter of Fundamental Rights and freedoms of Canada and the Charter of Fundamental Rights of the European Union [62]. It has been applied not only in the field of public law, but also in the field of civil law. In the specific measures to regulate carbon emissions, such as carbon emission quota system, some scholars also advocate the introduction of the principle of proportionality [63]. The principle of proportionality can be used as a methodological principle to improve the legal structure of carbon neutrality, to test the necessity of measures and to balance conflicting values. "Co-ordination" and "Value balancing" are two of the most important challenges facing the legal structure of carbon neutrality. "Co-ordination" requires harmonisation between the different branches of the legal system that make up carbon neutrality, such as environmental law and civil and commercial law, between international and domestic law, and between carbon neutrality legislation, justice and enforcement, the "Value balance" requires dealing with the multiple and even conflicting values in the "Double carbon" target, which is prominently reflected in the value conflict between economic development and environmental protection. The imbalance of development between the east and the west, between urban and rural areas, and the demand of current and future generations for the use of resources also need to be balanced, that is, the carbon-neutral legal structure needs to take into account the level of economic development in different regions, the needs of present and future generations should be balanced with the goal of reducing carbon emissions in terms of legislative provisions, judicial interpretation and law enforcement. "Effectively respond to the economic, financial and social risks that may accompany the green and low-carbon transition, prevent over-reaction and ensure safe decarbonisation," it said. The principle of proportionality can be used as a tool to achieve this adjustment. When formulating policies and legislations to optimize production capacity and eliminate backward industries, it is necessary to examine the appropriateness and necessity of measures and choose the scheme with the least impact on people's lives. At the same time, the principle of proportionality in a narrow sense is used to weigh the proportionality between the measures taken and the carbon reduction goals pursued, so that the measures taken are proportional to the goals achieved, avoid situations where overly aggressive measures have a major impact on people's lives [64].

IV. Principles of public participation: Foundations for the implementation of a carbon-neutral rule of law architecture

The principle of public participation is the basic principle of climate change law and even the whole department of Environmental Law. Article 5 of our country's environmental law stipulates the principle of public participation, in the chapter of "Information Disclosure and public participation", the rights of citizens, legal persons and other organizations to obtain environmental information, participate in and supervise environmental protection and the system of public interest litigation are stipulated, it establishes the basis for public participation at the legislative, judicial and law enforcement levels. The principle of public participation is also an important principle of international climate governance. Article 9 of the European Climate Act provides for a system of public participation to promote the participation of citizens, social partners and stakeholders, the European Commission has an obligation to facilitate the exchange of "Best practices" and other actions with civil society, academia, business and social partners, and can conduct public consultations and multi-level climate and energy dialogues [65]. Incorporating the principle of public participation into the legal structure of carbon neutrality is not only in line with the general rules of the environmental law sector, but also with the needs of international climate governance.

As a procedural content, public participation can promote the process of carbon neutrality justice, law enforcement and law-abiding through the power of social supervision, and promote the effective implementation of the rules in carbon neutrality legislation. The deepening of public participation can enhance the public awareness of green low-carbon life, and realize the participation of the whole people in the implementation process of the "Double carbon" goal. On the basis of practice, the principle of public participation and specific implementation mechanism have been embodied in some laws and regulations. For example, the Tianjin regulations on peak carbon and carbon neutrality provide for "The establishment of a long-term mechanism for departmental coordination, social interaction and public participation" [66], the regulations on the ecological and environmental protection of the Shenzhen Special Economic Zone include a special chapter on "Information Disclosure and public participation", which requires carbon trading institutions to establish a sound information disclosure system, publishing information on carbon trading [67]. The disclosure of carbon information is also covered in the administrative measures for the legal disclosure of enterprise environmental information. Most of the existing laws and regulations concerning the public are individual or compulsory activities such as advocating green consumption, low-carbon lifestyles and energy-saving behaviors. The public has access to public carbon information, there are still deficiencies in terms of participation in carbon-neutral decision-making and safeguards for the right to know. Incorporating public participation into the legal structure of carbon neutrality is conducive to improving the system of information disclosure and public participation related to carbon neutrality, and promoting public interest litigation with carbon information disclosure as the starting point, promoting "Dual carbon" targets at both the law enforcement and compliance levels.

5.3.2 *Establishing a Multi-Tiered and Core Legal Framework for Carbon Neutrality*

a. Special Legislation: the Core of the Carbon Neutrality Rule of Law Structure

"Carbon peak', 'Carbon neutrality" and other core concepts need to be integrated into our country's environmental legal system, to clarify the core terms of carbon neutrality, carbon emissions trading system and other basic content. A law to regulate carbon neutrality would solve the problem of policy rather than law in the legal structure of carbon neutrality, and there is no law to follow in carbon reduction and sequestration, this will make the governance system more structured and focused. The guidelines make clear the need for a law on peak carbon and carbon neutrality. Some experts and scholars have also suggested starting a special legislative process [68]. The "Guiding opinions on coordinating and strengthening the work related to climate change and ecological environment protection" points out that it is necessary to accelerate the promotion of legislation related to climate change and promote the promulgation and implementation of regulations on carbon emission trading [69]. However, there are different plans on how to choose the style of special legislation.

I. Special legislation to regulate carbon neutrality

China's mid-century long-term low greenhouse gas emission development strategy calls for "Studying and formulating special laws on carbon neutrality, revising the energy conservation law, the electricity law, the coal law, the renewable energy law and the circular economy promotion law as soon as possible, and enhancing the pertinence and effectiveness of relevant laws and regulations" [70]. In the State Council's 2022 legislative work plan, the energy law and the interim regulations on the administration of carbon emissions trading will be included in plans to formulate and revise laws and regulations [71]. A dedicated carbon neutrality legislation can fill the gaps in legislation at the national level and improve the fragmented and flat carbon neutrality legal structure.

II. Enacting special legislation on climate change

The special legislation of climate change has been practiced in some places, such as Shanxi and Qinghai. In addition, climate change can be used as a superordinate concept of carbon neutrality. The law on responding to climate change is one of the "Research projects" in the 2016 legislative work plan of the State Council. In 2021, the guiding opinions on coordinating and strengthening work related to climate change and ecological and environmental protection, we should take addressing climate change as a key area of the rule of law in ecological and environmental protection, and actively promote synergy between addressing climate change and environmental governance, ecological protection and restoration. Many scholars also advocate that the "Climate change response law" should be used to guide the existing decentralized dual-carbon legal system [72]. However, most of the existing local climate change legislation is around 2010–2011 and lacks carbon neutrality. The progress of climate change legislation at the national level has been slow and gradually stagnated, and it is also difficult to make breakthroughs in the short term. In addition, the legislation of carbon neutrality is not only the transformation of "Double carbon" policy into law, but also the comprehensive regulation of the green and low-carbon development of our economy and society, its effectiveness spills over into the entire legal system [73]. This connotation has gone beyond the current legislative practice of our country to respond to climate change, and can not be completely covered by the climate change response law.

III. The integration of carbon neutrality in the environmental code

According to the 2021 annual legislative work plan of the Standing Committee of the National People's Congress, the standing committee of the National People's Congress will study and start the codification of environmental codes, education codes and administrative basic codes, which are ripe for compilation in the field of administrative legislation. The codification of environmental law has frequently entered the discussion agenda. As an environmental code covering all matters related to the environment, it should naturally include provisions related to climate change, including provisions on peak carbon and carbon neutrality. Taking advantage of the development opportunity of codification of environmental protection law, peak carbon carbon and carbon neutrality will be systematically integrated into the environmental protection code [74]. The legislative plan related to carbon neutrality in the environmental code is to set up "Green and low-carbon development part", which is juxtaposed with pollution control part and natural ecological protection part. Green Low-carbon development will fill the gaps in the field of climate change and carbon neutrality legislation in our country. With its innovation, it carries "The most forward-looking and innovative part of the environmental code" [75], it is no less than the unique contribution of the independent compilation of personality right to the civil code and the rule of law in China. There are many discussions on the content of green low-carbon development, but it generally includes clean production, carbon peak carbon neutrality and international cooperation [76].

Compared with the integration of carbon neutrality in the separate law, the integration of peak carbon carbon neutrality in the environmental code is more comprehensive and can be reflected in both the general provisions and the specific provisions. The legislative process of the environmental code itself is a process of integrating various environmental protection specific laws, whether carbon neutrality is discussed as a separate chapter or as a section in a special chapter on climate change, it will be addressed under a holistic system, thereby reducing the fragmentation of governance structures under the current system. For example, the coordination of pollution reduction and carbon reduction can be reflected in the pollution control part, and the carbon sink function of forests, wetlands and other ecosystems can be integrated into the natural ecological protection part, so that the various laws related to carbon neutrality can be integrated and coordinated in the environmental code.

However, there are also some problems in reflecting the content of carbon neutrality in the environmental code. First, the environmental code takes a long time to legislate and may not be published in the short term. Compared with the formulation process of the Civil Code, our country has successively started the formulation of the civil code four times in 1954, 1962, 1979 and 2001, but the compilation of the Civil Code has not been officially started in the end [77]. In November 2014, the fourth plenary session of the 18th CPC Central Committee clearly proposed the compilation of the Civil Code [78]. From June 2016, the Standing Committee of the National People's Congress reviewed the draft of the general provisions of the civil law to December 2019, the general provisions and sub-parts of the Civil Code have undergone several reviews. The formulation and discussion process of the civil code is time-consuming and complex. However, the environmental code is still in the preparatory stage of the start-up, and the development work has not yet officially started. Leaving the legislation of carbon neutrality to the environmental code may not meet the needs of the rapid development of carbon-related products and technologies such as carbon finance and carbon trading. Secondly, the stability of the code makes it less convenient to amend the content of the environmental code than the separate law procedure. There are scientific uncertainties about climate change, its trends and impacts are not clear, and carbon-neutral technologies and clean energy are in a rapid development stage and will continue to change in the future, codification will reduce the flexibility of the mechanism and can not respond to the legislative needs arising from emerging changes. As far as the positioning of the environmental code is concerned, the moderate codification is also difficult to cover all the special environmental laws and the constantly developing regulations, "The codification of environmental law can not cover all the sources of environmental law, but can only choose the important parts that reflect the essence of environmental law to be integrated, and comprehensively stipulate the basic categories, systems and contents" [75]. Therefore, although the establishment of a green low-carbon part in the environmental code to integrate carbon neutrality related content can be used as a future development direction, it is still necessary to formulate a separate legislation for carbon neutrality in the current development.

In summary, considering the current situation of legislative practice, the needs of future development and the need to strengthen the supply of rules in the field of carbon neutrality, starting special legislation for carbon neutrality is the best measure to clarify the core of the carbon neutrality rule of law system. Special legislation on carbon neutrality can not only fill the gap in the supply of rules in the field of carbon neutrality, but also support judicial practice and law enforcement measures, moreover, it is more feasible to develop a green low-carbon code than to formulate a climate change response law and to wait for the integration of environmental code legislation.

b. Horizontal Coordination among Different Departmental laws

General Secretary Xi Jinping emphasized: "Achieving carbon peaking and carbon neutrality is a solemn commitment made by China to the world, and it also represents an extensive and profound economic and social transformation." Climate change exerts comprehensive and all-dimensional impacts on multiple industrial sectors, and will remain a long-term environmental issue. Therefore, it requires regulation by specialized departmental laws. The Guidelines also point out the need to "comprehensively review and repeal provisions in existing laws and regulations that are incompatible with the work of carbon peaking and carbon neutrality, and strengthen the connection and coordination among laws and regulations." [79] Establishing a coordinated legal framework for carbon neutrality not only requires a special legislation that takes the core position and governs the entire legal system for carbon neutrality, but also demands horizontal connection and coordination among other departmental laws. Such horizontal coordination can integrate all departmental laws related to carbon neutrality, align the legal structure for carbon neutrality with China's broader legal framework, and enable various departmental laws to collaborate with each other to form a synergistic effect. General Secretary Xi Jinping emphasized: "Achieving carbon peaking and carbon neutrality is a solemn commitment made by China to the world, and it also represents an extensive and profound economic and social transformation." Climate change exerts comprehensive and all-dimensional impacts on multiple industrial sectors, and will remain a long-term environmental issue. Therefore, it requires regulation by specialized departmental laws. The Guidelines also point out the need to "comprehensively review and repeal provisions in existing laws and regulations that are incompatible with the work of carbon peaking and carbon neutrality, and strengthen the connection and coordination among laws and regulations." Establishing a coordinated legal framework for carbon neutrality not only requires a special legislation that takes the core position and governs the entire legal system for carbon neutrality, but also demands horizontal connection and coordination among other departmental laws. Such horizontal coordination can integrate all departmental laws related to carbon neutrality, align the legal structure for carbon neutrality with China's broader legal framework, and enable various departmental laws to collaborate with each other to form a synergistic effect.

I. Harmonization with the Natural Resources Protection Act

Carbon sequestration is an important means to achieve peak carbon and carbon neutrality. In the absence of an environmental code or special legislation on carbon neutrality, the forest law needs to continue to improve the relevant content of the forestry carbon sink system and stipulate the forestry carbon sink trading mechanism. The wetland protection law, grassland law, Marine Environmental Protection Law and other relevant laws regulating ecosystems with carbon sink function should make corresponding provisions for carbon sink function.

In order to avoid duplication and conflict with the provisions in the special legislation of carbon neutrality, it is necessary to design the terms of convergence. For example, in the wetland protection law, "The water law of the People's Republic of China, the flood control law of the People's Republic of China, the law of the People's Republic of China on the prevention and control of water pollution, the marine environment protection law of the People's Republic of China, the Yangtze River Protection Law of the People's Republic of China, the fisheries law of the People's Republic of China, and the law of the People's Republic of China on the administration of the use of sea areas shall also apply to the protection, use and related management of wetlands in rivers, lakes and sea areas." [80] Linking wetland protection to laws of other departments. Similar design can be adopted in carbon neutrality related legislation to realize the connection and coordination between special laws on carbon neutrality and laws related to carbon neutrality, such as environmental protection law, Forest Law and renewable energy law. The linkage between different laws, regulations and policies can also be specified in carbon neutrality legislation. For example, Article 15 of the wetland protection law stipulates that "The preparation of wetland protection plans shall be in line with such plans as Comprehensive River basin plans and flood control plans". Special legislation on carbon neutrality could include specific provisions linking the dual-carbon goal to other laws.

II. Harmonisation with civil and commercial law

It is very important to include the "Dual carbon" target in civil and commercial laws. Even in the case of the environmental code, carbon neutrality still needs to be regulated by the above-mentioned laws. The green principle in the civil code provides the basis for the connection with the goal of "Double carbon" in concept, and the provisions of environmental and ecological damage compensation are an important implementation of the green principle.

Commercial law is also the focus of the implementation of the "Double carbon" goal. The pre-2030 Peak Carbon Action Plan also proposes to guide companies to fulfil their social responsibilities and encourage listed companies and Bond issuers to regularly publish information on their carbon emissions, in accordance with legal disclosure requirements for environmental information [81]. However, the disclosure system for "Dual carbon" information still comes from policy guidance and departmental regulations, the administrative measures for the disclosure of corporate environmental information according to law, there are no provisions in the company law for disclosure of carbon-neutral information. The provisions of the company law on corporate social responsibility also focus on the expression of article 5: "When a company engages in business activities, it must abide by laws and administrative regulations, abide by social ethics and business ethics, be honest and trustworthy, accept the supervision of the government and the public, and assume social responsibilities" [82], lack of supporting systems to implement corporate social responsibility. To achieve the goal of "Double carbon" in the laws and regulations, we need to make clear that green and low carbon is part of corporate social responsibility, and implement the disclosure system of carbon neutrality information.

Green Finance and climate finance could be incorporated into commercial law. Regulations on green investment and green finance are only sporadically found in local regulations and regulatory documents, such as the Huzhou Green Finance Promotion Ordinance and the Shenzhen Special Economic Zone Green Finance Ordinance, or there are relevant provisions in local ecological and environmental protection laws and regulations. The formation of a national-level system is conducive to unifying market standards and providing legal support for green finance. Integrating support for Green Finance, Green Investment and green credit into commercial law is needed to harmonize carbon neutrality with other sectoral laws. The practice of local legislation could serve as a blueprint for the development of specific provisions on green finance and green credit that could be integrated into commercial law.

c. Vertical Coordination among Local Legislation

A coherent and coordinated rule of law structure requires not only the horizontal cooperation of various department laws, but also the coordination of laws and regulations at different levels between local governments and between the central and local governments. Vertical coordination can make the structure of the rule of law more hierarchical, hierarchical, and the legal norms at the same level remain consistent without conflict.

In order to realize the coordination on vertical level, the local legislation and the central legislation should be integrated. First of all, local legislation needs to be more balanced. In the current local legislation, the eastern developed regions such as municipalities directly under the central government and special economic zones are in the forefront, while the midwestern sectional figure skating championships have few legislative provisions on carbon trading, carbon emission system and green finance. In July 2021, the National Carbon Market was launched, with most of the country's provinces participating in the first round of implementation [83]. Local legislation on peak carbon neutrality is no longer just for the eastern coastal provinces and municipalities, they need to cover all parts of the country.

Second, the style and content of local legislation needs to be co-ordinated. Although the local legislation reflects the local characteristics and conforms to the needs of local development, it is still necessary to unify the legislative form and style arrangement. There are great differences in the content and form of legislation among several different modes, such as carbon neutrality separate legislation, carbon neutrality into local ecological environment protection regulations and carbon neutrality into climate change legislation, the fragmentation of the governance structure at the local level is exacerbated. There is a big difference between the legislation before and after the dual-carbon targets were proposed, and amendments need to be made to incorporate peak carbon neutrality into existing climate legislation.

After the promulgation of the provisions at the national level, the local legislation should be revised in a timely manner, and the inconsistencies with the national provisions should be deleted and modified to achieve coordination and unity in legal responsibilities. For example, the administrative measures of Shenzhen municipality on carbon emissions trading set a fine of 50,000 yuan (US $7000) for falsely reporting, concealing or failing to report annual carbon emissions by key emitters, and a fine of 100,000 yuan (US $10,000) if the circumstances are serious, shanghai's trial measures for carbon emissions management and the national regulations for carbon emissions trading will limit fines to 10,000 yuan (US $1000) and 30,000 yuan (US $3000) [84]. If the standards are not unified, the punishment for the same illegal act will be different in different regions, which will not only damage the stability of the law, but also form a "Pollution haven" in regions with lower standards, it is not conducive to the implementation of the carbon emission information disclosure system. In order to improve the legal structure of carbon neutrality, it is necessary to do a good job of cohesion and coordination between local legislation and between central and local legislation.

The legal structure of carbon neutrality is facing challenges in three aspects: the rationality of the legal hierarchy, the coordination between various departments of domestic law, and the overall coordination between domestic law and international law. In general, the structure of carbon neutrality rule of law shows a state that legislation lags behind policy, central legislation lags behind local legislation, and there is a lack of overall coordination among various department laws. Due to the low level of laws and regulations directly related to carbon neutrality and the lack of special legislation at the core to govern the whole system, the carbon neutrality legal structure is fragmented and flat, there are legislative gaps in some of the content. In terms of domestic and international governance, there is no organic connection with the international climate change law constituted by the Paris Agreement and the UNFCCC.

China's demand for International Convention implementation and international cooperation and the demand for domestic response to climate change not only bring the need to establish a carbon neutrality legal structure, but also need to build a carbon neutrality legal structure with Chinese characteristics. To establish this model, it is necessary to take the dynamic system theory as the methodology, the Green Low-carbon principle, the risk prevention principle, the proportional principle and the public participation principle as the basic principles, and integrate local legislation and department regulations, supplementing the laws of higher rank, establishing a multi-level balance between local legislation and central legislation, and a system of coordination between domestic law and international law. With the independent and special legal provisions regulating carbon neutrality as the core, the detailed rules of carbon trading as the supplement, and the provisions of higher-level laws such as the Civil Code and the environmental protection law as the principle provisions, the hierarchy is clear, a wide-ranging rule of law structure. Coordinating the domestic and foreign legal structures, making a good connection between domestic laws and international treaties, exploring new forms of international cooperation and climate rules with their own characteristics, and combining with the development trend of international climate change negotiations, adhering to multilateralism and the principle of common but differentiated responsibilities. From the perspective of the "Global South", China, as the largest developing country, has not only adopted its own climate governance practices and innovative measures, but also demonstrated its firm determination to address climate change, it will also have a profound and lasting impact on the global climate governance system. China's legal practice in carbon neutrality is exploring a new development path for the Global South that takes into account both economic development and environmental protection. This practice is an important contribution to global climate governance, it will also provide valuable lessons for other developing countries.

References

1. Herrle (2018) Global order and global governance (trans: Lin X). China Renmin University Press, Beijing, pp 267–268
2. Alam S et al (eds) (2015) International law and global south [M]. Cambridge University Press, New York, p 5
3. Susskind LE, Ali SH (2015) Environmental diplomacy: negotiating more effective global agreements, 2nd edn. Oxford University Press, New York, p 17; Cullet P (2021) Differentiation. In: Rajamani L, Peel J (eds) The Oxford handbook of international environmental law, 2nd edn. Oxford University Press, Oxford, p 330
4. Takeura M (2007, 23 November) The world is polluting China [EB/OL]. Retrieved 22 August 2022, from https://cssn.cn/
5. Paris Agreement 55 ILM 740, (opened for signature 12 December 2015, entry into force 4 November 2016), art
6. People's Republic of China (n.d.) Main Report: Effectiveness of China's Implementation of Its Nationally Determined Contributions and New Goals and Measures [EB/OL]. p 7. Retrieved from china-embassy.gov.cn

7. Wenxian Z (2014) Rule of law and the modernization of national governance [J]. China Leg Sci 04:6. https://doi.org/10.14111/j.cnki.zgfx.2014.04.018
8. Jiang W (2021) On the legal framework for carbon peaking and carbon neutrality initiatives [J]. East China Law Rev 05:124. https://doi.org/10.19404/j.cnki.dffx.20210906.006
9. People's Republic of China (n.d.) Forest Law of the People's Republic of China [Article 1]
10. People's Republic of China (n.d.) Environmental Protection Law of the People's Republic of China [Article 6]
11. Supreme People's Court of the People's Republic of China. Typical Cases of the Judiciary Actively and Steadily Promoting Carbon Peaking and Carbon Neutrality [EB/OL]. (2023-02-17) [2023-08-26] Typical Cases of the Judiciary Actively and Steadily Promoting Carbon Peaking and Carbon Neutrality - Supreme People's Court of the People's Republic of China (court.gov.cn)
12. People's Republic of China (n.d.) Energy Conservation Law of the People's Republic of China [Article 7]
13. People's Republic of China (n.d.) Yellow River Protection Law [Article 87]
14. People's Republic of China (n.d.) Qinghai-Tibet Plateau Ecological Protection Law [Article 3, Article 8]
15. People's Republic of China (n.d.) Civil Code of the People's Republic of China [Article 9, Article 998, Article 1231]
16. The Central People's Government of the People's Republic of China. China's Policies and Actions on Addressing Climate Change [EB/OL]. (2021-10-27) [2023-08-21] China's Policies and Actions on Addressing Climate Change - White Paper - Chinese Government Website (www.gov.cn)
17. Xinhua News Agency. Ministry of Ecology and Environment: Strive to Launch the National Greenhouse Gas Voluntary Emission Reduction Trading Market as Early as Possible This Year [EB/OL]. (2023-06-29) [2023-08-21] Ministry of Ecology and Environment: Strive to Launch the National Greenhouse Gas Voluntary Emission Reduction Trading Market as Early as Possible This Year - Departmental Updates - Chinese Government Website (www.gov.cn)
18. Article 19 of the Guidelines on the Format for Mandatory Environmental Information Disclosure by Enterprises
19. Supreme People's Court. Typical Cases of Judicial Active and Prudent Advancement of Carbon Peaking and Carbon Neutrality [EB/OL]. (2023-02-17) [2023-08-26] Typical Cases of Judicial Active and Prudent Advancement of Carbon Peaking and Carbon Neutrality - Supreme People's Court of the People's Republic of China (court.gov.cn)
20. Supreme People's Court. Opinion on Strengthening and Innovating Environmental and Resource Judicial Work in the New Era to Provide Judicial Services and Guarantees for Building a Modernization with Harmonious Coexistence between Man and Nature [EB/OL]. (2021-10-08) [2023-08-26] Opinion on Strengthening and Innovating Environmental and Resource Judicial Work in the New Era to Provide Judicial Services and Guarantees for Building a Modernization with Harmonious Coexistence between Man and Nature - Gazette of the Supreme People's Court of the People's Republic of China (court.gov.cn)
21. Supreme People's Procuratorate. Interpretation of the Supreme People's Court and the Supreme People's Procuratorate on Several Issues Concerning the Application of Law in Handling Criminal Cases of Environmental Pollution [EB/OL]. (2023-08-09) [2023-08-26] Joint Interpretation by the "Two Supreme Organs" on Criminal Offenses of Environmental Pollution Issued - Supreme People's Procuratorate of the People's Republic of China (spp.gov.cn)
22. Supreme People's Procuratorate. Typical Cases of Procuratorial Organs Serving and Guaranteeing Carbon Peaking and Carbon Neutrality [EB/OL]. (2023-06-05) [2023-08-26] Typical Cases of Procuratorial Organs Serving and Guaranteeing Carbon Peaking and Carbon Neutrality - Supreme People's Procuratorate of the People's Republic of China (spp.gov.cn)
23. The Central People's Government of the People's Republic of China. China Officially Launches Comprehensive Evaluation of Green Loans, Green Bonds, etc., and Incorporates Them into Institutional Ratings — Financial Institutions Need to Embed the "Dual Carbon" Goals into

the Entire Business Process [EB/OL]. (2021-07-20) [2023-08-21] China Officially Launches Comprehensive Evaluation of Green Loans, Green Bonds, etc., and Incorporates Them into Institutional Ratings — Financial Institutions Need to Embed the "Dual Carbon" Goals into the Entire Business Process - Rolling News - Chinese Government Website (www.gov.cn)
24. Pingshan Administration of Shenzhen Municipal Ecology and Environment Bureau, Administrative Penalty Decision (No. SHPEEB-Pingshan Penalty [2020] No. 070). (May 14, 2020)
25. Department of Ecology and Environment of Inner Mongolia Autonomous Region. Administrative Penalty Decision of the Department of Ecology and Environment of Inner Mongolia Autonomous Region [EB/OL]. (2023-04-12) [2023-08-21] Administrative Penalty Decision - Penalty Information - Department of Ecology and Environment of Inner Mongolia Autonomous Region (nmg.gov.cn)
26. Measures for the Administration of Carbon Emission Rights Trading (Trial Implementation) [EB/OL]. (2020-12-31) [2023-08-27] Measures for the Administration of Carbon Emission Rights Trading (Trial Implementation) - Documents of State Council Departments - Chinese Government Website (www.gov.cn)
27. Ministry of Ecology and Environment. Report on the First Compliance Cycle of the National Carbon Emission Rights Trading Market [R]. 2022: 4
28. Cao W (2022) Carbon neutrality legislation: why it is possible and what can be done [J]. Oriental Law 06:188. https://doi.org/10.19404/j.cnki.dffx.20221122.001
29. Standing Committee of the Guangzhou Municipal People's Congress. Regulations of Guangzhou Municipality on Ecological and Environmental Protection [EB/OL]. (2022-01-22) [2023-08-21] Announcement No. 95 of the Standing Committee of the 15th Guangzhou Municipal People's Congress - Website of the Standing Committee of the Guangzhou Municipal People's Congress (rd.gz.cn)
30. Yixiang X, Jichen L (2022) On the construction of the legal system for carbon peaking and carbon neutrality [J]. J China Univ Geosci (Soc Sci Ed) 22(03):22. https://doi.org/10.16493/j.cnki.42-1627/c.2022.03.009
31. Hu Xiaoling. IIGF Perspective | Overview and Recommendations on the Development of Local Carbon Incentive Mechanisms under the Background of "Dual Carbon" [EB/OL]. (2022-04-20) [2023-08-27] IIGF Perspective | Overview and Recommendations on the Development of Local Carbon Incentive Mechanisms under the Background of "Dual Carbon" - International Institute of Green Finance, Central University of Finance and Economics (cufe.edu.cn)
32. Shenzhen Municipal Ecology and Environment Bureau. Measures for the Administration of Carbon Emission Rights Trading in Shenzhen [EB/OL]. (2022-07-01) [2023-08-27] Measures for the Administration of Carbon Emission Rights Trading in Shenzhen - Shenzhen Municipal Government Website (sz.gov.cn)
33. Shanghai Municipal People's Government. Interim Measures for Carbon Emission Management in Shanghai [EB/OL]. (2013-11-18) [2023-08-27] Interim Measures for Carbon Emission Management in Shanghai - Shanghai Municipal Government Website (shanghai.ov.cn).
34. Measures for the Administration of Carbon Emission Rights Trading (for Trial Implementation)
35. Ministry of Ecology and Environment of the People's Republic of China (2022, 14 March). Announcement of Typical Cases Concerning Fraudulent Practices in Carbon Emission Report Data [EB/OL]. Retrieved 27 August 2023, from https://www.mee.gov.cn/
36. All-China Environment Federation. Our Federation's "Public Interest Litigation Case Concerning Carbon Emission Data Fraud" Accepted for Filing in Beijing [EB/OL]. (2022-06-22) [2023-08-27] Our Federation's "Public Interest Litigation Case Concerning Carbon Emission Data Fraud" Accepted for Filing in Beijing_All-China Environment Federation (acef.com.cn)
37. Wang L (2020) Adoption and application of the dynamic system theory in the personality rights chapter of the civil code of the People's Republic of China [J]. Jurist 04:2. https://doi.org/10.16094/j.cnki.1005-0221.2020.04.001

38. Wilburg W, Li H (2015) Development of dynamic systems in the sphere of private law [J]. J Soochow Univ (Law Ed) 2(04):107–112. https://doi.org/10.19563/j.cnki.sdfx.2015.04.011
39. Civil Code of the People's Republic of China (Art. 998)
40. Zheng Y (2023) On the quantification of punitive damages for ecological and environmental harm [J]. J Southwest Univ Polit Sci Law 25(03):114–130. Chen H (2022) The issue of environmental rights in the compilation of China's environmental code: an analysis from the perspective of research methodology [J]. J Beijing Univ Aeronaut Astronaut (Soc Sci Ed) 35(03):52–59. https://doi.org/10.13766/j.bhsk.1008-2204.2022.0298
41. Hu X (2021) The impact of the "dynamic system theory" in the civil code on traditional civil adjudication methods [J]. Law Sci 10:145
42. Koziol H, Zhu Y (2009) Reconstruction of tort damages law: european experiences and trends [J]. Jurist 03:6
43. Ibid., p. 44
44. Wang C, Zhang Z (2023) On legislative guarantees for achieving the carbon neutrality goal [J]. Environ Impact Assess 45(03):25. https://doi.org/10.14068/j.ceia.2023.03.004
45. Central People's Government of the People's Republic of China. Opinions of the CPC Central Committee and the State Council on Fully, Accurately and Comprehensively Implementing the New Development Philosophy to Advance Carbon Peaking and Carbon Neutrality [EB/OL]. (2021-10-24) [2023-08-27]. Chinese Government Network (Central Government Documents). Retrieved from https://www.gov.cn/ (Title: Opinions on Fully, Accurately and Comprehensively Implementing the New Development Philosophy to Advance Carbon Peaking and Carbon Neutrality)
46. Supreme People's Court of the People's Republic of China. Typical Cases of the Judiciary's Active and Prudent Advancement of Carbon Peaking and Carbon Neutrality [EB/OL]. (2023-02-17) [2023-08-26]. Supreme People's Court of the People's Republic of China. Retrieved from https://www.court.gov.cn/ (Title: Typical Cases of the Judiciary's Active and Prudent Advancement of Carbon Peaking and Carbon Neutrality)
47. Xi J. Hold High the Great Banner of Socialism with Chinese Characteristics and Strive Together for Building a Modern Socialist Country in All Respects—Report at the 20th National Congress of the Communist Party of China [EB/OL]. (2022-10-16) [2024-02-25]. China Court Network. Retrieved from https://www.chinacourt.org/ (Title: Xi Jinping's Report at the 20th National Congress of the Communist Party of China)
48. Zhao J (2014) International rule of law and domestic rule of law from the perspective of global governance [J]. Soc Sci China 10:82
49. Wang L (2021) Dynamic system theory: toward a "middle path" in normative form [J]. Law Soc Dev 27(04):174
50. National Development and Reform Commission & National Energy Administration. Opinions on Improving Institutional Mechanisms and Policy Measures for the Green and Low-Carbon Transition of Energy [EB/OL]. (2022-01-30) [2023-08-27]. Chinese Government Network (Documents of State Council Departments). Retrieved from https://www.gov.cn/ (Title: Opinions on Improving Institutional Mechanisms and Policy Measures for the Green and Low-Carbon Transition of Energy)
51. National Forestry and Grassland Administration. Series Interpretation of Forests as the "Four Banks": Forests Are Carbon Banks [EB/OL]. (2022-04-22) [2023-08-27]. National Forestry and Grassland Administration Government Website. Retrieved from https://www.forestry.gov.cn/ (Title: Series Interpretation of Forests as the "Four Banks": Forests Are Carbon Banks)
52. Lee H, Romero J (eds) (2023) IPCC, 2023: Sections. In: Climate Change 2023: Synthesis Report. Contribution of Working Groups I, II and III to the Sixth Assessment Report of the Intergovernmental Panel on Climate Change [R]. IPCC, Geneva, Switzerland, p 42. https://doi.org/10.59327/IPCC/AR6-9789291691647
53. Civil Code of the People's Republic of China (Art. 1231)
54. Qinghai-Tibet Plateau Ecological Protection Law, Article 3

55. Supreme People's Court of the People's Republic of China. Several Provisions of the Supreme People's Court on Evidence in Civil Litigation of Ecological and Environmental Torts [EB/OL]. (2023-08-15) [2023-09-04]. Several Provisions of the Supreme People's Court on Evidence in Civil Litigation of Ecological and Environmental Torts - Supreme People's Court of the People's Republic of China (court.gov.cn)
56. Supreme People's Court of the People's Republic of China. Interpretation of the Supreme People's Court on the Application of Punitive Damages in the Trial of Cases Involving Ecological and Environmental Tort Disputes [EB/OL]. (2022-01-13) [2023-09-04]. Interpretation of the Supreme People's Court on the Application of Punitive Damages in the Trial of Cases Involving Ecological and Environmental Tort Disputes - Supreme People's Court of the People's Republic of China (court.gov.cn)
57. Lü Zhongmei's Research Group, Zhongmei L, Xiao Z et al (2018) An outline on the implementation of the "green principle" in the civil code [J]. China Leg Sci 01:12–14. https://doi.org/10.14111/j.cnki.zgfx.2018.01.001
58. Jin W (2015) Environmental law [M]. Peking University Press, p 101
59. Environmental Protection Law of the People's Republic of China, Article 5
60. United Nations (1994) United Nations Framework Convention on Climate Change [1771 UNTS 107]. Opened for signature 9 May 1992; entered into force 21 March 1994, Article 3.3
61. Wenxuan Y (2019) The evolution and application of the precautionary principle in the context of ecological civilization [J]. Jilin Univ J Soc Sci 59(05):107. https://doi.org/10.15939/j.jujsse.2019.05.fx3
62. Government of Canada (n.d.) The Canadian Charter of Rights and Freedoms [Article 15]; European Union (n.d.) Charter of Fundamental Rights of the European Union
63. Zhenliang C, Ruyi X (2022) Review of the proportionality principle in the carbon emission allowance system and its optimization path: a normative analysis based on three carbon trading legislative texts [J]. Acad Exchange 03:78–91
64. Qu Peiran, Zhu Yan. Frequent Supply Interruption Incidents in the "Coal-to-Gas" Transformation in Hebei [EB/OL]. (2023-01-16) [2024-02-21]. Frequent Supply Interruption Incidents in the "Coal-to-Gas" Transformation in Hebei (people.com.cn)
65. European Parliament and Council of the European Union. (2021, 30 June). Regulation (EU) 2021/1119 Establishing the Framework for Achieving Climate Neutrality ('European Climate Law')
66. Regulations of Tianjin Municipality on Promoting Carbon Peaking and Carbon Neutrality, Article 2
67. Shenzhen Municipal Bureau of Ecology and Environment. Regulations of the Shenzhen Special Economic Zone on Ecological and Environmental Protection [EB/OL]. (2021-07-08) [2023-08-19]. Regulations of the Shenzhen Special Economic Zone on Ecological and Environmental Protection - Municipal Laws and Regulations of Shenzhen (sz.gov.cn), Article 112
68. Wang J (2023, 1 March) Proposal of the Central Committee of the China Association for Promoting Democracy: Launch the Legislative Process of the "Law on Addressing Climate Change and Carbon Neutrality" as Soon as Possible [EB/OL]. Retrieved 27 August 2023, from https://www.thepaper.cn/; Wen W (2021, 26 March) The Time is Ripe for the Legislation of the "Carbon Neutrality Promotion Law". Retrieved 27 August 2023, from https://www.thepaper.cn/
69. Ministry of Ecology and Environment of the People's Republic of China. Guiding Opinions on Coordinating and Strengthening the Work Related to Addressing Climate Change and Ecological and Environmental Protection [EB/OL]. (2021-01-11) [2023-08-21]. Guiding Opinions on Coordinating and Strengthening the Work Related to Addressing Climate Change and Ecological and Environmental Protection (mee.gov.cn)
70. People's Republic of China (n.d.) Long-Term Low-Greenhouse-Gas Emission Development Strategy of China for the Mid-21st Century, p 21

71. Central People's Government of the People's Republic of China. Circular of the General Office of the State Council on Issuing the Legislative Work Plan of the State Council for 2022 [EB/OL]. (2022-07-14) [2023-08-21]. Circular of the General Office of the State Council on Issuing the Legislative Work Plan of the State Council for 2022 (Guobanfa [2022] No. 24)_ Government Information Disclosure Column (www.gov.cn)
72. Jinlei H (2023) The logical path for the construction of the legal system for carbon peaking and carbon neutrality: taking the "climate change response law" as the entry point [J]. J Sichuan Univ Sci Eng (Soc Sci Ed) 38(02):40–51
73. Cao W (2022) Carbon neutrality legislation: its feasibility and approach [J]. Oriental Law 06:195. https://doi.org/10.19404/j.cnki.dffx.20221122.001
74. Jiang W (2021) On the legal framework for carbon peaking and carbon neutrality actions [J]. Oriental Law 05:132. https://doi.org/10.19404/j.cnki.dffx.20210906.006
75. Zhongmin Z (2022) The compilation logic and normative expression of the green and low-carbon development volume in the environmental code [J]. Tribune Polit Sci Law 40(02):32–33
76. Wenxuan Y, Zhaoyu S (2023) The path of climate rule of law from the perspective of the systematization of environmental law [J]. J Northwest Univ (Philos Soc Sci Ed) 53(04):37–48. https://doi.org/10.16152/j.cnki.xdxbsk.2023-04-004
77. People's Daily (2016, 26 October) Historical Evolution of the Compilation of the Civil Code in New China [EB/OL]. Retrieved 21 August 2023, from https://www.npc.gov.cn/
78. People's Network. How to Achieve Carbon Peaking and Carbon Neutrality: Xi Jinping's Layout and Planning [EB/OL]. (2022-06-05) [2023-08-27]. How to Achieve Carbon Peaking and Carbon Neutrality: Xi Jinping's Layout and Planning - Exclusive Article - China Communist Party News Network (people.com.cn)
79. Central People's Government of the People's Republic of China. Opinions of the Communist Party of China Central Committee and the State Council on Fully, Accurately and Comprehensively Implementing the New Development Concept to Do a Good Job in Carbon Peaking and Carbon Neutrality [EB/OL]. (2021-10-24) [2023-08-27]. Opinions of the Communist Party of China Central Committee and the State Council on Fully, Accurately and Comprehensively Implementing the New Development Concept to Do a Good Job in Carbon Peaking and Carbon Neutrality_Central Government Documents_Chinese Government Network (www.gov.cn)
80. Wetland Protection Law of the People's Republic of China, Article 2.15
81. Central People's Government of the People's Republic of China. Notice of the State Council on Issuing the Action Plan for Carbon Peaking Before 2030 [EB/OL]. (2021-10-26) [2023-08-27]. Notice of the State Council on Issuing the Action Plan for Carbon Peaking Before 2030_Ecological Monitoring, Protection and Governance_Chinese Government Network (www.gov.cn)
82. Company Law of the People's Republic of China, Article 5
83. Ministry of Ecology and Environment of the People's Republic of China. Report on the First Compliance Cycle of the National Carbon Emission Rights Trading Market [R]. 2022: 4.There are no key emission units in the Tibet Autonomous Region that meet the inclusion criteria. Due to their participation in the local government's quota settlement for 2019 and 2020, Beijing Municipality, Tianjin Municipality, and Guangdong Province (excluding Shenzhen City) do not participate in the quota allocation and settlement of the first compliance cycle of the National Carbon Market
84. Shenzhen Municipal Bureau of Ecology and Environment. Measures for the Administration of Carbon Emission Rights Trading in Shenzhen [EB/OL]. (2022-07-01) [2023-08-27]. Measures for the Administration of Carbon Emission Rights Trading in Shenzhen (sz.gov.cn). Shanghai Municipal People's Government. Interim Measures for the Administration of Carbon Emissions in Shanghai [EB/OL]. (2013-11-18) [2023-08-27]. Interim Measures for the Administration of Carbon Emissions in Shanghai (shanghai.gov.cn). Central People's Government of the People's Republic of China. Measures for the Administration of Carbon Emission Rights Trading (for Trial Implementation) [EB/OL]. (2020-12-31) [2023-08-27]. Measures for the

Administration of Carbon Emission Rights Trading (for Trial Implementation)_Documents of State Council Departments Chinese Government Network (www.gov.cn)

Chapter 6
"Global South" and Plastic Pollution Control

As "Global South" countries grow increasingly interconnected in economic and political spheres, they must also pay special attention to strategies for enhancing cooperation in environmental governance; beyond the carbon-neutral governance discussed in the previous chapter, marine plastic pollution emerges as another critical issue that demands urgent attention. Global plastic production has maintained a steady upward trajectory, reaching a substantial 367 million tonnes as of 2020 [1]. However, the global average recycling rate for plastic remains extremely low, at only approximately 9%, with the vast majority of plastic waste either being sent to landfills, incinerated, or discarded without undergoing proper disposal procedures [2]. Plastic materials are inherently difficult to degrade naturally, enabling them to persist in the environment for extended periods and causing severe contamination of both soil and water resources. Plastic waste in landfills can seep into the ground, contaminating precious groundwater supplies, while the incineration of plastic releases toxic carcinogens known as dioxins—substances that pose significant risks to human health. Additionally, plastics and microplastics are frequently carried into the ocean via river systems and improper disposal from ships. Once in the ocean, plastics threaten marine life primarily through two harmful pathways: accidental ingestion, which can lead to internal damage or starvation, and entanglement, which restricts movement and impairs survival. Plastics also harm marine habitats by blocking sunlight essential for photosynthetic organisms, abrading and damaging delicate coral reefs, or acting as carriers for invasive species—all of which disrupt and damage the fragile ecosystem structure of these habitats [3]. The continuous growth in global plastic waste generation, coupled with the high mobility of plastic materials across borders and ecosystems, has solidified plastic pollution's status as a pressing, far-reaching global environmental problem that requires collective action.

Plastic waste possesses the dual attributes of being both a product (in its functional phase) and a waste (in its discarded phase), with the production and international trade of plastic products inherently intertwined with the generation of plastic

X. Dong, J. Gu, *The Belt and Road Initiative and the Global South*, Energy, Climate Change & Sustainability in the Global South,
https://doi.org/10.1007/978-981-92-0144-0_6

waste. Even in its waste stage, plastic waste continues to account for a certain proportion of global trade flows, reflecting its cross-border mobility. The world's massive plastic production volumes paired with extremely low recycling rates have led to vast quantities of plastic waste seeping into the environment—with the ocean being a particularly severely affected ecosystem—and this crisis has attracted widespread attention from the international community. Owing to disparities in technological capabilities and capital resources between nations, the global north-south plastic trade has given rise to an inherently unfair situation. Regrettably, the perspective dominated by the World Trade Organization's (WTO) free trade principles has not only failed to drive improvements to address this unfairness but has instead served to perpetuate and protect this inequitable status quo. In the key areas of source reduction of plastic waste and the control of plastic production and consumption, the regulatory rules rooted in a trade perspective—with WTO rules as the primary representative—hold significant importance for the effective source control of plastic pollution and the cultivation of sustainable production and consumption patterns worldwide. Therefore, exploring the integration of fragmented governance mechanisms and addressing the critical issue of justice in global plastic trade and pollution control is of profound significance for advancing comprehensive and effective global plastic pollution management.

6.1 Environmental Justice in Global Plastic Trade

Environmental justice originated from the "Environmental justice movement" in the United States, which originated from the dumping of toxic industrial waste in communities of color and low-income groups in North Carolina, is closely related to the pollution of solid waste. With the development of the environmental justice movement, it has experienced the development of horizontal and vertical dimensions, from environmental justice in domestic law to transnational and even global environmental justice. With the development of globalization, global environmental problems have emerged and become increasingly serious, and the issue of environmental justice between North and south countries has become prominent.

6.1.1 Trade in Waste Plastics Makes Developing Countries "Pollution Havens"

Between 1950 and 2017, five billion tonnes of plastic waste were produced worldwide. A large proportion of plastic waste enters the trade and flows between countries. The flow of plastic waste trade is from developed countries to developing countries. The United States, the European Union and Australia are important plastic exporters, and China used to be the largest recipient of plastic waste. In terms of consumption, developed countries consume far more products and produce far more plastics. Per capita plastic consumption in 2016 was 105.3 kg per person per year in the US, 98.66 kg in the UK and 81.16 kg in Germany, far higher than the 19.88 kg in India and 15.67 kg in China, 13.42 kg in Pakistan and 34.9 kg in Indonesia [4]. While goods and services are enjoyed in the developed world, plastic pollution is increasingly being passed on to the developing world. In 2016, before the import ban, plastic waste exports reached 14.1 million tonnes, with China accounting for 7.35 million tonnes, accounting for the majority of plastic waste exports [5]. Burning, landfilling, or dismantling these plastics causes serious air, water, and soil pollution.

The resource utilization of solid waste and the transfer of negative externality of the environment constitute the logic behind the flow of plastic waste. On the one hand, plastic waste has the value of resources, processing and recycling of waste plastics constitute an important industry, and even drive the economic development of some towns. Low Labour and waste-disposal costs in developing countries have encouraged developed countries to export plastic waste to the developing world, boosting local recycling industries. But on the other hand, from stacking to dismantling, plastics are associated with environmental pollution. Much of the movement of plastic waste is not just a reflection of the market, but a search for "Pollution havens". The acceptance of plastic waste in developing countries is not due to its comparative advantage in waste treatment technology, but rather to lower regulatory costs and environmental standards, which undertake waste at the cost of environmental pollution and damage to the health of local residents, is the transfer of environmental negative externalities.

In the global trade in solid waste, there is a race to the bottom, with plastic waste flowing to the least regulated places because of differences in regulation and treatment costs, these are often the least developed countries with the least capacity to deal with waste. The same environmental injustice applies to the plastics trade. Developing countries don't consume so many plastic products themselves, but bear the brunt of the damage to the environment and human health caused by the back-end disposal of plastic waste, even in the treatment of plastic waste at the same time by some developed countries accused of a large number of plastic waste discharged into the environment.

The problem of solid waste smuggling also persists, attracted by the low cost of waste disposal. In 2018 and 2019, under the framework of the World Customs Organization, China Customs initiated the fourth and fifth phases of Operation Terra. In the fifth phase of enforcement, China Customs reported 85 cases, accounting for 36.8% of the global total. On the one hand, this ratio shows the contribution of the Chinese customs in combating the smuggling of solid waste. On the other hand, it shows that developing countries represented by China have become important smuggling destinations for solid waste, both legal and illegal export routes for solid waste. In the "World System," developing countries are on the periphery, exporting raw materials and natural resources in exchange for high-end manufactured goods from developed countries, they are responsible for some of the solid waste and pollution generated by high per capita consumption in developed countries. Through this unequal exchange, a considerable part of environmental pollution is transferred from developed countries to developing countries in the form of international trade.

6.1.2 Trade in Waste Plastics Makes Developing Countries "Pollution Havens"

Waste plastics possess the dual characteristics of being both a product (in certain functional contexts) and a waste (when discarded), embodying overlapping and sometimes conflicting attributes. The Basel Convention explicitly defines waste as "a substance or article which is disposed of or is intended to be disposed of or which is required to be disposed of under National Law," while its preamble clearly states that "strict control measures shall be taken to protect human health and the environment from the adverse effects which may result from the generation and management of hazardous wastes and other wastes." From this formal definition and the broader context of the Convention's objectives, it is evident that the Basel Convention places greater emphasis on the inherent "waste" nature of such materials and the potential environmental harm caused by the improper handling of solid waste. However, waste plastics also exhibit distinct "resource" and commodity properties, with the most prominent manifestation of these attributes being observed in the field of international trade. Under the framework of WTO rules, solid waste—including waste plastics—is treated primarily as a tradable commodity rather than a pollutant that requires targeted reduction measures. Notably, solid waste is assigned specific customs codes to facilitate trade operations, and it even sustains a thriving market alongside well-developed upstream and downstream industrial chains dedicated to its processing and distribution. Restrictions imposed on the trade of such solid waste can even give rise to international trade disputes, as illustrated by the Brazil retread case, in which Brazil's implementation of restrictions on the import of second-hand tyres was deemed to violate the WTO's principle of national treatment.

Even with certain resource attributes, the environmental impact of solid waste can not be ignored. From the perspective of environment, the management of solid waste is a problem of distribution of negative externalities [6]. The concept of producer responsibility (EPR) and life-cycle management follows the logic that national laws provide for special management of solid waste, producers of solid waste are responsible for the solid waste they produce. This kind of control makes solid waste different from ordinary "Goods", although under certain circumstances solid waste can create a certain economic value. At the international level, the Basel Convention encourages on-site disposal of waste and favours national disposal of waste generated by the country itself.

6.2 The Fragmentation Phenomenon of Plastic Pollution Treatment

Fragmentation is an important phenomenon in the development of contemporary international law. As a part of global environmental governance, the governance system of plastic pollution is also fragmented, especially marine plastic pollution. The characteristics of transboundary of marine plastic pollution, the diversification of plastic pollution sources and the extensiveness of plastic pollution hazards have exacerbated this fragmentation. Domestic, regional and international efforts have taken the form of "Soft law" and "Hard Law". Many conventions and resolutions regulate marine plastic pollution from different perspectives. However, there is currently no legally binding agreement governing land-based pollution and the sources of plastic, the most important sources of marine plastic, leaving a gap in the governance of marine plastic pollution.

6.2.1 *Global Conventions*

a. Convention on the Protection of the Marine Environment

(1) United Nations Convention on the Law of the Sea (UNCLOS)

Part XII of the United Nations Convention on the Law of the Sea (UNCLOS) is specifically dedicated to the protection and preservation of the marine environment, with Articles 192 and 194 laying out the fundamental general obligations for safeguarding the marine environment as well as the key obligation to prevent, reduce, and control marine pollution originating from any possible source. With regard to specific pollution sources, land-based sources of pollution, pollution caused by dumping activities, and pollution from ships are explicitly addressed and regulated in Articles 207, 210, and 211 of the Convention respectively. Article 207 of UNCLOS sets forth detailed provisions for the control of pollution from land-based sources, stating that "States shall adopt laws and regulations to prevent, reduce and control pollution of the marine environment from land-based sources, including rivers, estuaries, pipelines and outfall structures"; it also specifically references provisions "Designed to minimize, to the fullest extent possible, the release into the marine environment of substances that are toxic, hazardous or harmful to health, in particular persistent substances". Given its toxic, persistent, and harmful characteristics to marine ecosystems and human health, pollution arising from plastic products clearly falls into the category of substances targeted by this article.

UNCLOS is the only marine environmental protection treaty that deals with land-based sources of pollution. However, UNCLOS does not explicitly propose specific measures to regulate marine plastic or microplastic pollution, but treats it as a kind of "Pollution" in general. Therefore, the general and more general obligations in UNCLOS need to be elaborated through more specialized international conventions.

(2) International Convention for the Prevention of pollution from ships (MARPOL)

International Convention for the Prevention of pollution from ships (MARPOL) MARPOL's regulation of plastic pollution is primarily aimed at preventing waste dumping. Annex 5 of MARPOL prohibits the dumping of plastics. MARPOL could provide an appropriate management path for waste originating at sea. The revision of MARPOL Annex V is an important improvement in the prevention and control of marine plastic pollution, but there are still scope limitations. MARPOL can not be used to regulate land-based pollution, which is an important source of plastics and microplastics in the oceans. Since the amendment of Annex V was proposed, its implementation has been questioned.

(3) Convention on the Prevention of Marine Pollution by Dumping of Wastes and Other Matter (London Convention, 1972)

The 1972 London Convention on the Prevention of Marine Pollution by Dumping of Wastes and Other Matter is specifically intended to regulate the dumping of wastes at sea, with its application scope covering all sea areas globally except for the internal waters of sovereign nations. To fulfill its regulatory purpose, the London Convention establishes a formal permit system and categorizes waste into three clear categories: the dumping of wastes listed in Annex I must be completely prohibited, the dumping of wastes in Annex II requires the obtainment of a special permit, and the dumping of wastes in Annex III only needs a general permit. The 1996 Protocol to the London Convention took a more rigorous step forward by adopting a "reverse list" approach, under which permits are required for the dumping of all non-listed waste. Importantly, plastics are not included in this "white list," so their dumping falls under regulatory control. Despite the strict restrictions it places on waste types, the London Convention has certain limitations in its application scope: geographically, its definition of "dumping" is limited to disposal at sea or in the seabed and subsoil, failing to regulate land-based sources of pollution. The Convention's definition of "sea" does not include internal waters, thus not regulating dumping within such waters. Yet, the fluidity of the ocean's water column allows plastic pollution to drift via ocean currents. Since the Convention only targets acts of "intentional disposal," it does not regulate the discharge of waste generated during production processes. Moreover, the London Convention has far fewer signatories than global conventions like UNCLOS or MARPOL, which further restricts its overall scope.

b. Convention on Waste Pollution

(1) Basel Convention

The Basel Convention on the Control of Transboundary Movements of Hazardous Wastes and Their Disposal stands as the most pivotal international convention in the global waste governance field, as it exerts regulatory oversight over both land-based pollution and marine pollution—addressing two critical sources of environmental harm. Among its core general obligations, the Basel Convention explicitly requires Parties "to ensure that the generation of hazardous and other wastes within its territory is reduced to a minimum, taking into account social, technical and economic aspects," thereby laying out fundamental general provisions for the control of waste at its source and the overall reduction of waste volumes. When it comes to waste disposal, Parties to the Convention bear the obligation "to ensure the provision of adequate disposal facilities for the environmentally sound management of hazardous and other wastes," ensuring that waste handling aligns with environmental protection standards.

Annexes II, VIII, and IX of the Basel Convention have undergone targeted amendments to enhance its regulatory scope: Entry Y48 has been added to Annex II (which covers other wastes controlled by the Convention), Entry A3210 specifically for "Plastic wastes and their mixtures" has been incorporated into Annex VIII (governing hazardous wastes controlled by the Convention), and Entry B3011 has been added to Annex IX—collectively, these amendments significantly expand the range of plastic wastes subject to the Convention's control. At meetings of the Convention's Open-ended Working Group of the Parties, participating States adopted dedicated resolutions focused on marine plastic and microplastic litter; these resolutions call for the active prevention and minimization of plastic litter generation and put forward a life-cycle approach to address plastic waste from production to disposal.

There are also well-documented criticisms regarding the limitations of the Basel Convention, such as its lack of specific, measurable targets and clear timelines for implementation, as well as its focus solely on regulating the transboundary movements of waste—failing to address the large volumes of plastic waste generated at the source, which is a root cause of global plastic pollution. While the Convention's new amendments represent an important step forward in strengthening plastic waste control and are expected to help drive countries to improve the recycling and environmentally sound, harmless disposal of plastic waste in the long term, there are also lingering doubts: some argue that the amendments may impose additional burdens on existing plastic recycling systems and could merely result in shifting plastic waste from one region to another, rather than achieving a fundamental reduction in overall plastic pollution.

The Conference of the Parties to the Basel Convention has adopted the Cartagena Declaration on the Prevention, Minimization and Recovery of Hazardous Wastes and Other Wastes to guide implementation. Beyond the Convention's legally binding provisions, the Basel Convention framework also includes a series of relevant non-binding soft law measures to support practical action. The Convention has issued detailed technical guidelines on the environmental management and disposal of plastic waste, covering key processes such as incineration, landfill, recycling, storage, and transportation—providing Parties with actionable guidance. Additionally, the Basel Convention has established a dedicated Plastic Waste Partnership and a specialized working group under its institutional framework to facilitate collaboration on plastic waste issues. The Conference of the Parties further adopted the Cartagena Declaration on the Prevention, Minimization and Recovery of Hazardous Wastes and Other Wastes and developed a corresponding road map to outline clear steps for advancing the Declaration's goals.

6.2.2 Regional Conventions Relating to the Protection of the Marine Environment

UNEP (United Nations Environment Programme) implements regional seas projects across multiple key marine regions, including the Caribbean, Mediterranean, North-West Pacific, South Asian, South-East Pacific, Baltic, Black, Red, and South Asian Seas; additionally, there are dedicated regional marine projects in the North-East Atlantic and other geographical areas. Most of these regional initiatives are supported by formal action plans, and a number of them have led to the signing of legally binding regional conventions focused on marine environment protection—all of which are directly or indirectly relevant to addressing and managing marine plastic pollution.

Among these regional efforts, the initiatives in Europe stand out as the most institutionally sophisticated and comprehensive. The most representative of these European frameworks include the Oslo-Paris Convention (OSPAR Convention) for the Protection of the Marine Environment of the North-East Atlantic, the Mediterranean Convention for the Protection of the Mediterranean Sea Against Pollution (commonly known as the Barcelona Convention), and the Baltic Convention for the Protection of the Marine Environment of the Baltic Region (referred to as the Helsinki Convention). Article 3 of the OSPAR Convention's main text explicitly addresses the prevention of pollution from land-based sources, Article 4 focuses on reducing pollution arising from dumping and incineration activities, and Article 5 is dedicated to preventing pollution from offshore operations; for each of these articles, the Convention has adopted detailed annexes that outline specific, actionable measures for implementation. Furthermore, OSPAR has developed and adopted a targeted Marine Litter Action Plan, which aims specifically to reduce marine litter through strategies such as systematic monitoring of marine litter levels, organized beach clean-up campaigns, and ongoing collection of relevant data and information to inform future actions. The Conference of the Parties to the Barcelona Convention has also adopted a Regional Plan for the Management of Marine Litter in the Mediterranean Sea, which proposes concrete actions including reducing pollution from both land-based and marine sources of waste, exploring the implementation of extended producer responsibility schemes, introducing specific measures to reduce "ghost nets" (abandoned, lost, or otherwise discarded fishing gear) from fisheries activities, removing existing marine litter from the Mediterranean, and conducting marine litter monitoring based on an ecosystem-based approach to ensure holistic protection. The Baltic Marine Environment Protection Commission, an institutional body established under the Helsinki Convention, adopted the Baltic Marine Litter Regional Action Plan in 2015, with the clear objective of achieving a significant reduction in marine litter within the Baltic region by 2025. The Helsinki Convention comprises seven distinct annexes; in Annex I, titled "Hazardous Substances," substances that possess the characteristics of being "persistent, may float, remain suspended, or sink to the bottom" are formally classified and regulated as "hazardous substances," with specific controls on their dumping and disposal—and this classification aligns closely with the environmental profile of plastics. Meanwhile, Annex III of the Convention sets forth specific, targeted measures to prevent land-based pollution, including provisions for the proper treatment of industrial wastewater and agricultural runoff, which are key contributors to marine plastic pollution.

In addition, the Black Sea region has developed and established a dedicated Action Plan on Marine Litter, which puts forward specific proposals including the establishment of regional expert groups to provide technical support, encouragement for exploring extended producer responsibility mechanisms and financial instruments to curb the use of single-use plastics, and the launch of targeted programmes such as measures to clean up existing marine litter deposits. For regional projects that have not yet formulated a specific action plan focused on marine debris, many still incorporate marine debris-related targets or relevant supporting measures within their broader action plans. In the Red Sea and Gulf of Aden region, although there is no standalone plan specifically addressing marine debris, the local marine debris problem has seen a significant increase in recent years; notably, the Action Plan for the Protection of the Marine and Coastal Environment in this region, under Section A ("Environmental Monitoring"), Paragraph 12(d), explicitly refers to the need to investigate the discharge of industrial and domestic wastes from land-based sources into the sea and to study the potential impacts of such wastes on human health. The Regional Seas Programme in South Asia, within the objectives outlined in its 2020–2030 Strategic Plan, puts forward the goal of "Ensuring effective waste management at all levels" and has further developed a specialized "Plastic-Free Rivers and Seas Plan," whose core aim is to reduce the volume of plastic waste entering the ocean via river systems.

When examining the measures outlined in these regional ocean plans, it is evident that relatively comprehensive and well-designed measures have been implemented in some marine areas; however, there remain significant disparities between different regions, and the existing measures fail to cover all global sea areas. In certain parts of Europe, for instance, well-established and systematic measures are already in place—these measures explicitly highlight multiple sources of plastic pollution, including land-based pollution, sea dumping, and ship-generated pollution, while also actively encouraging source reduction measures, regular pollution monitoring, and targeted garbage removal initiatives. In contrast, some sea areas lack any relevant action plan addressing marine plastic pollution altogether, or their existing action plans are primarily composed of declarative concepts with relatively general descriptions, failing to propose concrete, actionable implementation measures. Furthermore, the vast majority of these marine action plans are non-binding in nature, often containing terms such as "encouragement" and "recommendations" that reflect voluntary participation, thus lacking mandatory constraints to ensure compliance. These differences in the content and enforceability of ocean action plans have ultimately led to a phenomenon of "regional fragmentation" in marine plastic pollution governance, leaving gaps in areas that are not covered by effective regulatory measures.

6.2.3 Declarations, Policies and International Institutions

The hazards posed by marine plastics and the urgency of addressing this issue are widely recognized and emphasized in various international political declarations and global governance platforms. United Nations General Assembly Resolution 66/288, titled "The Future We Want," explicitly states that "The health of the oceans and marine biodiversity are negatively impacted by marine pollution… especially plastics, persistent organic pollutants, heavy metals and nitrogen compounds"; it further identifies shipping activities and land-based runoff as key sources of such pollution and makes a formal pledge to "significantly reduce marine debris" by 2025 [7]. This commitment aligns with Goal 14.1 of the 2030 Agenda for Sustainable Development, which sets out the target "To prevent and significantly reduce marine pollution of all types, especially from land-based activities, including marine debris and nutrient pollution."

The United Nations Environment Programme (UNEP) has undertaken substantial efforts to combat marine plastic pollution, with a key initiative being the adoption and promotion of the Global Programme of Action for the Protection of the Marine Environment from Land-Based Activities—an instrument designed to coordinate global action on land-sourced marine pollution.

The issue of marine plastic pollution has continued to receive sustained attention at sessions of the United Nations Environment Assembly (UNEA). In 2014, the first UN Environment Assembly formally listed ocean plastic waste pollution as one of the top 10 global environmental problems requiring urgent resolution. Subsequently, the second, third, and fourth sessions of the UN Environment Assembly all adopted special resolutions specifically focused on "Marine Plastic Debris and Microplastics." In 2017, the UN Environment Assembly adopted an additional resolution and established the Open-ended Ad Hoc Group of Experts on Marine Litter and Microplastics to provide technical expertise and guidance. In 2018, a UN Environment Assembly resolution went further, calling for the exploration of "legally binding governance strategies and approaches" and the potential development of a dedicated convention framework to address plastics and plastic pollution [8]. These resolutions collectively propose more effective methods to tackle the issue, emphasize the need to address both land-based and sea-based sources of plastic pollution, advocate for reducing waste generation at the source, promote the introduction of extended producer responsibility systems, and support the adoption of a life-cycle approach to minimize plastic waste from production to disposal. They also stress the importance of adopting "an integrated approach from source to sea" when addressing plastic pollution, "taking into account that rivers, runoffs or winds carry terrigenous plastic waste and microplastics from land into the ocean," and call for the inclusion of the land-sea interface in plans aimed at preventing marine plastic pollution. Additionally, the resolution adopted at the Thirteenth Conference of the Parties to the Convention on Biological Diversity (COP 13) highlighted the specific hazards of plastics and microplastics to marine ecosystems and issued voluntary guidelines to help mitigate the adverse impacts of marine litter; however, this resolution, like many others in this domain, lacks legally binding force to ensure mandatory compliance.

6.2.4 *Fragmentation of Global Environmental Governance Reflected in Marine Plastic Pollution*

Biermann et al. categorize fragmented governance into three distinct types: synergistic fragmentation, collaborative fragmentation, and conflictual fragmentation—these types are differentiated based on the degree of collaboration among institutions, the consistency of core terms, and the alignment of actors, ranging from high to low [9]. In the cases of "synergistic fragmentation" and "collaborative fragmentation," there exists a set of core mechanisms with which other associated mechanisms operate either closely or loosely, and the core terms used across these mechanisms are interrelated or at the very least non-conflicting. "Conflictual fragmentation," by contrast, arises when an issue area contains multiple sets of mechanisms that have minimal communication with one another, adopt divergent decision-making approaches, and employ principles and core terms that are clearly contradictory; in this scenario, the primary actors involved are drawn from these separate, unaligned mechanisms [8]. Biermann points to the Montreal Protocol as a typical example of "synergistic fragmentation" and the UNFCCC (United Nations Framework Convention on Climate Change) as an example of "collaborative fragmentation."

The governance of marine plastic pollution is notably characterized by both "collaborative fragmentation" and "conflictual fragmentation." Global ocean governance as a whole exhibits inherent fragmentation: there is a lack of effective coordination among national policies addressing marine plastic pollution, and significant imbalances exist between the policies implemented by different countries and regions. The globalization of the plastic industry has further exacerbated this fragmentation, ultimately leading to the ineffectiveness of current marine plastic governance efforts. A multitude of mechanisms have been established to address the problem of marine plastic pollution: from the law of the sea framework represented by the United Nations Convention on the Law of the Sea (UNCLOS), to hazardous waste management laws exemplified by the Basel Convention, and to the Convention on Biological Diversity (CBD) which focuses on biodiversity protection—each of these conventions' mechanisms addresses the issue of plastic pollution in some form. Additionally, the United Nations Environment Programme (UNEP) has developed a series of "soft law" resolutions that specifically target marine plastics and microplastics. At the regional level, several regional marine conventions, such as the OSPAR Convention and the Convention for the Protection of the Mediterranean Sea Against Pollution (Barcelona Convention), also incorporate provisions to tackle marine plastic debris.

6.3 Potential Conflicts Between Plastics Trade Measures and Other Mechanisms in the Context of the Negotiation of the Global Plastics Convention

6.3.1 Provisions on Plastics Trade in the Draft Global Plastics Convention

The INC5-1 text incorporates specific provisions intended to coordinate cooperation and alignment regarding chemicals of concern in plastics and plastic products with relevant multilateral environmental agreements—namely the Basel, Rotterdam, and Stockholm Conventions—as well as the Agreement on Technical Barriers to Trade (TBT). In contrast, the final draft of INC5-2 removed this coordination provision, limiting encouragement for cooperation with other treaty instruments solely to the level of general international cooperation; as a result, the issue of coordinating with various international multilateral environmental conventions was diminished or even entirely eliminated.

The draft of INC5-1 includes a detailed specific provision on trade measures for chemicals, polymers, related products, and plastic waste, which aims to regulate trade in plastic products. This provision also addresses the issue of harmonization with the Agreement on Technical Barriers to Trade, offering three alternative text options: export licensing requirements, information disclosure requirements, prior informed consent procedures, and the strictest option of banning imports of certain types of plastics—content that bears similarities to relevant provisions in the Basel Convention. Additionally, INC5-1 contains principle-based provisions consistent with Principle 12 of the Rio Declaration, requiring countries to regulate trade in plastics in accordance with "the internationally binding principles of the multilateral trading system as enshrined in WTO law." Despite the existence of widely varying levels of regulatory stringency across jurisdictions, trade in plastics has thus received explicit attention, with attempts made to harmonize such trade with international multilateral environmental agreements or international multilateral trade agreements. However, INC5-2 omitted this entire trade-related clause; the text now contains only a single brief reference to "International Trade," which echoes Principle 12 of the Rio Declaration by stating that "Trade Policy Measures for environmental purposes shall not constitute a means of arbitrary or unjustified discrimination or a disguised restriction on international trade." This reference appears in the section on basic principles as a general statement of principle and remains enclosed in pending square brackets (indicating unresolved status). It is therefore evident that the issue of plastic trade has been almost completely set aside at the final draft stage, a development that reflects the significant difficulty in reaching a consensus among all parties with differing interests.

6.3.2 Potential Conflicts Between Plastics-Related Trade Measures and WTO Rules

There exist potential conflicts between plastics-related trade measures and World Trade Organization (WTO) rules. One key category of such conflicts arises between the provisions of multilateral environmental conventions and WTO rules. The three major conventions governing solid waste and chemicals include specific restrictions on the transboundary movement of wastes and chemicals, and these provisions may conflict with the General Agreement on Tariffs and Trade (GATT). (1) Conflicts with the WTO's Most-Favored-Nation (MFN) Treatment Principle: Article 4.5 of the Basel Convention prohibits the import and export of wastes between its Parties and non-Parties, while a resolution from the second Conference of the Parties to the Basel Convention further requires OECD countries to refrain from exporting hazardous wastes to non-OECD countries. Additionally, Article 3 of the Stockholm Convention on Persistent Organic Pollutants (POPs) mandates that Member States obtain certification from importing states when exporting Convention-controlled organic substances to non-Member States. These trade restrictive measures stand in conflict with the WTO's MFN principle, which requires non-discriminatory treatment among trading partners. Notably, the production of certain additives used in plastic products is regulated under the Stockholm Convention, meaning this convention can also exert an impact on the production and circulation of plastics. (2) Conflicts with the WTO's National Treatment Principle: Articles 4.1(a) and (b) of the Basel Convention grant a Party the right to ban the import of hazardous substances and impose an obligation on it to ban the export of hazardous substances to another Party that has refused to import them—provisions that conflict with the WTO's National Treatment Principle, which requires equal treatment of domestic and foreign products.

The other category of potential conflicts involves environmental measures that countries may adopt under the authority of multilateral environmental conventions. With the amendment to the Basel Convention bringing plastics under its annex-based control, the import and export of plastic products could face conflicts with WTO rules. Under the amended Basel Convention, the transboundary movement of plastic waste added to the annexes must comply with the Convention's obligations, including adherence to the Prior Informed Consent (PIC) procedure, ensuring environmentally sound management, and meeting standard packaging and labeling requirements; Parties also retain the right to establish more stringent control measures beyond these baseline obligations. For instance, China's ban on the import of plastic waste aligns with the requirements set forth in the Basel Convention but has sparked controversies when assessed against WTO rules.

The conflict of rules reflects the conflict of value orientation between WTO rules and international environmental law rules.

The core of WTO rules is free trade. With the development of the times, although the WTO legal system contains more trade and non-trade issues, it has not changed the value orientation of trade free [10]. However, the core value orientation of international environmental law and the value orientation of free trade of WTO will conflict under certain circumstances.

6.4 The Solution to Fragmentation: Mechanism Interaction and Integration

The emergence of fragmentation in marine plastic pollution governance is a response to the natural and pressing trend of plastics and microplastics causing harm to the marine environment. As the International Law Commission (ILC) noted in its report on the fragmentation of international law, "The emergence of new categories of professional law is by no means accidental and responds to new technical and functional requirements." The ILC further emphasized that "Such deviations do not arise as legal-technical 'errors'; instead, they reflect the different pursuits and preferences of actors within a diverse (global) society." [11]

Owing to the fragmented management of existing governance mechanisms, the insufficient control over land-based sources of marine plastic pollution, loopholes in the implementation of existing rules, and the lack of effective coordination among various mechanisms, there has been a strong and widespread call for the establishment of new mechanisms specifically designed to address marine plastic pollution [12]. United Nations Environment Assembly resolutions have also explicitly proposed the development of a dedicated convention to regulate marine plastic pollution; however, five rounds of negotiations have so far failed to yield such a new treaty. At this juncture, where negotiations on a global plastics convention remain deadlocked, there is an urgent need to discuss the interaction and integration of governance mechanisms across multiple levels.

In academic studies focusing on the fragmentation of international law, concepts such as Regime Interaction, Regime Interplay, Interlinkage, and Integration have been put forward to address the problem of regime fragmentation. The interaction between different governance mechanisms can foster synergy and complementarity among them, thereby enhancing the implementation effect of international multilateral environmental treaties. By strengthening cooperation and interaction between these mechanisms, a meaningful synergy effect—where the combined impact exceeds the sum of individual efforts—can be achieved.

6.4.1 Relevant Mechanisms for Marine Environmental Protection

In the regulation of dumping at sea, we need to further expand the number of contracting parties to the London Convention. Marine environmental protection-related mechanisms have the advantage of being more specialized in monitoring and removing plastic already released into the ocean. At present, some of the regional seas projects involve the monitoring and removal of marine litter, but there are no uniform standards or coverage of the entire sea area. The establishment of a global monitoring system for marine plastic debris is conducive to providing technical support for the reduction and removal of marine plastic debris and a more comprehensive assessment of the impact of marine plastics and microplastics.

6.4.2 Chemicals and Waste Management Mechanisms

The 2018 amendment to the Basel Convention marks a significant improvement in the global waste management mechanism, though this mechanism still has scope for further refinement to achieve plastic pollution reduction throughout the entire life cycle of plastic products. Both the preamble and the general obligations of the Basel Convention explicitly include requirements for waste reduction, while its financial measures mandate that countries establish regional or subregional centres dedicated to providing training and facilitating technology transfer in the management and reduction of hazardous and other relevant wastes [13, 14, 15].

As a specialized international convention focused on hazardous waste management, the Basel Convention covers both marine and terrestrial environments, and its general obligations incorporate clear requirements for the source reduction of waste. The Basel Convention holds substantial potential to address marine plastic pollution by expanding the concept of "hazardous waste"—as clearly reflected in the amendments to its Annexes II and IX—and by extending its management scope from the transboundary movement of waste to encompass the full life cycle of plastic production and disposal. This evolution has solidified its position as a core mechanism for solving plastic and microplastic pollution, enabling comprehensive control of plastic waste across multiple critical aspects.

6.4.3 Trade-Related Mechanisms Under the WTO Framework

Charnovitz points out that "The WTO is no longer just an institution about free trade"; instead, it should take on more environmental protection functions—a view that aligns with the growing urgency of plastic pollution and the pressing need for collective action [16]. In a speech delivered at Geneva Trade Week, which focused specifically on the trade in plastics, Alan Wolff emphasized the pivotal role of trade in tackling plastic pollution, calling for greater transparency in trade-related measures, alignment with coherent domestic policies, and enhanced harmonization with international multilateral environmental conventions. [17]

The WTO Committee on Trade and Environment convened an informal dialogue in 2019 centered on the sustainable development of the plastics economy. Subsequently, at the 12th WTO Ministerial Conference, China and Fiji jointly proposed a WTO "Plastics Initiative" with the specific goal of reducing plastic pollution [18]. On November 17, 2020, China and Fiji, acting as conveners, launched an informal WTO dialogue focused on environmental pollution, with plastic pollution as a key priority area. In December 2020, China, together with 12 other WTO members including Fiji, Australia, Canada, and Thailand, submitted formal proposals to advance the informal dialogue on the theme of "Plastic Pollution and Sustainable Plastic Trade." The second session of this informal dialogue was held in March 2021, followed by the third session in June 2021 [19].

Even in the absence of a legally binding treaty, "soft law" initiatives within the WTO framework can still exert a meaningful impact. Such initiatives could highlight and promote the environmental value of responsible plastic waste management in trade, foster the formation of international practices in the field of plastic waste disposal and trade by scaling up effective national practices, reduce environmental pollution associated with the cross-border movement of plastic waste, and advance environmental equity between Northern and Southern countries in plastics-related trade. Furthermore, the WTO Plastics Initiative could propose targeted cooperation with environmental conventions in the solid waste field—such as the Basel Convention—to strengthen synergies between WTO rules and multilateral environmental conventions, creating a more cohesive global response to plastic pollution.

6.4.4 International Water Law Mechanisms

Studies have shown that plastics and microplastics carried by river systems represent a major and increasingly recognized source of marine plastic pollution, with large river basins like the Amazon and Mekong ranking among the world's top contributors of plastic emissions to the ocean. While international water law conventions do not contain specific references to plastic pollution, they include provisions that can be linked to the protection of marine ecosystems affected by such pollution. Article 21 of the Convention on the Law of the Non-Navigational Uses of

International Watercourses explicitly sets out "Obligations to prevent, control and reduce pollution" of international watercourses, and Article 24 further stipulates that watercourse States shall "Individually and, where appropriate, in cooperation with other States, take all necessary measures in respect of international watercourses for the protection and preservation of the marine environment, including estuaries." Notably, measures aimed at controlling and reducing the flow of plastics and microplastics from rivers into the ocean clearly fall within the scope of Articles 21 and 24 of this Convention. Similarly, the Convention on the Protection and Use of Transboundary Watercourses and Lakes emphasizes the prevention of marine pollution in its preamble, with a specific focus on protecting coastal areas from land-based sources of pollution; its Article 3, titled "Prevention, control and reduction of pollution," also calls for "Encouraging sustainable waste management, particularly the ecosystem approach"—a principle directly relevant to addressing plastic waste in transboundary water systems.

Among conventions regulating pollution from land-based sources, the Basel Convention primarily focuses on governing the transboundary movements of hazardous wastes. However, plastic and microplastic wastes that enter internal waters and territorial seas via water flows are not covered by the Basel Convention's regulatory framework. This omission creates a critical gap in the global management of river-borne plastic pollution. To address and fill this gap, the Convention on the Law of the Non-Navigational Uses of International Watercourses could be updated to explicitly include elements relating to the prevention, control, and treatment of plastic and microplastic pollution in international watercourses. Interaction between mechanisms: creating synergistic effects.

Biermann's description of "Collaborative fragmentation" makes several points: the alignment of core terms and objectives, the alignment of the scope of participants. A typical case of "Synergy" through the interaction of mechanisms is the interaction between the Basel, Rotterdam and Stockholm conventions. This synergy reduces the fragmentation of the law and administrative costs, and is a successful case of synergy [20]. First, cooperation among the three conventions through resolutions of the conferences of the parties, the ad hoc joint working group on enhancing coordination and cooperation among the Basel, Rotterdam and Stockholm conventions was established. Second, a clearing-house mechanism has been established between the three conventions to facilitate the exchange of information. The Basel and Stockholm conventions establish some of the existing convention regional centres as regional focal points for coordination activities in chemicals and waste management. In the design of the conferences of the parties, the conferences of the parties of the three conventions are held at the same time and place to facilitate communication and collaboration. A similar model could be used to create synergies in the treatment of marine plastic pollution.

6.4.5 *Justice in the Global South*

Justice is essential in dealing with plastic pollution. In order to ease the north-south contradiction and maintain environmental justice, we should adhere to the principle of sustainable development, the principle of common but differentiated responsibilities and multilateralism.

The first is the principle of sustainable development. The principle of sustainable development has been adopted as a basic principle by the WTO agreement and several multilateral environmental conventions, and is also reflected in the draft of the negotiation of the Global Plastics Convention. The principle of sustainable development does not simply mean limiting economic activity by preserving or protecting the interests of the environment, but also a development approach that emphasizes the fundamental importance of equity within the economy. It is not only the intergenerational equity between the present and future generations, but also the intragenerational equity between the north and the south. It takes into account the imbalances in economic development and the distribution of resources, as well as the benefits derived by developed countries from the historical exploitation of natural resources and the responsibilities arising therefrom. "Sustainable development" is not only aimed at meeting the needs of the environment, it also requires a reorientation of the world economic system for the common good of all mankind [21].

Second is the principle of "Common but differentiated responsibilities". This principle is fundamental to the UNFCCC and the Paris Agreement, and is embodied in a number of international multilateral environmental conventions. As a global environmental problem, plastic pollution is similar to climate change. Both of them are global environmental problems. The causes of environmental problems are closely related to daily production and life, and the long-term environmental impact has not been fully studied. Once carbon dioxide/waste plastic is released into the environment, it is difficult to collect and remove it. In developed countries, there are some similarities between historical emissions of plastic and historical emissions of carbon dioxide. Sticking to "Common but differentiated responsibilities" is the way to achieve transformational justice in the Global Plastics Convention.

Finally, there is multilateralism in the negotiating approach. Compared with the multilateral system, the small multilateral or bilateral negotiation mode has fewer members, which reduces the possibility of reducing the power balance of different negotiating parties among southern countries through cooperation and is more conducive to the power of great powers. Multilateralism is able to reach consensus through consultation and is more likely to produce an instrument that embodies procedural and substantive justice.

6.5 Conclusion

With the in-depth cooperation and exchange between the countries of the "Global South", there are different interpretations of the trade of plastic waste from different perspectives. From a trade perspective, the trade in plastic waste is the flow of second-hand resources and their allocation under market-based instruments in terms of treatment costs, whereas from an environmental and 'Global South' perspective, the trade in plastic waste is more likely to take place under the 'Global South', the trade of plastic waste makes developed countries transfer pollution at a relatively low price, and developing countries bear the negative externalities of waste that they have not consumed, resulting in environmental justice issues. Free trade as the core value orientation of WTO has potential conflicts with multilateral environmental conventions in terms of value level and specific rules, which not only does not help to balance the unfair phenomenon between the north and the south, but also makes it difficult to balance the unfair phenomenon between the two sides, on the contrary, it protects the unbalanced trade. As the global situation of plastic pollution becomes more serious, different multilateral mechanisms have taken measures to strengthen cooperation and play a role in plastic pollution control.

References

1. Tiseo I (2021) Global plastic production 1950-2020. Statista, 21 June 2021
2. Jambeck
3. United Nations Environment Programme (UNEP) and National Oceanic Atmospheric Administration (NOAA) (2011) The Honolulu Strategy, pp 6–8
4. The United States' contribution of plastic waste to land and ocean, law 2020
5. Brooks AL, Wang S, Jambeck JR (2018) The Chinese import ban and its impact on global plastic waste trade. Sci Adv 4:eaat0131. https://doi.org/10.1126/sciadv.aat0131
6. Louka E (2006) International environmental law: fairness, effectiveness, and world order. Cambridge University Press, Cambridge
7. United Nations General Assembly. (2011) The future we want [UN Doc A/RES/66/288]. Paragraph 163
8. United Nations Environment Assembly (2018) Marine litter and microplastics resolution [UN Doc UNEP/EA.3/Res.7], 20 January 2018
9. Biermann F et al (2010) The fragmentation of global governance architectures: a framework for analysis. Glob Environ Polit 9(4):22–31
10. Ma L (2015) The value orientation and judicial logic in the application of GATT general exceptions. East China Univ Polit Sci Law J 18(1):16–24
11. International Law Commission (ILC) (n.d.) Report on the fragmentation of international law. Paragraphs 247, 248
12. Simon N et al (2021) A binding global agreement to address the life cycle of plastics. Science 373:43–47. https://doi.org/10.1126/science.abi
13. Dauvergne P (2018) Why is the global governance of plastic failing the oceans? Glob Environ Change 51:22, p 29
14. Raubenheimer K, Mcilgorm A (2017) Is the Montreal Protocol a model that can help solve the global marine plastic debris problem? Marine Policy 81:322, pp 322–329

15. Tessnow-von Wysocki I, Le Billon P (2019) Plastics at sea: treaty design for a global solution to marine plastic pollution. Environ Sci Policy 100:94, pp 99–100.
16. Charnovitz S (2007) A new WTO paradigm for trade and the environment. Singapore Year Book Int Law 11:15–40
17. Wolff A (n.d.) Speech at Geneva Trade Week: the role of trade in tackling plastic pollution. World Trade Organization (WTO). https://www.wto.org/english/news_e/news20_e/ddgaw_30sep20_e.htm#fntext-1.
18. World Trade Organization (WTO) (2020) Informal dialogue on plastics pollution and environmentally sustainable plastics trade [WT/CTE/W/250]
19. World Trade Organization (WTO) (2021) Third session of the informal dialogue on plastics pollution and environmentally sustainable plastics trade. http://www.tbt-sps.gov.cn/page/cwto/listNewsContent.action?id=9530&DIC_AREA=
20. Morgan JC III (2016) Fragmentation of international environmental law and the synergy: a problem and a 21st century model solution. Vermont J Environ Law 18:146
21. Boyle B, Boyle A (2007) International law and the environment, 2nd edn (Trans. Li N, Wang YZ, Wang XG). Higher Education Press, Beijing

Chapter 7
The Global South and the Environmental Provisions of Free Trade Agreements

With the global rise in the negotiation and conclusion of Free Trade Agreements (FTAs), a notable trend of "WTO-plus" provisions has emerged. Horn defines "WTO-plus" provisions in FTAs as those that address issues or cover areas not regulated by existing WTO agreements—key examples include the interface between environment and trade, labour standards, and competition policy [1]. In the specific field of environmental governance, this emergence of "WTO-plus" provisions is particularly prominent, primarily due to the longstanding lack of comprehensive environmental content in core WTO rules. Environmental issues have garnered increasing attention in the framework of FTAs, with a steady expansion in the number of environmental clauses. This evolution has followed a clear trajectory: from scattered, isolated environmental clauses embedded in broader trade provisions, to the establishment of dedicated, standalone environmental chapters. Similarly, the treatment of the relationship between FTAs and multilateral environmental conventions has advanced—shifting from vague, general provisions that broadly reference such conventions, to detailed provisions tailored to specific environmental issues and direct, explicit references to relevant multilateral environmental conventions. Innovative institutional mechanisms introduced in modern FTAs—such as provisions on public participation in environmental decision-making, formal environmental consultation procedures, and the establishment of specialized Environmental Affairs Committees—have significantly strengthened the binding force of environmental provisions and enhanced their practical enforceability. Overall, environmental clauses in FTAs have undergone a transformative process of "moving from marginalization to centrality" [2]: they have shifted from being peripheral, secondary issues in trade negotiations to occupying a core position, with content becoming more specific and obligations assuming stronger legal binding force. Today, embedding detailed environmental provisions in bilateral Free Trade Agreements has become a widely adopted trend, serving as a strategic approach to break the

X. Dong, J. Gu, *The Belt and Road Initiative and the Global South*, Energy, Climate Change & Sustainability in the Global South,
https://doi.org/10.1007/978-981-92-0144-0_7

longstanding deadlock in multilateral trade negotiations that emerged after the Doha Round [3].

However, from the perspective of the "Global South," the approach of coordinating trade and environmental issues through the environmental provisions of Free Trade Agreements (FTAs) has inherent defects. To a significant extent, tensions between trade and environmental objectives remain deeply intertwined with the broader North-South divide in global governance [4]. Susskind and Ali explicitly identify conflicts between North and South countries as one of the three primary obstacles to effective global environmental cooperation, arguing that global inequalities are particularly acute in the realm of international environmental law [5]. While environmental clauses in FTAs do play a positive role in facilitating coordination between trade liberalization and environmental protection, they also carry the risk of exacerbating existing environmental injustice between the Global South and the Global North.

7.1 Reasons for the Rise of Environmental Clauses in FTAs

7.1.1 Multilateral Environmental Conventions Extensively Deal with Trade Measures

The issue of the interplay between trade and the environment first emerged in the international discourse following the 1972 Stockholm Environment Conference and further developed after the establishment of the World Trade Organization (WTO) in 1995. The earliest efforts to explore ways to balance trade and environmental objectives originated from the field of international environmental law, which adopted the concept of "sustainable development" as a key fulcrum for reconciling environmental protection and economic development. The widespread adoption and global recognition of the "sustainable development" concept can be traced back to the Brundtland Report—officially titled Our Common Future—issued by the World Commission on Environment and Development (WCED) in 1987. This influential report defines sustainable development as "development that meets the needs of the present generation without jeopardizing the ability of future generations to meet their own needs." In the Rio Declaration on Environment and Development (1992), the concept of sustainable development was clearly and systematically articulated. The Declaration emphasized both the fulfillment of the right to development and the critical principle that "environmental protection should become an integral part of the development process and cannot be viewed in isolation from it." The idea that trade and the environment should be mutually supportive first appeared in Agenda 21 (also adopted at the 1992 Rio Earth Summit), which explicitly calls on governments to support and encourage the formulation and implementation of policies that "make economic growth and environmental protection mutually reinforcing." [6]. Additionally, the elaboration of Principle 12 of the Rio Declaration—which addresses the relationship between trade and the economy—also incorporates this mutually supportive character, stating that "States should cooperate to promote a supportive and open international economic system that would lead to economic growth and sustainable development in all countries, to better address the problems of environmental degradation." [7].

Some multilateral environmental conventions inherently contain trade restriction provisions that may conflict with existing WTO rules. Notable examples include the Montreal Protocol on Substances that Deplete the Ozone Layer, the Convention on International Trade in Endangered Species of Wild Fauna and Flora (CITES), and the Basel Convention on the Control of Transboundary Movements of Hazardous Wastes and Their Disposal. Other multilateral environmental conventions do not contain provisions that directly conflict with WTO rules, but unilateral environmental measures adopted by individual countries to implement these conventions—such as carbon tariffs designed to meet domestic or international emissions targets—may still give rise to conflicts with WTO obligations. A broad range of multilateral environmental conventions include trade-related measures covering diverse areas such as climate change, biodiversity conservation, wildlife trade regulation, and solid waste management. The extensive integration of trade measures into multilateral environmental conventions reflects the deep-seated linkages between environmental issues and other domains of global governance. Environmental affairs are no longer confined to the narrow scope of environmental law alone; they have formed wide-ranging connections with areas such as international trade, cross-border investment, human rights, and general international law [8]. As noted in relevant legal and policy discourse, "the inherent and complex interrelationships between different environmental issues and between the environment and many other areas of socio-economic life" make it extremely difficult to address these issues in isolation [9]. For this reason, the coordination of trade and environmental objectives has become a focal point of discussion and debate not only within the framework of multilateral environmental conventions but also in the field of international trade law.

7.1.2 Stagnation of Trade and Environment Issues Under WTO Rules

There are two primary ways to promote the coordination of trade and environment within the WTO framework: one is through the Committee on Trade and Environment (CTE), and the other is via the WTO Dispute Settlement Mechanism. In the early years after the WTO's establishment, the issue of trade and environment saw a certain degree of progress. The Doha Ministerial Declaration explicitly called for "increased mutual support between trade and environment," providing a clear mandate for relevant WTO bodies to advance this coordination [10]. First, regarding the Committee on Trade and Environment (CTE): According to Paragraph 31 of the Doha Ministerial Declaration, the CTE's mandate includes reviewing the relationship between WTO rules and multilateral environmental conventions "with a view to strengthening mutual support between trade and the environment." This mandate also covers promoting negotiations between the secretariats of multilateral environmental conventions and WTO committees on matters such as information exchange, standards for observer status, and tariff reductions for environmental goods and services. Since its inception, the CTE has served as a dedicated forum for facilitating communication among officials from national trade and environment departments, secretariats of multilateral environmental conventions, and international environmental organizations [11]. For instance, the secretariats of several key multilateral environmental conventions—including the Montreal Protocol—have been granted observer status at CTE meetings, allowing them to participate in WTO discussions, hold regular meetings with WTO bodies, and engage in systematic information exchange. However, as the Doha Round of multilateral trade negotiations stalled, progress on trade and environment issues also came to a halt. The CTE's work has further faced criticism for failing to achieve significant substantive progress in harmonizing trade and environmental objectives; instead, some of the most important contributions to this area have come from the WTO Appellate Body through its jurisprudence [12]. Additionally, the Environmental Goods Agreement (EGA), which was launched in its first round of negotiations in July 2014 with the goal of promoting free trade in environmental goods and establishing a unified list of such goods, has encountered persistent difficulties since negotiations began and has yet to reach a final agreement.

At the judicial level, the Appellate Body's jurisprudence on trade-environment disputes has faced challenges even as it has evolved. The GATT itself contains very few rules directly related to the environment; these are concentrated in three areas: the GATT Preamble, subparagraphs (B) and (G) of Article XX ("General Exceptions"), and the absence of explicit provisions regulating the relationship between GATT/WTO rules and multilateral environmental conventions. During the GATT era, the application of general exceptions in early GATT Commission rulings was extremely restrictive—so much so that these exceptions were almost "unenforceable." [13]. However, in judicial practice spanning from the GATT period to the WTO era, the application of these two general exceptions (subparagraphs B and G) underwent a breakthrough development. For example, the introduction of the "Balancing Test" in the Korea—Beef case lowered the standard for "necessity" in applying GATT Article XX (B) from the strict "minimum trade restriction" requirement of the GATT period. Meanwhile, the use of "evolutionary interpretation" in the Shrimp—Sea Turtle case expanded the scope of application of the term "exhaustible natural resources" under Article XX (G). These developments gradually relaxed the WTO's criteria for invoking exceptions in trade-environment disputes. In the Shrimp—Sea Turtle case, the WTO Appellate Body further cited external treaties such as the United Nations Convention on the Law of the Sea (UNCLOS) and the Convention on Biological Diversity (CBD), establishing a precedent for multilateral environmental conventions to influence WTO jurisprudence. Such progress in Appellate Body jurisprudence is widely viewed as the "only concrete path to trade-environment balance within the WTO" beyond the CTE's work. However, simply expanding the scope of exceptions is no longer sufficient to meet countries' needs for balancing trade and environmental interests. By its literal meaning, "General Exceptions" are not positive, proactive rules but rather special, exceptional allowances for protecting certain important interests. This inherent nature means that "General Exceptions" permit only minimal deviations from GATT/WTO legal obligations [14]—a constraint that has led panels and the Appellate Body to subject the application of Article XX to critical examination and restrictive interpretation. Some scholars argue that this overly strict interpretation overemphasizes the "exception" aspect of Article XX while ignoring its "generality," resulting in rigid application of the GATT clause that fails to keep pace with the evolving international economic landscape. Two key challenges further undermine progress in this area [15]: First, pressing ongoing environmental issues—such as climate change, biodiversity loss, and high seas conservation—and the periodic renewal of multilateral environmental conventions continue to challenge WTO mechanisms that are already lagging behind. Second, the rise of anti-globalization sentiment and the shutdown of the WTO Appellate Body have directly threatened the viability of the WTO Dispute Settlement Mechanism itself. Since late 2019, the Appellate Body has been in a state of "shutdown" due to the United States' persistent blocking of new judge appointments. The vacancy of Appellate Body judges has left the body unable to finalize decisions on pending disputes, leading to a backlog of cases and severely undermining the WTO's dispute settlement capacity. The paralysis of the Appellate Body has also made it impossible to adopt reports from expert panels, giving rise to "invalid appeals." This situation risks pushing the Dispute Settlement Mechanism away from a "rules-based" system and toward a "power-based" one [16], ultimately threatening the mechanism's very existence. Against the backdrop of an ongoing crisis within the WTO system—with the CTE, environmental negotiations, and the Dispute Settlement Mechanism all mired in difficulties—progress on coordinating trade and environment has also come to a standstill.

7.1.3 The Rise of Regional and "Small Multilateral" Mechanisms

The rapid development of environmental clauses in FTA is based on the rise of regional mechanisms and the increasing attention to environmental issues. The slow progress of the WTO multilateral mechanism has led countries to shift their negotiating activities to regional and bilateral mechanisms, leading to a rapid increase in the number of FTAs. The crisis of the multilateral mechanism itself has promoted the rise of FTA, a "Small multilateral" mechanism. Multiple multilateral negotiation processes had stalled, and the withdrawal of the major powers from treaties and international institutions had shaken respect for international law. Some powers tend to withdraw from international organizations or paralyze the functions of international organizations [17]. At the same time, the emerging institutions under bilateral or small multilateral arrangements have become powerful competitors of multilateral international organizations, and have an impact on multilateral mechanisms and the trend of "Overhead". In climate governance, for example, some scholars argue that, to some extent, "It should be more efficient to discuss climate change in FTAs than in climate change negotiations alone" [18]. The rise of small multilateralism reflects the real needs of the international community and is more efficient than multilateral mechanisms in decision-making. Compared with multilateral trade agreements, regional trade agreements have a limited number of members, which makes it easier for members to reach agreement on environmental issues, and the high degree of consensus that is already present in the formation of regional trade agreements will also make negotiations smoother [19].

7.2 Coordination Between FTAs and Multilateral Environmental Conventions: Development Above WTO Rules

The lack of conflict clauses between WTO rules and multilateral environmental conventions, and the lack of attention to environmental issues have been criticized and controversial. Experts, academics and negotiating members have proposed different "Fine-tuning" or more radical changes to WTO rules to harmonise the WTO with multilateral environmental conventions, including the prioritization of certain multilateral environmental conventions by drawing on the NAFTA approach, amending Article 20, adding provisions on multilateral environmental conventions and providing conditional exemptions from parties' obligations under the WTO, to allow them to fulfill their obligations under multilateral environmental conventions, to formulate interpretative rules to clarify the text of WTO rules, etc. [20, 21, 22]. Although WTO rules have not been modified, similar legislative techniques have been put into practice and developed in regional free trade agreements. In the preamble of the FTA, the text, the specific setting of environmental clauses, and the coordination mechanism with multilateral environmental conventions have been improved. This refinement is based on the "General exception" to WTO rules, the "Sustainable development" mentioned in the preamble and the "Mutually supportive nature of trade and environment" in the Doha ministerial declaration, building on this, further deepening and innovation has been undertaken to create synergies and cooperation with multilateral environmental conventions in order to balance trade and environmental values, address applicable priorities with multilateral environmental conventions, mutually reinforcing effects.

7.2.1 *The Perfection of the Preface and Objectives*

Clarifying Environmental Protection in the Preamble

The WTO Preamble explicitly sets out "Sustainable Development Goals" and calls for the proper use of resources while "seeking to protect and preserve the environment"—a provision that reflects an inherent balance between environmental protection and trade liberalization values. This value balance has been further deepened in some Free Trade Agreements (FTAs). For example, the preambles of both the Comprehensive and Progressive Agreement for Trans-Pacific Partnership (CPTPP) and the United States-Mexico-Canada Agreement (USMCA) address the goal of achieving "high levels of environmental protection" and sustainable development through mutually supportive trade and environmental policies. Notably, the GATT Convention's Article XX ("General Exceptions") specifically references public health, environmental protection, and the preservation of exhaustible natural resources in its preamble. This preamble expresses a commitment to preserving the flexibility of parties with regard to "public health, safety, the environment, the protection of exhaustible biological or non-biological natural resources, the integrity and stability of the financial system and public morals"—amounting to a reaffirmation of the purpose and scope of the general exceptions [23]. Some FTAs also directly address their relationship with multilateral environmental conventions in their preambles. For instance, the United States-Singapore Free Trade Agreement states: "Recognizes the importance of pursuing these objectives in a manner that is compatible with the protection and enhancement of the environment, including regional environmental cooperation and the implementation of multilateral environmental conventions." [24]. Compared with the WTO Preamble, FTA preambles more explicitly define the "mutually supportive" relationship between trade and the environment and use more specific language to articulate environmental protection commitments.

Reconfirmation of Principled Terms in the "Background and Objectives" Clause

AFTAs that include a dedicated environment chapter typically feature a "Background and Objectives" clause at the start of this chapter—functioning as a de facto preamble for the environment-related provisions. In the language outlining the goals of the environment chapter, most clauses incorporate principled concepts for harmonizing trade and environment, with the principle of "mutual support" being particularly prominent. The "mutual support" principle has a basis in the Doha Ministerial Declaration and the jurisprudence of the WTO Appellate Body, but it is not explicitly enshrined in the WTO Agreement itself. In contrast, this principle is widely adopted in FTAs: it is referenced not only in preambles but also in the substantive body of FTA texts. "Mutually supportive" often appears in the "Background and

Objectives" clause at the beginning of the environment chapter, where it is paired with the concept of sustainable development. This pairing serves as an opening statement of trade policy objectives, sets an overarching tone for addressing the trade-environment nexus, or is integrated into conflict clauses that regulate the relationship between the FTA and multilateral environmental conventions. For example, Article 20.2 ("Objectives") of the CPTPP states: "The objective of this chapter is to promote mutually supportive trade and environmental policies" and proposes "enhanced capacity of parties to address trade-related environmental issues, including through cooperation." [25]. It can be inferred from this article that specific requirements for "mutual support" include cooperative measures between the parties. Article 20.3 ("General Commitments") of the CPTPP further re-emphasizes the importance of mutually supportive trade and environmental policies and practices in enhancing environmental protection and promoting sustainable development—effectively elevating "mutual support" and sustainable development to the status of general obligations for parties.

In addition, influential soft law documents in international environmental law are often invoked in the "Background and Objectives" clause of FTA environment chapters. For instance, Article 16.1 ("Background and Objectives") of the China-South Korea Free Trade Agreement states: "The parties recall the Stockholm Declaration on the Human Environment of 1972, the Rio Declaration on Environment and Development of 1992, Agenda 21 of 1992, the Johannesburg Plan of Implementation on Sustainable Development of 2002 and the outcome document of the Rio + 20 Summit of 2012, 'The Future We Want'." Similarly, the chapter on sustainable development in the ECLAC (Economic Commission for Latin America and the Caribbean)—related FTA (Article 22.1, "Background and Objectives") also recalls soft law documents such as the Rio Declaration on the Environment, Agenda 21, and the Johannesburg Plan of Implementation for Sustainable Development.

From the perspective of purposive interpretation, while the legal effect of such recall statements is relatively limited and the invoked soft law lacks formal legal binding force, these provisions reflect the parties' recognition of basic principles agreed upon in international environmental law and demonstrate an intention to promote coordination between trade and environment [26]. The citation of these "soft laws" also signifies recognition of the core principles embedded in them—such as the principle of sustainable development and the principle of common but differentiated responsibilities. When interpreting the FTA preamble, these soft law principles will be given greater consideration.

In essence, the "Background and Objectives" clause can be viewed as the preface to the environment chapter: it more clearly articulates the purpose of the environment-related provisions and plays a similar interpretive role for these clauses. In judicial practice, the preamble of a specific article or chapter often has a more direct impact on interpretation than the preamble of the entire agreement. For example, the application of GATT Article XX inevitably requires interpretation of its own preamble. Similarly, when interpreting FTA texts, the context and objectives outlined in the "Background and Objectives" clause can be used to clarify the contracting parties' intentions, facilitating the selection of interpretive methods that are more compatible with the obligations of multilateral environmental conventions.

7.2.2 Improvement of Conflict Clauses: Cooperation, Priority, Balance and Exception

WTO rules do not contain provisions specifying rules for preferential application when conflicts arise with other international conventions. The closest analogous conflict clause is the "General Exception" in GATT Article XX, which operates in the form of an exemption: it allows a state party to deviate to a certain extent from its WTO obligations, effectively granting precedence to other rules in specific circumstances without constituting a breach of WTO rules. This lack of explicit conflict rules in the WTO framework is partially ameliorated in Free Trade Agreements (FTAs). There are roughly two types of clauses in FTAs that can be categorized as conflict-related clauses: one is the same "General Exception" clause as GATT Article XX, and the other is the "Multilateral Environmental Agreement (MEA) - specific clauses" that regulate the relationship with multilateral environmental conventions within dedicated environment chapters or standalone environmental clauses. The approaches adopted by MEA-specific provisions to address the relationship with MEAs can be broadly divided into three categories: provisions that promote "mutual support" between trade and environmental regimes, provisions that facilitate mutual cooperation among parties, and provisions that either grant precedence to certain multilateral environmental conventions or require a balance between trade and environmental obligations. As for the "General Exception" clause, some FTAs incorporate the jurisprudence of the WTO Appellate Body and provide further interpretation of the environmental aspects of the "General Exception."

From Conflict Clauses to Cooperation Clauses: The Development of "Mutual Support"

The idea of using "mutual support" as a tool to reconcile trade and environmental agreements did not originate in trade agreements; it first emerged in multilateral environmental conventions. The principle of "mutual support" was first embodied in the textual provisions of the Rotterdam Convention and was also explicitly expressed in the Stockholm Convention. The preamble to the Rotterdam Convention states that "Trade and environmental policies should be mutually reinforcing in order to achieve sustainable development," clarifies that "Nothing in this Convention shall be construed to imply any change in the rights and obligations of Parties under any existing international agreement applicable to the international trade in chemicals or to the protection of the environment," and adds that "The above statement is not intended to establish a hierarchy between this Convention and other international agreements." [27]. The "mutual support" framework developed in multilateral environmental conventions typically includes three core components: first, a value-oriented recognition that different values (such as trade liberalization and environmental protection) not only need to coexist but can also complement each other; second, a confirmation that obligations under the environmental convention do not derogate from other rules, often stated through language like "The provisions of this Convention shall not derogate from or increase the obligations of Parties under other international rules"; and third, an emphasis that the convention is not subordinate to other international rules, establishing a parallel (rather than hierarchical) relationship between different agreements. Such clauses are widely regarded as a new development in harmonizing trade and environment, as their focus on coordination and mutual support helps mitigate potential conflicts between trade and environmental regimes and facilitates the search for pragmatic solutions. However, they have also faced criticism: some argue that these conflict clauses not only fail to resolve existing conflicts but also lay the groundwork for future conflicts, with their practical impact remaining unpredictable. A key flaw is that they do not specify which treaties should take precedence in case of inconsistency—failing to serve the traditional purpose of conflict clauses—and lack a clear definition of what "mutual support" entails in practice, creating obstacles to their implementation [28].

In the evolution of FTAs, the type of "mutual support" provisions governing the relationship with multilateral environmental conventions has undergone significant development. The principle of "mutual support" has been separated from the preamble or "Background and Objectives" clause of the agreement and transformed into a standalone, specific clause dedicated to coordinating the relationship between parties. These clauses are usually formulated using verbs such as "recognize" and "emphasize," with one or two paragraphs highlighting the importance of mutual support between trade and environment, and acknowledging the parties' commitment to fulfilling their obligations under the multilateral environmental conventions to which they are party.

As traditional FTA provisions have evolved, they have also moved beyond the "mutual support" framework that merely "confirms obligations under multilateral environmental conventions" to become more concrete and enforceable. In some FTAs, the phrase "mutual support" is followed by additional terms related to negotiation and cooperation, aiming to facilitate information exchange and collaborative action. The introduction of an obligation to exchange information has enriched the practical meaning of "mutual support." For example, the EU-Vietnam FTA stipulates that "Parties shall consult and cooperate to respect common interests in trade-related environmental issues" and that "Parties shall exchange information with the Commission on Trade and Sustainable Development on the ratification or amendment of multilateral environmental treaties, other relevant information, and the agenda." The use of the modal verb "shall" here indicates the highest level of mandatory obligation. Through such provisions, "mutual support" is embodied in specific obligations to negotiate, cooperate, and exchange information, significantly enhancing its operability [29]. Paragraph 3 of Article 24.4 ("Multilateral Environmental Conventions") of the EU-Canada Free Trade Agreement further specifies the scope of information exchange when outlining the duty to consult and cooperate. This scope includes: "1. Implementation of multilateral environmental conventions to which one Party is a party; 2. Ongoing negotiations on multilateral environmental conventions; 3. Views of Parties on becoming parties to other multilateral environmental conventions"—[30] covering three scenarios: multilateral environmental conventions that have already been acceded to, those under active negotiation, and those that parties may consider joining in the future.

The development of complementary terms (such as cooperation obligations) and information exchange obligations has completed the operationalization of "mutual support," providing clear guidance on what actions are conducive to achieving "mutual support." Through robust information exchange and cooperative communication, parties can better avoid the emergence of conflicts; if conflicts do arise, these mechanisms also facilitate negotiated solutions. However, in terms of their design, such clauses still do not clearly specify treaty precedence and prioritize cooperation over conflict resolution. Although their aim is to address the relationship with multilateral environmental conventions, they differ fundamentally from traditional conflict clauses—making them appropriately describable as "cooperation clauses" based on their purpose.

Giving Precedence to Certain Multilateral Environmental Treaties

Conflict clauses that grant precedence to specific multilateral environmental treaties first appeared in the North American Free Trade Agreement (NAFTA) and were subsequently widely adopted in FTAs signed by the United States, with limited application in FTAs signed by Canada. NAFTA explicitly provides for the primacy of selected multilateral environmental conventions in cases where the agreement's provisions are inconsistent with specific trade-related obligations under a range of multilateral environmental agreements. NAFTA lists the priority multilateral environmental conventions, including CITES (Convention on International Trade in Endangered Species of Wild Fauna and Flora), the Montreal Protocol, and the Basel Convention. This arrangement is generally viewed as granting multilateral environmental conventions higher application priority under certain conditions, with its requirement for "least inconsistent means" bearing similarities to the WTO's "necessity test." This innovative approach has been praised in numerous academic studies and has even been cited as a reference for improving the relationship between the WTO and multilateral environmental conventions.

When NAFTA was renegotiated and updated to form the USMCA (United States-Mexico-Canada Agreement), the scope of application of this precedence provision was further expanded. In addition to the existing priority conventions under NAFTA—CITES, the Montreal Protocol, and the Basel Convention—the International Convention for the Prevention of Pollution from Ships (MARPOL), the Convention on Wetlands of International Importance Especially as Waterfowl

Habitat (Ramsar Convention), the Convention on the Conservation of Antarctic Marine Living Resources, and the Convention of the Inter-American Tropical Tuna Commission were added to the list. Notably, the Basel Convention was excluded from the five newly added conventions. In its FTA with Chile, Canada also stipulated that CITES, the Montreal Protocol, and the Basel Convention should take precedence in cases of inconsistency with specific trade obligations [31]. However, it added a requirement that parties must adopt "equally effective and reasonable means" and choose "the least inconsistent means with the provisions of this Agreement." [32].

The precedence clause—which directly specifies how to resolve inconsistencies between treaty obligations—is the type of provision most closely aligned with traditional conflict clauses. In practice, however, a clause indicating a clear precedence relationship may not always be the most effective means of promoting the application of multilateral environmental conventions. Although such clauses appear to directly stipulate a priority order, the accompanying interpretation standard of "least inconsistent means" has yet to be tested and refined through practical application.

"Balanced Trade and Environmental Obligations" Clauses

The phrase "balance of trade and environmental obligations" is frequently used in FTAs signed by the United States and Canada. These clauses require parties to seek a "balance between trade and environmental obligations" when their obligations under the FTA are inconsistent with those under a specific environmental convention. Compared with provisions that grant precedence to MEAs, balanced provisions maintain greater neutrality between trade and environmental values. The use of such balanced clauses is often accompanied by the listing of "covered agreements"—a specific set of multilateral environmental conventions. For example, some FTAs include the same list of "covered agreements" as the USMCA and specify that while parties must seek a balance, this balance shall not prevent a party from taking measures to fulfill its specific obligations under the "covered agreements." However, these clauses also include a caveat: the purpose of such measures shall not be to impose a "disguised restriction on trade." In essence, such balanced clauses integrate three distinct elements to achieve a reconciliation of trade and environmental objectives: first, in the event of a conflict, parties bear an obligation to strike a balance between their environmental obligations and their obligations under the trade agreement; second, this balance cannot be used as a pretext to avoid fulfilling obligations under the specified environmental conventions—effectively granting a degree of priority to obligations under the listed multilateral environmental conventions; and third, to limit potential abuse of this priority, the clause explicitly excludes "disguised restrictions on trade," leaving room for case-by-case review to ensure compliance.

Further Interpretation of the "General Exception" Clause

TFTAs also build on and extend the "General Exception" clause that WTO rules use to coordinate conflicts between trade and environment. Most FTA exception clauses directly adopt the WTO's general exception framework. However, some FTAs have further refined the "General Exception" to clarify its meaning and enhance its compatibility with environmental measures. For example, the "General Exception" clause in the CPTPP fully incorporates the "General Exception" provisions of GATT 1994 and then amends them: in paragraph 2, it explicitly states that the measures covered by GATT 1994 Article XX (B) include "environmental measures necessary for the protection of human, animal or plant life or health," and clarifies that GATT 1994 Article XX (G) applies to "measures relating to the protection of exhaustible biotic and abiotic natural resources"—reaffirming the applicability of the "General Exception" to environmental measures. The interpretation of GATT Article XX (G) in the CPTPP follows the findings of the WTO Appellate Body in the Shrimp-Turtle case, which expanded the scope of "exhaustible natural resources" to include biological resources. The general exception clause in the Regional Comprehensive Economic Partnership (RCEP) adopts the same formulation. The general exception clause in the China-South Korea Free Trade Agreement uses identical wording but adds an important qualification: "The application of such measures shall not constitute arbitrary or unreasonable discrimination between parties or a disguised restriction on trade in goods." Notably, "unreasonable discrimination" and "disguised restrictions on trade" are elements that would already be considered when interpreting the preamble of GATT Article XX; their explicit inclusion in the FTA clause serves to reinforce these constraints.

This further interpretation of the "General Exception" clause in FTAs transforms WTO Appellate Body jurisprudence into formal convention provisions. While this represents little substantive progress in terms of content, it constitutes an improvement from the perspective of legal sources. WTO Appellate Body jurisprudence does not operate under a strict "stare decisis" (precedent-following) principle, nor is it a formal source of law—meaning its binding effect between contracting parties is limited. Although many concepts and approaches developed in earlier jurisprudence (such as the "balancing test" in the Korea—Beef and Brazil—Retreaded Tyres cases, and the two-stage review process first established in the US—Gasoline case and later followed in the Shrimp-Turtle case) are invoked and reaffirmed in subsequent cases, creating a de facto "precedent-following" practice, WTO case rulings do not possess the status of formal legal sources. By confirming the consensus formed in WTO jurisprudence through explicit FTA provisions, FTAs help foster broader consensus on these exception rules and strengthen compliance with them.

7.2.3 *Invoking Multilateral Environmental Conventions in General Clauses*

Multilateral environmental conventions do not appear in the text of WTO rules. Although some MECS have been invoked in dispute settlement cases such as shrimp-sea turtle and retreaded tyres in Brazil, their role is limited. FTA broadens the scope of invoking multilateral environmental conventions. Multilateral environmental conventions appear directly in the text of FTA. The interpretation of environmental-related terms and the coordination of environmental protection obligations and free trade have a positive effect. In the expansion of FTA's environmental content from environmental clauses to environmental chapters, these substantive obligation clauses account for a large part of the content and have an important impact on the relationship between FTA and multilateral environmental conventions.

Reference to Certain Multilateral Environmental Conventions and Transformation of Convention Obligations into Part of FTA Obligations

In a series of "high-level" Free Trade Agreements (FTAs) led and dominated by developed countries, environmental clauses have been further expanded and structured into dedicated environment chapters. The scope of these chapters is broad, covering key environmental issues such as climate change, the marine environment, biodiversity conservation, and more—reflecting a growing integration of environmental governance into trade frameworks. Within these environmental chapters, a number of provisions directly reference Multilateral Environmental Conventions (MECs) and explicitly recognize the obligations arising from MECs as part of the FTA's commitments, thereby linking trade obligations to international environmental norms.

The Comprehensive and Progressive Agreement for Trans-Pacific Partnership (CPTPP) is a typical example of an FTA that extensively invokes MECs. It covers a wide spectrum of multilateral environmental conventions across core areas of international environmental law, including ozone layer protection, climate change, fish stocks conservation, biodiversity conservation, marine pollution prevention and control, and wildlife trade. Notably, the CPTPP not only cites legally binding MECs such as the United Nations Convention on the Law of the Sea (UNCLOS), the Montreal Protocol on Substances that Deplete the Ozone Layer, the International Convention for the Prevention of Pollution from Ships (MARPOL), and the Convention on International Trade in Endangered Species of Wild Fauna and Flora (CITES) but also invokes non-legally binding soft law instruments, such as the Code of Conduct for Responsible Fisheries. The United States-Mexico-Canada Agreement (USMCA) has similarly incorporated an expanded environment chapter, addressing issues including ozone layer protection, marine environmental protection, air quality, marine litter, trade and biodiversity, invasive alien species, wild fish conservation, and marine species conservation. In many of these areas, the USMCA broadly cites similar multilateral environmental conventions—for instance, in provisions related to the protection of endangered species and sustainable forest management. The Korea-United States Trade Agreement and the United States-Peru Free Trade Agreement define the scope of obligations requiring direct compliance with multilateral environmental conventions in a manner fully consistent with the USMCA, and these conventions are specifically listed in annexes to the agreements. However, it is noteworthy that two major categories of conventions—those addressing climate change and biodiversity, which occupy pivotal positions in international environmental law and involve the participation of numerous parties—are not mentioned in these FTAs.

Through this direct invocation of MECs, environmental obligations are formally integrated into the trade agreement, meaning they are treated as an integral part of the FTA's commitments. When interpreting the FTA, the obligations of parties under multilateral environmental conventions are explicitly considered within the context of the trade framework. For example, CPTPP Article 20.5 and 20.6 set out parties' obligations to reduce the production of substances harmful to the ozone layer and prevent marine pollution from ships; these provisions explicitly indicate their connection to relevant multilateral environmental conventions (such as the Montreal Protocol and MARPOL) and specify that future amendments to these conventions and protocols will also apply to the FTA. The CPTPP further clarifies compliance with MEC-related obligations in its wording: "A Party shall be deemed to be in compliance with the provisions of Annex 20-B if it maintains one or more of the measures listed in Annex 20-B to meet its obligations under MARPOL or maintains any subsequent measures that provide an equal or higher level of environmental protection as compared with one or more of the measures listed." [33]. Additionally, CPTPP Article 20.17, paragraph 2, directly states in its substantive text: "Each Party shall adopt, maintain and enforce laws, regulations and any other measures to fulfil its obligations under the Convention on International Trade in Endangered Species of Wild Fauna and Flora (CITES)." Such provisions effectively consolidate parties' compliance obligations under multilateral environmental conventions with their obligations under the trade agreement. They also allow parties to adopt stricter environmental protection standards than those required by the MECs themselves, thereby reinforcing and strengthening the obligations set forth in the multilateral environmental conventions.

Using MEAs to Interpret Terms in Trade Agreements

The invocation of multilateral environmental conventions can serve as a practical tool for interpreting the language of trade agreements, effectively aligning the provisions of trade agreements with the content and objectives of multilateral environmental conventions. One common approach to this alignment is the direct introduction of identical concepts from multilateral environmental conventions into trade agreements; by referencing these conventions, the terms used become a shared interpretive tool for both trade agreements and multilateral environmental conventions. For example, Paragraph 2 of Chapter 20.16 (Environment) of the CPTPP directly stipulates that the term "illegal, unreported and unregulated fishing" shall be understood to have the exact same meaning as it does in Paragraph 3 of the International Plan of Action to Prevent, Deter and Eliminate Illegal, Unreported and Unregulated Fishing (IPOA-IUU 2001)—a document adopted by the Food and Agriculture Organization of the United Nations (FAO) in Rome in 2001. This provision explicitly adopts the same concept as that used in relevant multilateral environmental conventions, ensuring terminological consistency. Another approach involves interpreting newly introduced terminology in trade agreements by referencing documents from multilateral environmental conventions. Paragraph 3 of Article 20.16 of the CPTPP, for instance, sets out an obligation for all parties to seek "to implement a fisheries management system that regulates the harvesting of wild marine fish." It further clarifies that such a management system "should be based on the best available scientific evidence and internationally recognized best practices in fisheries management and conservation, as reflected in the relevant provisions of international instruments aimed at ensuring the sustainable use and conservation of marine species." The interpretation of the term "best practices" in this context explicitly includes reference to key multilateral environmental and fisheries instruments: the United Nations Convention on the Law of the Sea (UNCLOS), the Agreement for the Implementation of the Provisions of the United Nations Convention on the Law of the Sea of 10 December 1982 Relating to the Conservation and Management of Straddling Fish Stocks and Highly Migratory Fish Stocks (United Nations Fish Stocks Agreement), the Code of Conduct for Responsible Fisheries of the FAO, the Agreement to Promote Compliance with International Conservation and Management Measures by Fishing Vessels on the High Seas (Compliance Agreement), and the 2011 Plan of Action for Illegal, Unreported and Unregulated Fishing. Similarly, Article 24.10 ("Prevention and Control of Pollution of the Marine Environment") of the USMCA references the London Convention on the Prevention of Marine Pollution by Dumping of Wastes and Other Matter; meanwhile, Article 24.18(3) of the USMCA, which addresses "best practices" for achieving sustainable fishery management, explicitly refers to instruments such as UNCLOS and the Code of Conduct for Responsible Fisheries—reflecting an obligation to invoke multilateral environmental conventions when interpreting trade agreement provisions. This method of cross-referencing is highly conducive to ensuring consistency in the connotation and scope of application of environment-related terms and concepts across different legal frameworks. Ultimately, it facilitates coordination in the interpretation of multilateral environmental agreements and multilateral trade agreements, reducing ambiguity and promoting coherent implementation of both sets of obligations.

7.2.4 The Institutional Innovation of FTA in Coordinating Environmental and Trade Issues: Cooperative Consultation as an Obligation

EStrengthened information exchange through cooperation with the secretariats of Multilateral Environmental Conventions (MECs) stands as an important means of reconciling potential conflicts between WTO rules and MEC obligations. While the WTO has practically established the Committee on Trade and Environment (CTE) and advocates for cooperation in this regard, such cooperative efforts lack explicit authorization in formal WTO rules. In contrast, within Free Trade Agreements (FTAs), cooperation is elevated to the status of a binding treaty obligation, and more comprehensive institutional mechanisms are established to facilitate it. FTA Environment Committees are typically established on the basis of dedicated environmental provisions in the agreement. Critically, cooperation with the secretariats of multilateral environmental conventions or relevant international organizations is incorporated into the text of trade agreements as a substantive, enforceable obligation. For example, in its chapter on fisheries subsidies and combating illegal, unreported, and unregulated (IUU) fishing, the USMCA explicitly proposes to collaborate with Regional Fisheries Management Organizations (RFMOs) and Regional Fisheries Management Arrangements (RFMAs), laying the groundwork for institutional-level coordination. Similarly, the EU-Canada Free Trade Agreement (CETA) includes a "Cooperation" clause in Article 24.12, which calls for cooperation with the WTO, the United Nations Environment Programme (UNEP), the Organisation for Economic Co-operation and Development (OECD), and multilateral environmental conventions—all with the goal of harmonizing trade and environmental policies.

Compared to the WTO's Committee on Trade and Environment (CTE), the Environment Committees established under FTAs have expanded functions, including assuming certain roles in dispute settlement processes. The Environment Committee established by the CPTPP, for instance, is tasked with both deliberative and consultative functions. This Committee is required to regularly report to the CPTPP Free Trade Agreement Committee on the implementation of the environment chapter and to provide a dedicated forum for information exchange and cooperative activities among parties. The Committee convenes every 2 years, and its decisions and reports are made publicly available to ensure transparency. Within 5 years of the CPTPP's entry into force, the Environment Committee also bears the responsibility of reviewing the implementation and application of the environment chapter, with a requirement to submit its findings to the contracting parties and the FTA Committee. The CPTPP further enhances cooperation by establishing special focal points and three-tiered consultation procedures for addressing environmental matters: basic environmental consultations, consultations involving high-level representatives, and ministerial-level consultations. These focal points serve as central conduits for information exchange between parties. As specified in Article 20.19, paragraph 3 of the CPTPP, the Environment Committee also has the function of "deliberating on and seeking resolution of" matters referred to it through high-level representative consultations. In terms of supervisory functions, the CPTPP Environment Committee's role is significantly expanded compared to the WTO CTE: it not only operates under more detailed substantive provisions but also assumes responsibility for monitoring the implementation of environmental clauses—representing a clear advantage in enforceability design over the CTE.

Cooperating with multilateral environmental conventions is also explicitly designated as a responsibility of Environment Committees under many FTAs. For example, CETA establishes a Commission on Trade and Sustainable Development, which is tasked with reviewing the content of the environment and sustainable development chapters, providing advice during consultation processes, and establishing expert panels when dispute-related matters are referred to it. This Commission integrates multiple functions, including facilitating cooperation, conducting deliberations, supporting dispute resolution, proposing bodies to consider multilateral environmental conventions, and strengthening cooperative ties with MECs [34]. In the EU-Japan Economic Partnership Agreement (EPA), the Commission on Trade and Sustainable Development similarly holds responsibilities for reviewing the implementation of the environment chapter and enhancing cooperation with multilateral environmental treaty bodies. Additionally, this Commission is mandated to engage in liaison with civil society organizations on matters related to the implementation of environmental obligations [35]. By embedding specific provisions in FTAs that define Environment Committees' responsibilities to cooperate with multilateral environmental conventions, the task of managing the relationship between the WTO and MECs is transformed from a non-binding policy advocacy goal into one of the formal, mandatory obligations of FTA parties.

7.3 Characteristics and Influence of Trade and Environment Coordination Mechanism Under FTA

7.3.1 Emphasis on Coordination and Promotion Rather than Conflict

The relationship between trade and the environment is often expressed in terms of coordination and support, focusing on the synergy rather than the conflict. Provisions in the "Mutually supportive" category are sometimes referred to as "Ensuring that trade and environment are mutually supportive", "Promoting trade and the environment as mutually supportive" or "Recognizing that economic development, social development and environmental protection are interdependent and mutually supportive components of sustainable development". First, it acknowledges that trade and the environment can be reconciled. Expressions such as "Recognizing" or "Promoting" imply that trade and the environment are already in some mutually supportive state, just in need of improvement and maintenance. The relationship with MECS is often dominated by "Recognition of the role of MECS in protecting the environment" and "Reaffirmation of obligations under MECS", it does not deal directly with conflicts and priorities. From the value orientation on the emphasis on integration and coordination, emphasizing cooperation and trade and environment to promote each other.

In terms of substantive obligations, the obligations of multilateral environmental conventions have been confirmed and strengthened in FTA. These rules either supplement the original rights and obligations, or form a confirmation of the rules of the existing multilateral environmental conventions, which is a gradual rather than a conflict relationship. Even part of the soft law in the form of FTA environmental clauses have been "Hardening", with a stronger binding force. Procedurally, the information disclosure, environmental consultation and dispute settlement mechanisms established by the FTA also provide a stronger monitoring platform for multilateral environmental conventions. With the linkage between FTA provisions and multilateral environmental conventions, procedural public participation, information disclosure and dispute settlement mechanisms can also be used to promote the implementation of multilateral environmental convention obligations.

7.3.2 Different Citation Preferences May Affect the Implementation of Multilateral Environmental Conventions

The manner in which Free Trade Agreements (FTAs) address multilateral environmental conventions exerts a two-way influence: it not only shapes the development of FTAs and international trade rules but also impacts the implementation and focus of multilateral environmental conventions themselves. On one hand, FTAs reinforce the obligations outlined in multilateral environmental conventions through dedicated environmental provisions and by leveraging the economic benefits of trade liberalization. Consequently, multilateral environmental conventions that are more frequently invoked in FTAs and that establish deeper, more extensive linkages with trade frameworks tend to be implemented more effectively—thereby shifting global attention toward the specific types of environmental issues these conventions address.

The frequency with which different multilateral environmental conventions appear in FTAs, as well as which countries advocate for their inclusion, varies significantly. This preferential pattern of invocation is closely tied to the underlying interest relationships between countries. FTAs led by developed countries typically feature more detailed environmental clauses and chapters, with stronger connections to multilateral environmental conventions. In contrast, the Regional Comprehensive Economic Partnership (RCEP)—which includes a large number of developing country parties—lacks both a dedicated environment chapter and standalone environmental clauses, and hardly invokes any multilateral environmental conventions. It only emphasizes sustainable development and mutual support in its preamble, and includes a single article in the "General Provisions and Exceptions" chapter that addresses the relationship with the Convention on Biological Diversity (CBD) (recognizing parties' rights and obligations under the CBD) [36]. Overall, RCEP maintains an approach to environmental issues that is similar to the WTO's framework. Developed countries such as the European Union (EU), the United States, and Canada exhibit distinct preferences when invoking multilateral environmental conventions in their FTAs. The EU places particular emphasis on climate change: its bilateral FTAs with Japan, Vietnam, and Singapore all explicitly address collaboration to advance the implementation of obligations under the UNFCCC (United Nations Framework Convention on Climate Change), the Kyoto Protocol, and the Paris Agreement. An earlier EU FTA with South Korea also referenced the UNFCCC, the Kyoto Protocol, and the Bali Road Map, and incorporated extensive climate-related provisions. Through academic analysis of climate change provisions in EU FTAs, scholars have observed that the EU achieves "issue linkage" by embedding climate change issues into trade agreements. Leveraging its economic and trade advantages, the EU uses this approach to export its institutional rules in the climate change field and strengthen its voice in global climate governance [37]. In terms of environmental clause design, the EU frequently adopts "Trade and Sustainable Development" as the title for its environmental chapters—used in FTAs with Singapore, South Korea, Canada, and Vietnam—which integrates trade, environmental, and labor issues, with wording that places greater emphasis on sustainable development.

The United States, which is not a party to the Kyoto Protocol or the Convention on Biological Diversity (CBD), adopts a more conservative stance on climate change and biodiversity issues. When signing FTAs, the U.S. often avoids invoking multilateral environmental treaties such as the UNFCCC and CBD, even when the agreements include provisions related to climate change and biodiversity protection. For example, both the CPTPP (in which the U.S. was an initial negotiating member) and the USMCA (a "high-level" FTA with robust environmental protections) emphasize the importance of climate change and biodiversity. However, neither agreement establishes textual links to, or references, the UNFCCC, CBD, or their associated protocols—nor do they use these conventions as reference points for interpreting specific terms in the agreement. In the area of solid waste management, the U.S. approach has even shown "backsliding": from NAFTA to the USMCA, the Basel Convention was removed from the list of conventions eligible for priority application. This trend partly reflects the challenges inherent in coordinating trade and environmental rules, as well as the fragility of such coordination: in areas where conflicting interests are truly acute, the effectiveness of "coordination" mechanisms diminishes significantly. The absence of the UNFCCC and CBD from U.S. FTAs represents a deliberate evasion, underscoring the underlying conflicts of interest between major powers. In contrast, conventions such as CITES (Convention on International Trade in Endangered Species of Wild Fauna and Flora) and the Montreal Protocol are frequently cited in various FTAs. This is largely due to their proven implementation effectiveness or the fact that they involve less contentious interest conflicts. This phenomenon reveals a critical reality: environmental issues do not receive attention proportional to the extent of ecological damage they cause or the future threats they pose. Instead, the design of environmental clauses in FTAs is heavily influenced by developed countries, reflecting their ability to shape institutional frameworks. As a "trade tool" that reinforces the environmental preferences of economic powers, FTAs carry the risk of sidelining the environmental concerns of developing countries. Another key dynamic lies in enforcement capacity: multilateral environmental conventions generally lack strong enforcement bodies, resulting in weak implementation. In contrast, some FTAs feature relatively comprehensive enforcement mechanisms, including public participation, consultation procedures, and dispute settlement systems. In practice, there have been instances where developed countries exploit their influence in FTAs and the linkages between FTAs and multilateral environmental conventions to erode obligations under the latter. Specifically, there is a risk that countries may "interpret" the obligations of multilateral environmental treaties in ways that are more favorable to their national interests within the FTA framework—ultimately reducing their own compliance responsibilities.

7.3.3 The Use of Environmental Clauses Is Unbalanced Between North and South Countries

Against the backdrop of the widespread emergence of environmental clauses in Free Trade Agreements (FTAs), a hidden North-South imbalance has emerged. Some scholars have pointed out that environmental provisions are not evenly distributed across all FTAs; instead, they appear in large numbers in FTAs signed between developed and developing countries. Specifically, the average number of environmental provisions in North-South Regional Trade Agreements (RTAs)—which stands at 10—has surpassed that in North-North and South-South RTAs, and this average has increased rapidly in recent years [38]. A notable example is the EU-Vietnam FTA, which includes a comprehensive environment chapter covering topics such as the relationship with multilateral environmental conventions, climate change, biodiversity conservation, sustainable forest management, fishing, and the conservation of high seas living resources. This chapter not only invokes multilateral environmental conventions but also references soft law instruments like the Code of Conduct for Responsible Fisheries; it even requires consideration of non-environment-specific frameworks such as the OECD Guidelines on Corporate Social Responsibility. As the scope of "soft law" invoked in such FTAs expands, the voluntary environmental obligations initially undertaken by developing countries take on greater binding force. Additionally, mechanisms such as eco-labelling and environmental impact assessment systems are exported through FTAs, often without fully accounting for the technological and financial capacity constraints of developing countries. This phenomenon has led to the "spillover" of environmental rules from developed countries (such as Europe and the United States) to the broader international community, while the environmental governance of Global South countries has been shaped by the "internalization" of these externally driven rules.

The support for developing countries' rights—an emphasis embedded in both multilateral environmental conventions and WTO rules—has also been undermined. The WTO Preamble explicitly states its commitment to "Taking into account different levels of economic development" and "Ensuring that developing countries, in particular the least developed countries, share in the growth of international trade in a manner commensurate with their level of economic development." In contrast, neither the CPTPP nor the USMCA—both of which include developing-country signatories—guarantees adequate representation of developing countries' interests. Only the RCEP, which counts a large number of developing countries among its parties, proposes to consider additional flexibility for Least Developed Countries (LDCs) and includes provisions for assisting LDCs. While the concept of "common but differentiated responsibilities" has been incorporated into many multilateral environmental conventions, this fundamental principle—which holds a pivotal position in climate change governance—has not been emphasized in most FTAs. Some scholars have noted that FTAs are increasingly becoming "a new institutional carrier for developed countries to compete for the right to set the agenda on climate issues." This trend is not limited to climate change; it also applies to other environmental issues such as biodiversity conservation, fishery resource management, and solid waste control. On one hand, negotiations on multilateral environmental conventions—which typically emphasize the historical environmental responsibilities of developed countries and the principle of common but differentiated responsibilities—remain fraught with difficulties. On the other hand, environmental chapters in bilateral or "small multilateral" FTAs have grown in prominence, with environmental issues being integrated into FTA negotiations. Unlike multilateral environmental conventions such as the UNFCCC and the Basel Convention, these bilateral or small multilateral FTA environmental provisions do not stress "common but differentiated responsibilities" or acknowledge the historical overuse of resources by developed countries. By separating these regional mechanisms from the WTO and multilateral environmental conventions, the bilateral or small multilateral context allows developed countries to set aside their historical environmental responsibilities and bypass the procedural influence that Global South countries wield within multilateral frameworks.

FTAs also exert a certain impact on the stability of the WTO regime, particularly amid the rise of "small multilateral" free trade arrangements such as the CPTPP and RCEP. The growing prominence of regional free trade agreements (including the CPTPP and RCEP) signals a decline in the relative importance of the traditional global free trade system, as many economies increasingly prioritize bilateral or small multilateral free trade frameworks [39].

However, even large regional multilateral trade agreements like the CPTPP or RCEP—which boast numerous signatories—can hardly replace the WTO's regime and status. Both the CPTPP and RCEP explicitly state in their preambles that they are established "on the basis of their respective rights and obligations under the Marrakech Agreement Establishing the World Trade Organization." Article 1 of the RCEP clarifies that it is an FTA established pursuant to Article 24 of the GATT and Article 5 of the GATS; Article 1 of the CPTPP includes an identical stipulation. Most FTAs first ground their rights and obligations in the GATT (a core component of WTO rules). FTA texts also incorporate a large number of WTO rule provisions: for example, the "Exceptions" section in most FTAs almost completely adopts the exceptions outlined in GATT 1994 and the GATS. Other basic provisions—such as national treatment and most-favored-nation treatment—are also aligned with GATT 1994, which explicitly states that such provisions "shall be incorporated into and become part of this agreement with such modifications as may be necessary in particulars." In their conflict clauses and final clauses, FTAs usually include specific provisions confirming that regional free trade agreements do not undermine parties' rights and obligations under the WTO. For instance, Article 20 (Final Clauses), Paragraph 2 of the RCEP clearly states: "This Agreement coexists with the WTO Agreement, and the rights and obligations of the Parties under this Agreement shall be recognized without prejudice to their respective rights and obligations under the WTO Agreement." Regardless of the underlying motivations, FTA texts do not seek to weaken or replace the WTO. On the other hand, WTO rules themselves provide legal space for the formation of FTAs: both Article 24, Paragraph 4 of the GATT and Article 5 of the GATS elaborate on the conditions for establishing free trade areas, and the conclusion of separate bilateral or multilateral free trade agreements by WTO members is explicitly authorized under WTO rules. In essence, FTAs are built on the foundation of a series of WTO rules—including GATT 1994, the TRIPS Agreement, and the GATS. The boundaries of FTA parties' rights and obligations are consistent with WTO rules, and their operational models and legal sources are inseparable from the WTO framework. While FTAs may erode the WTO system to a certain extent, they cannot replace WTO rules.

As a global multilateral mechanism, the WTO possesses unique advantages that FTAs cannot replicate. First, from the perspective of environmental governance effectiveness: the rise of environmental clauses and chapters in FTAs does not mean that trade and environmental issues can be resolved by bypassing the WTO and relying entirely on regional agreements. Ecosystems such as marine and atmospheric systems are open and interconnected, making environmental problems inherently transboundary (and often global) in nature—regional governance alone is unlikely to achieve optimal results. Second, the WTO's emphasis on and protection of developing countries' interests reflects a commitment to fairness in the social dimension of sustainable development, which aligns with the principle of "common but differentiated responsibilities" enshrined in multilateral environmental conventions. Thus, even with the rapid development of FTAs, exploring ways to balance trade and environmental objectives under WTO rules remains indispensable.

7.4 China's Response to the Rise of FTA Environment Clause

7.4.1 *Conform to the Trend and Perfect the Environmental Clause of Our FTA*

From the quantity change and development trend of FTA Environment Chapter and Environment Clause, it is the general trend to add environment clause in FTA. In the practice of our country, the environment-related content in the trade agreement has grown from nothing, from the preamble to the substantive clause, and then expanded to the specific chapter, from the declarative content to some of the entity's obligations and consultation procedures. As of December 2021, our country has signed 20 FTAs, of which 5 FTAs contain environmental chapters [40]. Compared with the developed countries in Europe and, the FTA signed by our country is less in the use of environmental chapters and environmental clauses, the principle content is more than the actual obligation clause, and generally does not involve the invocation of multilateral environmental conventions. As the negotiation of free trade agreement continues to advance and our country applies to join CPTPP, it is very important to study the environmental clause. Our country can conform to the trend, actively design environmental rules in FTA, form environmental terms with its own characteristics, and strengthen the construction of cooperative mechanisms related to environmental protection, we should improve procedural clauses such as public participation and environmental impact assessment.

7.4.2 *Using FTA Environmental Clauses to Promote the Implementation of Multilateral Environmental Conventions*

References to multilateral environmental conventions and recognition of obligations under multilateral environmental conventions in FTAs constitute a reinforcement of multilateral environmental conventions. Cooperative mechanisms such as the environmental committees established in FTAs can serve as an additional platform for advancing the implementation of multilateral environmental conventions and cooperation. Our country actively participates in the negotiation, conclusion and implementation of multilateral environmental conventions, and is a party to the multilateral environmental conventions commonly cited in CITES, the Montreal Protocol, the UNFCCC, CBD and other FTAs. Reaffirm or emphasize that the obligations under these multilateral environmental conventions have no bearing on our compliance obligations. Our country can use the cooperation and information exchange provisions in the FTA to promote cooperation between our country and other parties under the FTA in the field of the environment and to strengthen capacity-building to improve the level of the environment, the promotion of environment-friendly products and clean production technology, etc., to better serve our country's implementation work. For the areas where China has a strong ability to implement the convention, and where environmentally friendly products and technologies are in the leading position or have a strong voice, relevant multilateral environmental conventions can be embedded in the FTA, so as to strengthen the implementation of multilateral environmental conventions.

7.4.3 Emphasizing the Protection of the Rights and Interests of Developing Countries

The inequality of the world political and economic structure is also reflected in the environmental issues. First, historical inequities in the use of resources create difficulties for developing countries in balancing their own development and sustainable growth patterns. Global environmental problems such as climate change and marine pollution caused by the exploitation and utilization of natural resources by the northern countries are shared by the international community, including the southern countries. At the same time, under the deterioration of the environment, the northern countries that have realized the upgrading of technological production methods require "High-level environmental protection", and the environmental rules formulated by the southern countries restrict the development and utilization of resources. Second, the uneven distribution of the global industrial chain allows the northern countries to obtain high-value products, while the southern countries mainly export their own resources or use them as contract manufacturers at relatively low prices, the waste treatment bases bear the negative environmental externalities of the northern countries' exports. Finally, national strength affects the setting of environmental political agenda, and the international community is more likely to pay attention to the ecological and environmental issues that the northern countries are concerned about and ignore the ecological and environmental issues that are important to the southern countries [41]. Under the multilateral agenda, whether multilateral environmental conventions or WTO rules, there are supportive and protective measures for developing countries based on this north-south imbalance, however, in bilateral or regional free trade agreements, support and protection measures for developing countries and least developed countries have been weakened. Although the model of embedding environmental clauses in FTAs commonly used in developed countries in Europe and the United States has promoted the relationship with multilateral environmental conventions and the implementation of obligations under multilateral environmental conventions, however, there are defects in balancing the obligations of the north and south countries. In the agenda of our FTA negotiations, we also need to pay attention to this tendency to dissolve the original obligations of developed countries through bilateral mechanisms, return to the emphasis on differential treatment for developing countries in multilateral environmental conventions and WTO rules in terms of principles and concrete measures.

First of all, we need to emphasize the social equity attribute of the principle of "Sustainable development" from the perspective of the principle of "Sustainable development" which connects trade and environmental issues. The principle of "Sustainable development" has become a principle governing the relationship between trade and the environment in several FTAs. In some of the FTAs signed by the European Union, the environment chapter is entitled "Trade and sustainable development", there is a special "Sustainable development" clause. However, the emphasis on sustainable development in FTA is mainly on the balance between economic development and environmental protection, and the attribute of sustainable development in social equity dimension has not been fully paid attention to. The principle of sustainable development does not simply mean limiting economic activity by preserving or protecting the interests of the environment, but also a development approach that emphasizes the fundamental importance of equity within the economy [42]. It is not only the intergenerational equity between the present and future generations, but also the intra-generational equity between the north and the south. It takes into account the imbalances in economic development and the distribution of resources, as well as the benefits and responsibilities that developed countries have historically derived from the exploitation of natural resources. "Sustainable development" is not only aimed at meeting the needs of the environment, it also requires a reorientation of the world economic system for the common good of all mankind. Sustainable development is a balance between trade and the environment and between the equal sharing of the fruits of development. In order to implement the principle of sustainable development in FTA, we need to emphasize the attribute of sustainable development that focuses on the balance between north and south countries, increase technology transfer support from developed countries to developing countries, and provide assistance to least developed countries.

Secondly, the principle of common but differentiated responsibilities should be incorporated into the multilateral environmental conventions while strengthening the linkages with them. The principle of common but differentiated responsibilities, set forth in the Stockholm and Rio Declarations, is an important principle in international environmental law, several multilateral environmental conventions such as the Framework Convention on climate change and the Basel convention embody the principle of common but differentiated responsibilities. It is consistent with the principle of "Common but differentiated responsibilities" in international environmental law that WTO protects the rights and interests of developing countries and advocates the fair sharing of the fruits of economic growth among countries. "Common but differentiated responsibilities" should not be evaded or dissolved in the context of bilateral or "Small multilateral" negotiations. In the negotiations, our country can actively promote the embodiment of the principle of "Common but differentiated responsibilities" in the environmental provisions of the FTA, in response to the developed countries through the FTA framework to the "High Level" of environmental protection in the name of the tendency to create green barriers to safeguard their own rights and interests.

7.5 Conclusion

In the mode of dealing with the relationship with multilateral environmental conventions, the use of FTA clauses to coordinate and avoid conflicts has been greatly developed compared with the text of the WTO agreement. From the development of environmental content, the emphasis on environmental protection has moved from the preamble to the body of the treaty, from the more significant content of the declaration of purpose and purpose to the provisions with substantive obligations, the general concept of dealing with "Multilateral environmental conventions" has given way to the distinctive branches of climate change, biodiversity, fisheries protection and so on, the content has also been expanded from environmental clauses to special environmental chapters. In terms of implementation, some agreements have introduced special review and dispute settlement mechanisms, and introduced tools in domestic environmental law such as environmental impact assessment and public participation, which have increased the effectiveness and enforcement of environmental provisions, it also helps the effective implementation of multilateral environmental conventions. Both technological development and value orientation reflect increased attention to environmental issues, a significant development for the vision of "Mutually supportive trade and environment". The FTA places more emphasis on establishing synergies with multilateral environmental conventions rather than indicating a preferential relationship in the conflict of rules, and forms the progressive development of rules through the recognition and invocation of obligations under multilateral environmental conventions, better strengthen the obligations in multilateral environmental conventions. However, there is also a risk that the FTA will serve as a tool for developed countries to weaken the multilateral mechanism, weaken their historical environmental responsibility, and export their own institutions. A preference for incorporating the content of multilateral environmental conventions could lead to a selective emphasis on environmental issues, to the detriment of developing countries. From the perspective of the "Global South", multilateral mechanisms remain indispensable to avoid the FTA expanding the gap between the voice of the south and that of the north in environmental governance. On the other hand, the FTA rule-making process needs to respect different national conditions, taking into account the "Common but differentiated responsibilities" and other basic principles of international environmental law.

References

1. Horn H, Mavroidis PC, Sapir A (2010) Beyond the WTO? An anatomy of EU and US preferential trade agreements. World Econ 33(11):1565–1588
2. Zhao Y (2013) An empirical study on environmental rules under the BIT and FTA frameworks: a text-based analysis. Int Econ Trade Res 29(09):103
3. Zhou Y (2015) The United States' strengthening of environmental provisions in free trade agreements and its impacts. Contemp Int Relat (04), p 1

4. Xiao-mei E (2006) Unilateral PPM environmental trade measures and WTO rules: conflict and coordination. Law Press China, Beijing, p 141
5. Susskind LE, Ali SH (2015) Environmental diplomacy: negotiating more effective global agreements, 2nd edn. Oxford University Press, New York, pp 16–17
6. Agenda 21 (adopted at United Nations Conference on Environment and Development) A/CONDF.151/26/Rev.1 (1992)
7. United Nations Conference on Environment and Development (1992) The Rio Declaration on environment and development [A/CONF.151/26, Vol. I]
8. Agius MF (2014) Interaction and delimitation of international legal orders. Koninklijke Brill NV, Leiden
9. Hirst A (2018) Global order and global governance, Chinese edn. China Renmin University Press
10. World Trade Organization (WTO) (2001) Doha Ministerial Declaration [Para. 31]. http://www.wto.org/english/thewto_e/minist_e/min01_e/mindecl_e.doc
11. Cima E (2021) From exception to promotion: re-thinking the relationship between international trade and environmental law. Koninklijke Brill NV, Leiden, pp 174, 185
12. Birnie P, Boyle E (2007) International law and the environment, 2nd edn (Trans. Li N, Wang Y, Wang X). Higher Education Press, pp 673, 42, 43
13. Charnovitz S (2007) The WTO's environmental progress. J Int Econ Law 10(3), pp 685–706, pp 695–696
14. Zeng LL, Chen WD (2001) On the WTO General exceptions clause (GATT Article XX) and China's appropriate countermeasures. Leg Forum (04), pp 32–49
15. Liu XH (2018) A critique of misunderstandings in the application of the WTO General exceptions clause. East China Law Rev (04), pp 72–82
16. Du B (2021) WTO dispute settlement after the appellate body shutdown. Nanjing Univ Law Rev (01), pp 101–113
17. Farah PD et al (2023) Introduction: mapping the crisis of multilateralism. In: Gruszczynski L et al (eds) The crisis of multilateral legal order: causes, dynamics and implications. Routledge, New York, p 8
18. Zhao YY (2022) A study on the rule of law of "small multilateralism" in climate change. J Int Econ Law (02), p 121
19. Zheng LL, Liu C (2015) A study on the conflict and coordination model of environmental issues: taking the Trans-Pacific Partnership Agreement as an example. Pacific J 23(04), pp 66–74, 72
20. Liu Y (2003) On the conflict between WTO rules and multilateral environmental treaties and its resolution: some reflections on WTO trade and environment negotiations. Foreign Econ Manag (01), pp 7–12
21. Qi H (2004) Treaty law issues in the relationship between the WTO and multilateral environmental agreements (MEAs). J Beijing Technol Bus Univ (Soc Sci Edn) (03), pp 71–75
22. Bian YM (2008) An analysis of trade measures in multilateral environmental treaties. Int Commercial Law Rev 9(00):9–34
23. Preamble Comprehensive and Progressive Agreement for Trans-Pacific Partnership (CPTPP)
24. United States-Singapore Free Trade Agreement (n.d.) Preamble
25. Comprehensive and Progressive Agreement for Trans-Pacific Partnership (CPTPP) (n.d.) Article 20.2
26. EU-Canada Comprehensive Economic and Trade Agreement (CETA), 2017
27. Rotterdam Convention on the Prior Informed Consent Procedure for Certain Hazardous Chemicals and Pesticides in International Trade (2004) Preamble. (Entered into force 24 February 2004)
28. Liao SP (2008) A study on the fundamental issues of treaty conflicts. Law Press China
29. European Union-Vietnam Free Trade Agreement (2020) Article 13.5. https://eur-lex.europa.eu/legal-content/EN/TXT/PDF/?uri=OJ:L:2020:186:FULL&from=EN#page=132
30. EU-Canada Comprehensive Economic and Trade Agreement (CETA) (n.d.) Article 24.4
31. The United States-Mexico-Canada Agreement (USMCA), Art 24.8

32. Canada-Chile Free Trade Agreement (n.d.) Article A-04. https://international.gc.ca/
33. Comprehensive and Progressive Agreement for Trans-Pacific Partnership (CPTPP) (n.d.) Articles 20.5, 20.6, 20.17, 20.16, 20.19
34. EU-Canada Comprehensive Economic and Trade Agreement (CETA) (n.d.) Articles 24.12, 24.13
35. EU and Japan's Economic Partnership Agreement (EPA), Art 16.12, 16.13
36. Article 17.10 of the Regional Comprehensive Economic Partnership Agreement (RCEP)
37. Hongyan C (2020) Free trade agreements: a new path to enhancing China's institutional discourse power in global climate governance. Law Sci 2020(02), pp 156–171, p 160
38. Yamin Z. Green governance in global value chains: status adjustment and relationship reconstruction between northern and southern countries. Chin J Int Polit (J China Foreign Aff Univ), pp 49–80, pp 55–56, p 58
39. Wei S (2019) WTO failure: dilemmas and disagreements. J Shanghai Bus Sch 20(05), pp 58–74, p 73
40. Ministry of Commerce of the People's Republic of China (n.d.) China Free Trade Zone Service Network. http://mofcom.gov.cn
41. Hurrell A (2018) Global order and global governance. China Renmin University Press, pp 267–268
42. Birnie P, Boyle E (2007) International law and the environment, 2nd edn (Trans. Li N, Yanzhi W, Xiaogang W). Higher Education Press, p 42

Index

X. Dong, J. Gu, *The Belt and Road Initiative and the Global South*, Energy, Climate Change & Sustainability in the Global South,
https://doi.org/10.1007/978-981-92-0144-0

The manufacturer's authorised representative in the EU is Springer
Nature Customer Service Centre GmbH, Europaplatz 3, 69115 Heidelberg,
Germany. If you have any concerns regarding our products, please
contact ProductSafety@springernature.com

Printed and bound by CPI Group (UK) Ltd, Croydon, CR0 4YY
07/10/2026
02229352-0003